Foundations of Educational Leadership

Foundations of Educational Leadership provides a fresh and research-based perspective on educational leadership, exploring 10 specific aspects of "glocalization" in which educational leaders must be literate in order to establish and sustain relevant and useful educational experiences for students in their schools. In addition to covering traditional concepts such as culture, instructional leadership, professional ethics, and politics, well-known authors Brooks and Normore also introduce several conventionally neglected, cutting edge concepts like spirituality, holistic health, and information leadership. This important book emphasizes how a framework of learning, literacy, leadership and reflection is critical to the preparation and practice of educational leaders. *Foundations of Educational Leadership* ensures aspiring and practicing leaders will be prepared to influence processes and outcomes for creating a more just and equitable environment for all students.

Key Features:

- Each chapter focuses on what leaders need to *learn*, the concepts with which they need to be *literate*, how to *lead* in the area, and aspects on which they should *reflect*.
- Discussion sections at the end of each chapter include prompts, questions, and activities suited for engaging ideas, alone, or with classmates.
- Includes eResources featuring PowerPoints for instructors.

Jeffrey S. Brooks is Professor of Educational Leadership at Monash University, Australia.

Anthony H. Normore is Professor of Educational Leadership and Department Chair of Graduate Education at California State University, Dominguez Hills, USA.

Foundations of Educational Leadership

Developing Excellent and Equitable Schools

Jeffrey S. Brooks and
Anthony H. Normore

Routledge
Taylor & Francis Group
NEW YORK AND LONDON

First published 2018
by Routledge
711 Third Avenue, New York, NY 10017

and by Routledge
2 Park Square, Milton Park, Abingdon, Oxon, OX14 4RN

Routledge is an imprint of the Taylor & Francis Group, an informa business

© 2018 Taylor & Francis

Library of Congress Cataloging-in-Publication Data
A catalog record for this book has been requested.

ISBN: 978-0-415-70934-7 (hbk)
ISBN: 978-0-415-70935-4 (pbk)
ISBN: 978-1-315-88559-9 (ebk)

Typeset in Sabon and Helvetica Neue
by Florence Production Ltd, Stoodleigh, Devon, UK

Visit the eResource: www.routledge.com/9780415709354

Contents

Preface   *vii*

Acknowledgments   *x*

1   Educational Leadership: From Classic to Cutting Edge   1

2   Political Leadership   26

3   Economic Leadership   42

4   Cultural Leadership   54

5   Moral Leadership   72

6   Pedagogical Leadership   91

7   Information Leadership   107

8   Organizational Leadership   133

9   Spiritual and Religious Leadership   151

10   Temporal Leadership   166

11   Holistic Health Leadership   179

12   Bringing It All Together: Dynamic and Synergistic Leadership   195

Index   *199*

Preface: Why Do We Need Another Book on Educational Leadership?

The odds are good that you found this book on a website, in a bookstore or on the shelves of a library. Look at the other titles on those virtual or physical shelves—there are a lot of books on educational leadership and even more on leadership in general. Do we really need another one? The answer is yes—because this book both introduces new information to the foundation of educational leadership and also takes an uncommon re-examination of classic ideas. Today's leaders need to be conversant with what we know, but they also need to be engaged in ongoing learning about what we still *don't* know if their practice is going to be relevant, thoughtful and student-centered in today and tomorrow's dynamic educational environments. To this end, our goal in this book is not to offer up a list of "what works," because what works in one space will not work in another. It is rather a book that seeks to present what has worked in certain places at certain times, coupled with a recognition that leadership is about taking this information, considering how it might make a positive impact in a particular context and then employing conceptual, technical and relational skills to support change in the best interests of students and educators. Put differently, this is not a book designed to tell leaders what to do—it is a book designed to introduce leaders to ideas that should empower and inform their leadership and to make them aware of possibilities they can consider as they make leadership in their own way, built on their strengths and buoying their weaknesses.

One of our central assumptions is that leadership is learned. Moreover, if leadership is learned then that learning must continue through the entire career of a leader AND it must account for the fact that we are constantly learning new things that should inform leadership in education. That means that leadership *is* learning—it is understanding the past but also keeping current, reading, viewing, sharing, critiquing, reflecting and creating. One of the oft-cited maxims among educational leaders is that if you don't read, you can't lead. We agree, but would expand it—if you don't learn, you can't lead. We believe that the continuing education of our leaders is imperative to education. This book is written in the spirit that education and leadership are always changing, and that the art and science of leadership is in one sense about what leaders do with information from the past, information about their context and information that shapes the way they think about the future. We also believe that leadership is fundamentally about advocating for equity, understanding education as a simultaneously local and global phenomenon, and about putting students and educators' interests at the forefront of the work.

Who Should Read This Book?

Do you train, study or teach educational leaders? We mean this book to be a useful resource for you and something that can guide you and your students through some of the central concepts of educational leadership. In addition to organizing the knowledge base in educational leadership into engaging chapters, the book includes several pedagogical and andragogical features designed to help you interact with students in meaningful ways, including discussion prompts that can be used face to face or online and a companion web site of complementary resources. This book is designed for course use in educational leadership preparation programs, but will also be helpful for professional development and self-development.

Are you an aspiring educational leader? If you are considering applying for educational leadership positions or if you are sure that leadership is in your future, this book is for you. On these pages we will introduce you to cutting-edge and classic research-based ideas related to educational leadership. We write about what you should know and help you think through the kind of dispositions, knowledge and skills you should develop as you look forward to influencing education in a new way.

Are you an educational leader? If you are already in a formal or informal leader in your organization, then this book is for you. We will help you look at the familiar in new ways and deepen your understanding of the ways that you can influence important teaching and learning issues, and the ways that these influence the ways you can, and cannot lead in your organization.

How Is the Book Organized?

This book is organized into 12 chapters, each of which is structured in a similar manner:

Chapter 1: Educational Leadership: From Classic to Cutting Edge
Chapter 2: Political Leadership
Chapter 3: Economic Leadership
Chapter 4: Cultural Leadership
Chapter 5: Moral Leadership
Chapter 6: Pedagogical Leadership
Chapter 7: Information Leadership
Chapter 8: Organizational Leadership
Chapter 9: Spiritual and Religious Leadership
Chapter 10: Temporal Leadership
Chapter 11: Health and Holistic Leadership
Chapter 12: Bringing It All Together: The Dynamic and Synergistic Leader

Each chapter begins discussing what leaders need to *learn* in the area, the concepts with which they need to be *literate*, how to *lead* in the area, then aspects of the area on which leaders should *reflect*. We discuss this approach in more detail at the end of Chapter 1. At the conclusion of each chapter, we include a discussion section with a collection of prompts, questions and activities suited for engaging ideas alone or with classmates. The book ends with a chapter that urges leaders to bring everything together as they approach their preparation and practice.

Beyond the Book: Introducing an eResource

In addition to the print book, we have developed presentations for each chapter that features input from the authors and from leading scholars and practitioners from around the world. In accordance with our belief that the knowledge base of educational leadership is always expanding, the site will be updated periodically, with new resources and features added as our knowledge of new issues expands. Considered together, through the book and website, we invite you to a conversation about educational leadership—one in which each of us has something important to learn and contribute. We invite you to an ongoing and dynamic conversation that will challenge and deepen your understanding about what leadership is, and what it is not.

Acknowledgments

The authors thank educational leaders from around the world who have shared their insights and expertise in practice and research. In particular, we thank the many students, colleagues and collaborators who have enriched and challenged our thinking around the issues in this book. Jeff is especially appreciative of the patience, love and support of Team Rainbow: Melanie, Holland, Bronwyn, Clodagh and Jürgen. Tony likewise thanks his family and friends for their steadfast backing of his work.

We reserve the highest praise for our editor at Routledge, Heather Jarrow. Without her encouragement, counsel and patience this book would not have happened.

CHAPTER 1

Educational Leadership: From Classic to Cutting Edge[1]

Leadership can help people and organizations accomplish great things, and it can plunge them to disaster. Leadership can help people and organizations behave in an ethical manner that benefits all, or compel them to be jaded, cynical or distrustful and focused on self-preservation or aggrandizement. Leadership can help improve the conditions for teaching and learning in a school and it can crush students and teachers as well. What is it that allows some leadership to be positive and other leadership to be negative? In order to begin an answer to this central question, we need to understand leadership— and more specifically leadership in *education*—in a broader perspective. In this book, we focus on the positive side of educational leadership but do so without avoiding the dark side of leadership—those aspects that undermine positive change. We find that this "eyes wide open" approach to understanding leadership is often absent in the dominant discourses that frame the study and practice of leadership. The bottom line is that leadership is a hammer—and a hammer can build or destroy.

We have examined classic and cutting-edge thinking about educational leadership, and our analysis pointed to 10 specific areas where leaders can make a difference in their organizations. Some of these are familiar, while others are under-represented in the traditional canon of ideas in the field. In this book, we do not pretend to offer a definitive statement about leadership, but rather seek to introduce new ways of thinking about "old" ideas while also offering some new areas relevant to twenty first century leadership. The 10 areas we have identified are: a. political leadership, b. economic leadership, c. cultural leadership, d. moral leadership, e. pedagogical leadership, f. information leadership, g. organizational leadership, h. spiritual and religious leadership, i. temporal leadership and j. health and holistic leadership.[1] Further, at the end of the book, we explore the nature of each of these aspects of education and the synergy between them through a concluding reflective chapter.

TEN IMPORTANT AREAS OF EDUCATIONAL LEADERSHIP PRACTICE

In this chapter, we will briefly explain 10 areas of practice with which educational leaders must be knowledgeable and conversant. This will in turn enable them to lead education in a more informed manner and then reflect on their leadership as something manifest both in the immediate context, and also in the context of national and global movements in education. In that sense readers will see us refer frequently to the concept of globalization and glocalization throughout the book. There is also a strong emphasis on leadership that promotes the values of equity and social justice. In the subsequent sections, we briefly touch on some of the concepts in each chapter, and then conclude this Introduction by explaining the developmental way we view educational leadership.

Political Leadership

Scholars of the politics of education have long argued that "educational leaders and school administrators find themselves in a continually contentious arena and vie for ways of balancing, directing, controlling, manipulating, managing, and surviving their edgy environments" (Lindle & Mawhinney, 2003, p. 3). Several researchers therefore suggest that educational leaders must develop a working understanding of politics, a base of knowledge that can also be called political literacy. Cassel and Lo (1997) cite Denver and Hands' (1990, p. 263) definition of political literacy as "the knowledge and understanding of the political process and political issues which enables people to perform their roles as citizens effectively" (pp. 320–321). Further, educational politics is commonly characterized as "the study of power, influence, and authority in the allocation of scarce and valued resources at various levels of the education sectors" (Johnson, 2003, p. 51). Considered in glocal perspective, this suggests that a politically literate educational leader is familiar both with various formal and informal processes by which people engage local and national issues and the outcomes and consequences of said processes. Fyfe (2007) argued that with community involvement and social and moral responsibility, political literacy is considered a core element that underpins effective education for citizenship. In recent years, interest has grown within the international community surrounding disengagement of young people from conventional political processes and structures (Berman, Marginson, Preston, McClellan & Arnove, 2003; Held, 2006; Sassen, 2006; Slaughter, 2004; Turner, 2002). Moreover, in relation to educational leaders, political literacy means developing an understanding of how to act as empowered participants in these processes that influence local, national, and international decisions and policies. Mitchell and Boyd (2001) explain this orientation by arguing that globalization "is fundamentally changing the parameters of political deliberation throughout the industrialized world, raising the stakes for education policy and changing the ground rules for its adoption and implementation" (Mitchell & Boyd, 2001, p. 60).

Among other important political dynamics particularly important for educational leaders to understand is the way that glocalization changes the nature of (de)centralized authority. Mitchell and Boyd (2001) explain that globalization causes

> "a simultaneous centralization and devolution of authority in ways that sharply reduce the power of professionals and middle-level officials in all types of organizations. The process is occurring in governments, corporations, and the public

bureaucracies responsible for developing and delivering public services such as education" (p. 71).

School leaders have been characterized as middle-level leaders (Spillane, Diamond, Burch, Hallett, Jita & Zoltners, 2002). As such, it is important for them to consider the precise forces that surround them. A political perspective focused on a closed-system school (Wirt & Kirst, 1997), district, provincial, state and/or national is a fine beginning, but ignores the basic reality that a school is embedded in a world political culture (Fowler, 2000). Further, "continued globalization of educational policy is sure to bring individual preferences, democratic redistribution of authority, and individual rights to personal liberty and diversity of opportunity back to the top of the political agenda" (Mitchell & Boyd, 2001, p. 74). These leaders need to generate a discourse constructed around new global alliances and extending the boundaries of political expression and participation. Based on assertions by Fyfe (2007), their "political interests, aspirations and actions presents a challenge to the relevance and effectiveness of existing educational programs intended to prepare them for political life" (p. 1).

Economic Leadership

For many educational leaders, the extent of their preparation with regard to economics has to do with balancing a school budget. However, educational leaders should also understand the economic realities of schools in relation to larger local and global trends. Schools are intended to educate and prepare students to enter into and thrive in a global economy (Spring, 1998). The literature is replete with commentary that state education and education reform initiatives are driven by the global economy (e.g., Barro, 2000; OECD, 2003; Sachs, 2005; Stevens & Weale, 2003). Much of the educational discourse around economic literacy has centered on the need for educators to focus on a "renewed attention to the technical importance of reading and math skills. The new economic environment can only be accessed successfully by individuals who can read fluently, compute efficiently, and do both with understanding" (Mitchell & Boyd, 2001, p. 73). These skills, in particular, are emphasized as a broader recognition of the need for students to participate in a knowledge-based economy that demands increasingly sophisticated and specialized capabilities (Stromquist, 2002). At the very least, educational leaders must have a basic understanding of microeconomics and macroeconomics, which would include literacy in the area of global economics. As Johnson (2003) explains in this distinction: "macroeconomics focuses on the economy as a whole: gross production, overall employment, and general price levels" (Heilbroner & Galbraith, 1990; Heilbroner & Thurow, 1994). "Microeconomics is concerned with the activities of individual consumers and producers" (p. 51). Additionally, Spring (2008) notes that "government and business groups talk about the necessity of schools meeting the needs of the global economy" (p. 331).

Yet Spring (1998) also cautions against a single-minded focus on global economics as the driver, education, as such an orientation, reduces "citizens to good workers and consumers" (p. xi). Further, emphasizing global economic viability in education may exacerbate global inequities, including: a. transnational brain drain/brain gain dynamics that would concentrate an inordinate amount of technical and conceptual expertise in a few affluent centers (Friedman, 2005; Spring, 1998), and b. a potentially negative impact on human and educational rights, due to extreme inequality with respect to access of quality educational materials and educators (Spring, 1998; Willinsky, 1998). Economic literacy for educational leaders, then, extends beyond technical expertise with budgets and encompasses an understanding of the opportunities and challenges provided by a rapidly globalizing economy.

Cultural Leadership

Educational leadership literature tends to emphasize school and organizational dynamics as a means of understanding culture (Cunningham & Gresso, 1993; Deal & Peterson, 1991, 1999). Kilmann, Saxton, and Serpa (1986) defined organizational culture as "the shared philosophies, ideologies, values, assumptions, beliefs, expectations, attitudes, and norms that knit a community together" (p. 89). There is a substantive body of research suggesting that leaders can influence organizational culture (Collins, 2001; Fullan, 2001; Schein, 1992). From this perspective culture is manifest in behavioral norms, hidden assumptions, and human nature. According to Saphier and King (1985), the 12 norms of school culture that affect school improvement are: (a) collegiality; (b) experimenta- tion; (c) high expectations; (d) trust and confidence; (e) tangible support; (f) reaching out to the knowledge bases; (g) appreciation and recognition; (h) caring, celebration, and humor; (i) involvement in decision making; (j) protection of what's important; (k) traditions and (l) honest, open communication. Leadership plays a role in establishing and sustaining norms related to these cultural dynamics. While these concepts are certainly important, the glocal perspective demands a rethinking of focus on these ways of understanding leadership.

It is important for school leaders to understand that people in a glocalized world exist in multiple cultures simultaneously, and the particular cultures of which each person is part have a profound effect on education (Spring, 2008). While this assertion is hardly novel, a growing body of research indicates that "cultures are slowly integrating into a single global culture" (Spring, 2008, p. 334). This global culture, connected most obviously by technology and interconnected multinational economic webs, is also merging a world knowledge base that in turn influences what and how topics are taught (Lechner & Boli, 2005). However, understanding that people are connected through a developing global culture is only part of the complexity educational leaders must understand. In addition to an awareness of such a macro culture, leaders must also under- stand two specific micro cultures as well, subculture dynamics and propriespect: Research indicates that subcultures have a strong influence on leadership practice in schools (Wolcott, 2003). Subcultures in schools often develop naturally around content areas, grade levels, and among educators and students who share specific values not fully held by the larger group. Educational leaders must be mindful of how their practice and decisions helps create an environment where subcultures can collaborate synergistically, or potentially pit them in adversarial stances (Brooks & Jean-Marie, 2007).

Propriespect is the notion that each person constructs a unique cultural experience rather than necessarily adopting or assimilating group and/or organizational values and norms. Put differently, everyone has an individual culture. Wolcott (1991) suggested the concept "as a complement to the global reference to all the information aggregated within an entire cultural heritage" and recognized a "need to specify the particular information that any particular human, who must therefore be a member of a particular subset of human groups, actually knows" (p. 257). Thinking of culture in this way is very similar to the widely recognized notion that each student learns differently, and that educators and educational leaders who individualize their practice can have the most positive influence on a student. Understanding culture in terms of propriespect, an educational leader will understand and value the importance of individual histories, values and beliefs in addition to those that espoused in plenum. Indeed, leaders with this kind of literacy might be said to practice a culturally relevant leadership, similar in some ways to culturally relevant pedadgogy (Ladson-Billings, 1995a, 1995b), an approach to education centered on individual children's culture. As a final note about culture, educational leaders must understand that each of these forms of culture are nested within each other in a unique manner for each person (see Figure 1.1). Certain people will interact and share certain values, beliefs, and norms at various levels, but each experiences glocal culture in a discrete manner.

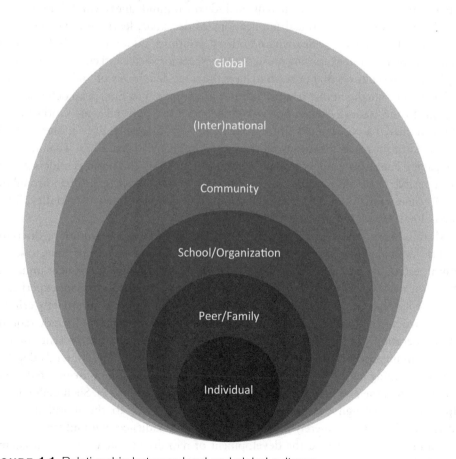

FIGURE 1.1 Relationship between local and global cultures

Moral Leadership

In this section, we argue that use of a moral literacy approach to analyzing and interpreting social events, social justice, equity and equality builds amity, harmony, and trust among stakeholders, positioning educational leaders to make risky, yet transformational and ethically responsible decisions for the benefit of morally literate school communities, morally literate nations, and a morally literate world (Paul-Doscher & Normore, in press). Since public life in democracy is interwoven by social values, opportunities to engage in moral literacy interpretations enable the public to come to grips with the common good for the greater society. Moral literacy promotes development of knowledge and moral virtues in students, and helps to develop skills for moral reasoning. To become moral agents, educators need to acknowledge and honor the importance of assuming responsibility to be informed before making moral judgments—whether locally, nationally or globally. Tuana (2003, p.8) asserts that social imperatives must be taken into account. She states, "Our sense of ourselves, as well as what others think of us, often rests on the extent to which we live up to these virtues" (p. 8). Consequently, developing skills for moral reasoning is necessary, whereby students, and those who teach them, develop the skills and dispositions to identify the critical values at play. Tuana further maintains that such skills include open-mindedness, careful attention to others' views, considering ethical implications of decisions, learning how to evaluate strengths and weakness of our own and others' positions, taking responsibility for our actions and beliefs, and exercising fairness and respect for social and cultural differences.

While some cultures do not seem to have the same definitions of "fairness" or "respect" (e.g., in fundamentalist Islamic cultures as compared to European definitions, or adhering to the Geneva conventions as guidelines for "civilized war"), other moral virtues are shared across many cultures (Normore & Paul-Dosher, 2007). These include honesty, fairness, respect, responsibility, and caring (Christians, 2003; Tuana, 2003). By engaging education leaders in such a discourse, analysis can harness understanding of responsible leadership and learn the reflective practices that can filter throughout school systems and connect to morally literate citizenship (Kohn, 1997; Malley, 2005; Tuana, 2003; Widdowson, 1995).

Morally literate citizenship requires exposure to media representation, discourse about the dominant hegemony, and dealing with moral relativism as it pertains to social, cultural, economic, and political issues. Tuana (2003) asks, "what stronger argument is there for making moral literacy a component of our formal educational experience" (p.4)? Media often engage in language practices that legitimize or alternately criticize existing structures of power (Merrill, 1990; Ranly, 1992). But, moral literacy requires the consideration of alternative discourses and subversive texts that present counter-points to an unexamined or dominant consensus. Christians (2003) contends that "on those invigorating occasions when the moral contours of the taken-for-granted world are illuminated, the news media enhance our social dialogue" (p. 8). Such dialogue can help penetrate through the political and economic surface to the moral dynamics underneath. Rather than merely providing readers and audiences with information, the press' aim is, or ought to be, the development of morally literate citizens (Christians, Ferre, & Fackler, 1993).

As private citizens, professional educators, and public servants, our University students will need to make numerous moral decisions throughout their lives and how these decisions have impact on not only their immediate surroundings but also on the larger global community. These decisions are often based on exposure to media texts in which students can theorize, engage in news discourse, and grapple with their own personal and professional codes of ethics. However, in these contexts, many educators (e.g., teachers, teacher educators, school leaders, leadership educators, etc.) are so occupied with trying to defend basic working conditions and what they perceive to be the gains of "progressive" education under fierce accountability policies that they often fail to see the bigger picture of authentic teaching and learning experiences—those that truly prepare students as responsible citizens on the global stage. We argue that educational leaders and those who prepare them must consciously and intentionally take the actions that s/he believes are in the best interests of the students, while modeling the importance of caring and just relationships and understanding that his/her decisions have consequences across entire systems. Doing this will afford the educational leader the opportunity to cooperate with all the stakeholders in the community, assuring that the school will reflect the communities' intended goals—to assist young people in fully realizing their potential, with the understanding that they are connected to others through a web of national and international inter-relationships of which they may not even be conscious, but one that exists nonetheless. We will next discuss the role of *pedagogical literacy* and *information literacy* and how these literacies play a vital role for understanding glocalization. We acknowledge that literacies are common to all disciplines, to all learning environments and to all levels of education and recognize the disparities in learning styles and in the nature and development of literacy in different countries.

Pedagogical Leadership

In the context of literacy being understood as an evolving concept, we argue that a particular form of literacy, pedagogical literacy, is an important cognitive tool for a developed conceptualization of pedagogical content knowledge and that, by extension, being *pedagogically* literate is an integral feature of being a professional educator. We further argue that literacy can empower learners to "design their own representations of knowledge rather than absorbing representations preconceived by others; that it can be used to support the deep reflective thinking that is necessary for meaningful learning; and that it enables mindful and challenging learning" (Maclellan, 2008, p. 1986). With powerful connections to the other literacies, pedagogical literacy is a reflexive concept in which learning (through a knowledge-transforming model) about pedagogical content knowledge, teaching and learning, and assessment and evaluation, is the essential means through which the pedagogical reasoning develops (Ludwig & Herschell, 1998). According to the Organization for Economic Cooperation and Development (OECD), in its functional form literacy is less the ability to read and write and more the ability to comprehend and use written script to serve the purposes of everyday life at home, at work, in the community, and in the world. Critical literacy, underpinned by different theoretical perspectives (see Robinson & Robinson, 2003), involves the "analysis and critique of the relationships among texts, language, power, social groups and social practices, and shows us ways of looking at texts to question and challenge the attitudes, values and beliefs that lie beneath the surface" (Maclellan, 2008, p. 1987).

A strong movement from psychological models of learning (i.e., reading and writing) to a more contextual approach has been under way in recent years. Contextual approach redefines literacy as a set of social and cultural practices (Maclellan, 2008). According to Ludwig and Herschel (1998), "Recent examinations of literacy teaching and learning practices have drawn on multiple perspectives that recognize a complex socio-cultural interaction between teacher/parent and student/child" (p. 7). These authors further assert that sociological, linguistic, philosophical and pedagogical perspectives must be addressed if educational leaders are to adequately account for the multiple practices that make up students' literacy experiences. Furthermore, Gee (1991) reiterated that literacy practices are intricately related to demands of work, identity and citizenship and are clearly implicated in an educational agenda concerned with social justice. It is within this context that teachers and education leaders will need to ask, "How is effective instruction conducted to students with diverse backgrounds and how do students learn about and use multiple literacies in the complex, dynamic and interactive environments of the home, the classroom, and beyond?"

Researchers (e.g., Ludwig & Herschel, 1998; Freebody & Luke, 2003) alerted educators to the fact that international community groups have reacted to the literacy situation as one in crisis due to a "climate where fair and equitable practices are competing for space with powerful economic rationalist considerations." (Ludwig & Herschel, 1998, p. 7). Community demands range from calls for "back to the basics" through to "progressive" personal growth models of curriculum and pedagogy. As a response, "skills", "growth and heritage" and "critical-cultural" approaches to literacy have been vigorously debated (Ludwig & Herschel, 1998). In many sites, literacy educators seem faced with two basic options: that of "competencies", "basic skills" and "accountability" on the one hand, and that of "experience", "process" and "personal empowerment" on the other (Freebody & Luke, 2003). To be pedagogically literate, educators must be able to access and use the specialized written documents of pedagogical knowledge (Olson, 2001, 2003), thereby allowing them to hypothesize as to reasons for the success or otherwise of pedagogical practices. Pedagogical literacy is therefore the fundamental competence of being able to read, understand and criticize the documents and other information that make up the professional knowledge base of teaching and learning. Since information is expanding at an unprecedented rate, and enormously rapid strides are being made in technology for storing, organizing, and accessing the ever-growing wave of information (Picciano, 2006; Tansley, 2006), we argue that information literacy must also play an equally vital role in the preparation of educational leaders if these leaders are to effectively take their place as responsible citizens in the world.

Information Leadership

The combined effect of the rapid growth of information is an increasingly fragmented information base, a large component of which is available only to people with money and/or acceptable institutional affiliations. In the recent past, the outcome of these challenges has been characterized as the "digital divide" between the information "haves" and "have nots" along racial and socio economic lines that seem to widen as time passes (del Val & Normore, 2008). The digital divide addresses issues concerning equal opportunity, equity and access that have an effect on the development of marginalized and otherwise disadvantaged students in education systems (del Val & Normore, 2008; Selwyn, Gorard, & Williams, 2001). As a result, those with limited access become less prepared for the increasingly global market that is emerging in the twenty first century. Research (e.g., Carvin, 2006; Hage, 2005; Picciano, 2006; Tansley, 2006; Welner & Weitzman, 2005) clearly indicates that this is a global phenomenon that has caused a widening equity gap in primary, secondary and higher education across all continents. Consequently, information literacy has become more critical than ever as discourses about the knowledge economy focus on the necessity of educating ALL students with skills for the global workplace.

To be "information literate", school leaders and those who prepare them will need to know why, when, and how to use all of these tools and think critically about the information they provide. To do so will enable educators to interpret and make informed judgments as users of information sources. It will also enable them to become producers of information in their own right, and thereby become more powerful participants in society. This is part of the basic entitlement of every citizen, in every democracy in the world, to freedom of expression and the right to information (Abdelaziz, 2004). It is instrumental in building and sustaining democracy. These skills are viewed by many policy makers and educators as critical to the creation of an equitable global "Information Society" in which both developed and developing nations can share in social and economic development. Information literacy aims to develop *both* critical understanding *and* active participation.

We contend that information literacy forms the basis for lifelong learning and should be introduced wherever possible within national curricula as well as in tertiary, non-formal and lifelong education. Drawing on the work of Reich (1990), Mitchell and Boyd (2001) suggest that "under the influence of the new information technologies (IT), machines can easily outthink and outperform anyone whose academic skills do not include understanding as well as efficiency" and that "Managing the productivity of information-age machinery will require workers who have a more comprehensive and a subtler grasp of both reading and mathematics than has heretofore been expected of public school students" (p. 73). Information literacy is concerned with teaching and learning about the whole range of information sources and formats. Thus, the various technologies of public communication (i.e., print, Internet, television, radio, etc.) ought to engender information literacy. As a result, information literacy is a social process for understanding, finding, evaluating, communicating and using information—activities which may be accomplished in part by fluency with IT, in part by sound investigative methods, but, most important, through critical discernment and reasoning.

Using print media as an integral part of the educational leadership experience, for example, can stimulate the moral imagination and help produce information literate citizens. Research on media representations provides comment on the media coverage directed at various social, cultural and political issues. Texts, film, television and books have focused on analyses of public debates during political campaigns, assessment processes of schools and education policies, and social and cultural issues (Shapiro, 1989; Smith, 1999; Taylor, 1997). Studies have reported that media, such as film, newspapers and magazines, influences popular beliefs about current affairs (Giroux, 2002). For example, Thomas (2006) cited a study that investigated the content, effect, and intent, or influence, of Brisbane newspaper reports on the issues of entrance to tertiary education. A strong correlation between content of press items and public opinion was found, together with evidence of agenda setting involving the selection and omission of items and preferential media access to public elites. As such, it reflects the emphasis on news found in much of the work on media discourse and questions the ability of journalists and news reporters to adequately inform the public and policy makers on national and global issues (Afflerbach & Moni, 1994). Tuana (2003) argued, for example, that "the news media . . . in striving to provide interesting sound bites about human cloning has often been ethically irresponsible in failing to adequately explain the science of cloning" and "politicians debating cloning legislation often do not acknowledge the full range of scientific options that are available" (p. 3). Media knowledge—as an integral form of information literacy and communication is always a form of social practice (Giroux, 2002). Researchers (e.g., Thomas, 2006) have argued that the press constructs a hegemonic consensus within a framework given by "the powerful and the privileged of society who are seen by the press to be legitimate spokespersons for society . . . depicting reported crises as a symbol of moral decay . . . the work ethic and moral order" (p. 34). Thomas emphasized the ideological dominance to the process of hegemonic struggle—a struggle in which the news media can work to give hegemonic consent to the maintenance of existing political, social, and economic arrangements. According to Fairclough (1995, p. 49):

> theorization of news as discourse highlights the discursive nature of media power and its influence on knowledge, beliefs, values, social relations and social identities through its particular ways of representing the world, its particular constructions of social identities and its particular constructions of social relations.

As suggested in the research (e.g., Abdelaziz, 2004; Burkhardt, MacDonald, & Rathemacher, 2005; Correia, 2002) information literacy initiates, sustains, and extends lifelong learning through abilities which may use technologies but are ultimately independent of them. As information is increasingly codified in digital forms (Correia, 2002), new skills are needed to operate the technology to search for, organize, manage information and use it to solve problems and create new knowledge and cultural products. Since the Internet is a common information and communication tool globally, IL is often understood as digital literacy in which computer literacy, media literacy and media education are integral components. As Abdelaziz (2004, p. 3) claims:

> Introducing new media technology—let alone the kinds of "critical thinking" and the new pedagogies associated with IL– is almost bound to meet with considerable inertia, if not overt resistance . . . Still, a vigorous IL campaign could result in the long run in the emergence of an "information culture."

Organizational Leadership

More than ever, leaders are expected to be change agents in their respective organizations. Yet, leadership turnover continues to rise and organizations continue to struggle in their efforts to confront the fearsome adaptive challenges of the global age (Clark, 2007). We contend that educational leaders need to understand theories of organizations, socialization patterns, and how their leadership practices influence organizational dynamics. Teachers and administrators who understand the politics in schools can operate more successfully to facilitate change. However, possessing the skill set is necessary to identify and influence common social patterns that affect their work in school organizations. Research on organizational dynamics, socialization, behavior and learning (e.g., Barth, 2003; Bolman & Deal, 2007; Clark, 2007; Collins, 2001; Harvey & Drolet, 2004; Hoban, 2002; Normore, 2006; Senge, Smith, Kruschwitz, Laur, & Schley, 2008; Shafritz & Ott, 2005) identified several social patterns common to organizations. Among these are patterns of organizational culture, diversity, values and goals. Goals, derived from the organization's mission and strategic planning process, provide purpose and direction for organizational members and work groups. Goals have the most impact on people's behavior if they are clear and owned by individual members and/or by the collective (Fullan, 2001; Senge et al, 2008). Of course, people differ with respect to the way they respond to and internalize organizational goals. Some of these differences have little influence on organizational life, while others have a substantial affect. Diversity may be in terms of personality, motivation, cognitive style, leadership/followership style, gender, ethnicity, class, age, competency, seniority, organizational function, and so on. Understanding and appreciating these differences is necessary for successful collaboration. Senge and colleagues (2008) maintain that a revolution is underway in today's organizations. According to these authors, organizations around the world are boldly leading the change from dead-end business-as-usual tactics to transformative strategies that are essential for creating a flourishing, sustainable world. Today's most innovative leaders, educational and otherwise, are recognizing that, for the sake of organizations and our world, we must implement revolutionary—not just incremental—changes in the way we live and work.

Other important organizational processes requiring attention include communication, decision making, conflict management, and bureaucratic social patterns. Earle and Kruse (1999) discuss the importance of bureaucratic social patterns, which are characterized by a fixed division of labor, hierarchy of offices, explicit rules, and specialized job training. When translated to school systems these authors contend that certain political, social communal patterns, and patterns of inequality based on social class, race, and gender unfortunately, yet predictably, influence organizational norms. Each of these patterns describes a variety of often unexamined social patterns that affect how students experience the practices of schooling; on the complexity of school change and how understanding these patterns can help create collaborative school organizations of promise and optimism. By working collaboratively across boundaries, organizations are already exploring and putting into place unprecedented solutions that move beyond just being "less bad" to creating pathways that will enable us to flourish in an increasingly interdependent world (Senge et al., 2008).

The "iceberg metaphor" (see Clark, 2007) has sometimes been used to make a distinction between the visible formal organization and the informal features of organizational life lying hidden below the water, which also require examination. According to Clark, if we pay attention to things like goals, roles, communication, and decision-making processes we will have a good grasp of the dynamics of organizational life (the above-the-water features). However, our actual behavior (and the behavior of others) in organizations doesn't always follow the logical, rational, systematic, and linear contours expected. Sometimes the irrational, the rational, the covert, the political (both intentional and unintentional), the nonlinear, or the unconsciously motivated seems to occur and may be quite disruptive to the organization (Clark, 2007). Full organizational literacy also requires that we gain an understanding of these under-the-water organizational features as well.

School organizations are meaningfully connected to the external environment (customers, suppliers, vendors, government, competition, etc.) such that change in one of these external areas is likely to affect conditions inside the organization as well. Furthermore, the functional units of schools (departments, divisions, etc.) are connected to one another in such a way that events taking place in one part of the system affect other parts of the school operations as well. The big picture created by this "systems perspective" (see Clark, 2007; Senge et al., 2008) is the foundation for developing and maintaining a collaboratively interdependent organization. The systems perspective should guide organizational design, work design, strategic planning, communication, compensation plans, decision-making procedures, problem solving, and so on.

In his path-breaking contribution to the study of leadership and organizational change Clark (2007) studied large-scale organizational change in business, healthcare, government, education, and the nonprofit sector and unveiled the "Power Curve of Change" framework and EPIC system for change management (Evaluate, Prepare, Implement, Consolidate) for leaders who are charged to lead high-stakes change initiatives in their organizations. Clark argues for a strategic-level road map for the every-day needs of leaders who must respond to all types of adaptive challenges to remain competitive and healthy. He further iterates that in order for leaders—and those who prepare and train them—to effectively step up in their roles as organizationally literate, they will need to develop the indispensable competency of leading change in a permanently and profoundly different age. Change rarely fails for lack of strategy—that only the discretionary efforts of people can make change happen—and this requires leadership and energy management.

All education leaders need a conceptual road map for successfully navigating the roles they play in the various school organizations of which they are a part. If educators have little understanding of organizational processes, they may fail to influence effectively and may even inadvertently inhibit organizational effectiveness. Organizational literacy is necessary for education leaders to make a contribution and obtain satisfaction in joining with others in tasks that clearly see the interconnectedness of the organization to the larger world.

Spiritual and Religious Leadership

Leaders should be mindful of differences and similarities with respect to the spiritual/religious orientation of stakeholders and of how these things influence their own leadership behavior. Importantly, religion and spirituality are not one and the same. As Dantley (2005) explains

> "spirituality inspires creativity, inquiry, and transformative conduct. Our spirit enables us to connect with other human beings; it underpins our ability to take steps to dismantle marginalizing conditions while simultaneously creating strategies to bring about radical changes to less-than-favorable circumstances. Our spirituality is the core of who we are. It is the place of our authentic selves or the genuine persons that we are. It is the place where motivation and inspiration live. Our spirituality connects our lives to meaning and purpose" (p. 654).

Dantley (2005) further clarifies the relationship of spirituality to religion by suggesting that religions help give order and systematic meaning to spiritual experiences: "religion is built upon the premise that order, continuity, and stability are essential to any civil society" (p. 653). Yet other researchers have noted that religion can mean a systematic devotion to many things. For example, Bracher, Panoch, Piediscalzi and Uphoff (1974) explain that "the broad definition envisions religion as any faith or set of values to which an individual or group give ultimate loyalty . . . Buddhism, Taoism, Ethical Culture, secularism, humanists, scientism, nationalism, money, and power illustrate this concept of religion" (p. 5). Furthermore, this list emphasizes the need for spiritual and religious literacy to include a sensitivity and understanding of religious diversity (Uphoff, 2001), in its many forms.

Skepticism is sometimes expressed about the legitimacy of spirituality in the workplace, especially in public education (Fairholm, 1997). However, Thompson (2004) attests that spiritual-based leadership does not challenge the separation of church and state delineated in the United States Constitution's Establishment Clause. Klenke (2006) offers the following explanation:

> Spirituality is often defined by what it is not. Spirituality . . . is not religion. Organized religion looks outward; depends on rites and scripture; and tends to be dogmatic, exclusive, and narrowly based on a formalized set of beliefs and practices. Spirituality, on the other hand, looks inward, tends to be inclusive and more universally applicable, and embraces diverse expressions of interconnectedness (p. 59).

Research maintains that spirituality is the ability to lead from deeper levels of experience, meaning, and wisdom (Thompson, 2004). Fairholm (1997) concurs stating that "Spirituality does not apply to particular religions, although the values of some religions may be part of a person's spiritual focus. Said another way, spirituality is the song we all sing. Each religion has its own singer" (p. 29). Fairholm (1997) argues that as individuals begin to differentiate religion from spirituality, the role of spirituality within individual and organizational life becomes clear. He concludes:

Our spirit is what makes us human and individual. It determines who we are at work. It is inseparable from self. We draw on our central values in how we deal with people every day. Our values dictate whether we set a good example, take care of people, or try to live the Golden Rule. Our spirituality helps us think and act according to our values (p. 77).

Spirituality's role in aligning a leader's actions with their values is a distinctive characteristic not shared by religion. Religion guides by specific doctrine whereas spirituality is generic and affords the leader a dynamic quality capable of capitalizing on the diverse belief systems operating within an organization (Riaz & Normore, 2008).

Given these definitions of spirituality and religion, the literate educational leader will be sensitive to the notion that, regardless of religion, and even in the absence of an espoused religious denomination, all people can have spiritual experiences.

Temporal Leadership

As Hall (1959) pointed out, "temporality . . . is tied into life in so many ways that it is difficult to ignore it" (p. 45). Yet understanding this important and neglected aspect of educational leadership can help leaders more successfully design and implement meaningful change in schools. In the most basic sense, temporal literacy has to do with being able to read and understand the history, present and future of people and institutions. Several leadership scholars have noted the importance of understanding the history of an organization (Fullan, 2001; Deal & Peterson, 1991; Schein, 1992). Without an astute understanding of the history of a school and community, leaders run the risk of getting the school stuck in the rut of policy churn, a cycle of action that yields no substantive or continuous improvement (Hess, 1999). This understanding of history should inform educational leadership practice as leaders seek to implement various school reforms (Brooks, 2006). Yet a solid understanding of an organization and community's history should inform contemporary practice by suggesting which types of change were successful and which failed. Moreover, considered in glocal perspective, an understanding of history at local, national, and global levels—and an understanding of how all of these histories have been and continue to influence one another (Friedman, 2005)—allows a leader to avoid repeating the mistakes of the past.

It is also important for educational leaders to understand the future. Traditionally, the orientation for this understanding has been strategic planning (Kaufman & Herman, 1991), yet educational researchers in globalization studies suggest that a more appropriate approach might be found in future trends (Green, 1997). There is ample evidence that strategic planning was never effective in business, and that educators likewise have reaped little, if any, benefit from the process, despite ongoing enthusiasm for the approach (Mintzberg, 1994). As an alternative to strategic planning, future trends instead look at longitudinal data and, rather than looking at them in isolation (treating the school as a closed system), integrates these data with other longitudinal data to promote connected leadership via a future trends framework. Marx (2006a, 2006b) identified sixteen distinct future trends of immediate concern to educational leaders:

1. For the first time in history, the old will outnumber the young. (Note: This aging trend generally applies to developed nations. In underdeveloped nations, just is opposite is true: the young will substantially outnumber the old.)
2. Majorities will become minorities, creating ongoing challenges for social cohesion.
3. Social and intellectual capital will become economic drivers, intensifying competition for well-educated people.
4. Technology will increase the speed of communication and the pace of advancement or decline.
5. The Millennial Generation will insist on solutions to accumulated problems and injustices, while an emerging Generation E will call for equilibrium.
6. Standards and high-stakes tests will fuel a demand for personalization in an education system increasingly committed to lifelong human development.
7. Release of human ingenuity will become a primary responsibility of education and society.
8. Continuous improvement will replace quick fixes and defense of the status quo.
9. Scientific discoveries and societal realities will force widespread ethical choices.
10. Common opportunities and threats will intensify a worldwide demand for planetary security.
11. Polarization and narrowness will bend toward reasoned discussion, evidence, and consideration of varying points of view.
12. International learning, including diplomatic skills, will become basic, as nations vie for understanding and respect in an interdependent world.
13. Greater numbers of people will seek personal meaning in their lives in response to an intense, high-tech, always-on, fast-moving society.
14. Understanding will grow that sustained poverty is expensive, debilitating, and unsettling.
15. Pressure will grow for society to prepare people for jobs and careers that may not currently exist.
16. Competition will increase to attract and keep qualified educators.

Marx (2006, Winter) explains the importance of these trends:

all organizations, especially education systems, are of this world, not separate from it. To earn their legitimacy, they need to be connected with the communities, countries, and world they serve. Unless they are constantly scanning the environment, educators will soon find themselves isolated . . . and out of touch . . . Understanding these forces is the key to un-locking rigidity and reshaping our schools, colleges, and other institutions for the future. In a fast-changing world, looking at tomorrow and seeing it only as a little bit more or a little bit less of today won't cut it as we move into the future. As educators and community leaders, we need to use powerful trends data, coupled with imagination, as we plan ahead. A challenge will be to not only develop a plan but to turn it into a living strategy—a strategic vision that will help us lead our students, schools, and communities into an even more successful future (p. 4).

Health and Holistic Leadership

We also cover several aspects of health and holistic leadership, being mindful of the need for leaders to care for themselves and for others. This often-neglected aspect of leaders' work demands more attention, and we have endeavored to introduce key concepts in this area. In this chapter, we iterate that health and Holistic leadership proffer seven fundamental assumptions about the nature of effective leadership:

1. Successful outcomes result from an orientation toward development.
2. The healthiest and most productive development is done collaboratively.
3. The leadership unit shapes the context of collaboration.
4. The core leadership unit is the individual, which makes every participant a leader within his or her own sphere of influence.
5. The intrinsic desire for meaningful purpose suggests that every individual wants to realize his or her best potential.
6. Holistically-led collaboration requires that the participant's right to self-determination be respected.
7. The exercise of self-determination in a way that realizes the individual's best potential, results from an iterative process that must be supported.

Discussions of health and holistic leadership vary in terms of which aspects of humanity appear to warrant our focus and sustained attention. For example, based on her academic background in organizational learning and social work, as well as her experiences with leadership training in a variety of organizations, Julie Orlov (2003) states that holistic leadership is "being able to lead from the mind, the heart, and the soul" (p. 1). Clearly, there is no reference to the physical (i.e., the body) aspect of holistic leadership development. In stark contrast, Sinclair (2007), in her treatise on how to become an enlightened leader, emphasizes the importance of paying attention to the body for gaining new insights for leadership. Alternatively, Taggart (2010), a self-described student of leadership for over 20 years and creator of a leadership consulting organization, omitted any references to mind, body, and spirit in presenting his model of holistic leadership. Therefore, we may infer that the apparent lack of consensus regarding holistic leadership may be the result of authors' use of different terminology, at least to some extent.

We introduce two educators who share shared poignant and relevant experiences that were shared through the lens of growth and self-reflection about two leadership development projects in the United States (e.g., teacher leadership, youth leadership). Engaging learners and leaders in authentic learning experiences (e.g., self-reflection, ethics of responsibility, moral literacy, spiritual development and connectedness) signifies critical steps toward a holistic educational approach to moral and leadership development. As initially highlighted by the educators, these projects were intended to engage in critical reflection and to cultivate development of morally literate and responsive leaders in education. Participants ranged from PK-12 teachers, administrators, to higher education faculty, community and youth leadership. The process of reflecting critically on shared experiences, as both inquirers and respondents (see

Lincoln et al., 2011), presents a series of discussion questions for health and holistic leadership development.

FROM LITERACY TO LEADERSHIP: A DEVELOPMENTAL APPROACH

In the preceding sections, we discussed several forms of literacy that research suggests are necessary to be educational leaders in the twenty first century. However, it is important to recognize that the bodies of knowledge of each of the domains exhibit certain qualities that are important for those who prepare and practice educational leadership to consider. In particular, we argue that (a) each of these areas has ecological and dynamic qualities and that (b) educational leaders must understand and take responsibility for the way their unique agency enhances their ability to influence each of these domains and to translate literacy into leadership.

Each domain of knowledge is constantly changing, and as concepts emerge in one literacy domain they necessarily influence others (Capra, 2003). Some of these relationships are immediately observable, while others are more opaque. Knowledge is protean, in a constant state of revision, refinement, and critique as new ideas and empirical evidence emerges (Kuhn, 1962). This basic idea has permeated the knowledge base(s) of educational leadership for some time and the notion that knowledge in educational leadership can be viewed from multiple perspectives simultaneously, each of which evolves over time, is widely accepted (English, 2002, 2003a, 2003b, 2006).

All forms of leadership we name in this book are interconnected. As such, "the more we study the major problems of our time, the more we come to realize that they cannot be understood in isolation. They are systemic problems, which mean that they are interconnected and interdependent" (Capra, 1996, p. 3). We must move from shallow ecology toward a paradigm of deep ecology (Capra, 1996) in our understanding of leadership, the fundamental difference between the two being that the shallow ecologist focuses on issues as part of an isolated and closed system, and the deep ecologist conceives issues as a meta-system of several interconnected systems. This ecosystem includes not only physical aspects of existence such as the environment and sustainable resources, but also the interconnected and inter-related nature of societies, ideas, the future and past, and between the other various forms of literacy we have described above. Put differently, "these areas stretch across the boundaries of nation-states and continents with the local and the global becoming enmeshed" (Spring, 2008, p. 334).

The implications of glocalization are profound, and the consequences of not understanding the way that the local and global are interconnected will increase over time. As Senge (2008) suggested, there is an understanding gap between the implications of this interconnectivity and our understanding of this interconnectivity.

For educational leaders, it is important to consider how this understanding gap limits educational resources they provide students and their school systems. It should also give educational leaders and those who prepare them cause for concern, as their lack of understanding may not be preparing prospective leaders for the world in which they will lead.

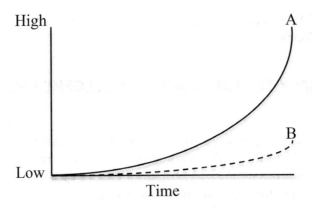

FIGURE 1.2 Relationship between (A) the implications of interconnectivity, and (B) our understanding of interconnectivity.

Note. Adapted from "Educating for systems citizenship," address by P. Senge, June 2008, Systems thinking and dynamic modeling for K-12 education conference: Wellesley, MA.

As a final note about these ten areas of educational leadership, it is important to mention that educational leaders are uniquely positioned to influence each of these domains in that they help shape the conceptualization and practice of education in various settings. This assertion is based on a belief that "at the core of most definitions of leadership are two functions: providing direction and exercising influence. Leaders mobilize and work with others to achieve shared goals" (Leithwood & Riehl, 2003). Understanding, practicing, and studying educational leadership as a glocal endeavor is complicated, but imperative if we are to provide students with an engaging and relevant educational experience. This approach to leadership demands that educational leaders develop new skills, and broaden their understanding of the way local and global forces are enmeshed in an increasingly sophisticated manner.

AN EDUCATIONAL LEADERSHIP DEVELOPMENT FRAMEWORK

We think of leadership development as something that occurs in four cyclical stages: learning, literacy, leadership and reflection. Together, these four stages make up the educational leadership development framework:

Learning: For each topic an educational leader must face, they should first *learn* as much as possible about the topic. This means staying in touch with best practices and current relevant research.

Literacy: As an educational leader's knowledge grows, they must then become *literate* in how the specific issue looks in their school and educational setting. This means gathering information on their specific context and identifying the strengths and weaknesses of their school community in relation to that issue. This entails understanding and analysis of human and educational resources, organizational dynamics and identification of possible ways leaders might influence the issue through leadership, management and administration.

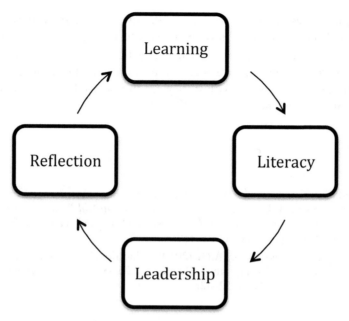

FIGURE 1.3 Cyclical Approach to Educational Leadership Development

Leadership: The *leadership* stage represents moving from thought into action. In order to positively, intentionally and proactively influence various dynamics in a school, action is required. We discuss various strategies for approaching this work, with a particular emphasis on how the specific conceptual, technical and interpersonal skills needed to effect change.

Reflection: Once leaders have started to act, they must reflect on their actions and on the way chance is influencing the organization. The reflection stage emphasizes not only personal reflection, but the ongoing collecting and analysis of relevant data that will help educators determine if the change is having the desired change at the appropriate organizational level. The reflection stage is also crucial in making sure that leadership in a school is not characterized by random acts of improvement and is instead a coherent system that refreshes itself with new information at the learning stage.

This cyclical approach to leadership allows leaders great flexibility and encourages both reflective practice and a dynamic approach to their work. Furthermore, we recognize that this approach is in keeping with current research that suggests educational leaders (a) work in dynamic and fluid educational settings where personnel and policies change, (b) should sometimes lead and sometimes follow, depending on the situation, and (c) should adapt as new information and research becomes available. Educational leaders must understand and take responsibility for the way their unique agency enhances their ability to influence each of these domains and to translate learning and literacy into leadership.

As a final note about our perspective on educational leadership, we suggest that it is important to focus on how educational leaders can influence processes and outcomes for both equity and excellence. This means that educational leaders must not only focus on academic measures of success such as grades or standardized achievement scores, but they must also balance such efforts by being advocates on issues of access, process and outcomes for traditionally or systematically under-represented or marginalized people. In the following chapters, we begin our examination of key concepts that leaders must learn about and be literate with if they are to practice leadership and ultimately reflect on what they have done.

NOTE

1   The introduction is taken from the original article (with minor changes) by the same two authors, that was published in the SAGE journal, *Educational Policy: An Interdisciplinary Journal of Policy and Practice*. The authors substantially expanded the ideas from their article into chapters. The original source is as follows:

> Brooks, J. S., & Normore, A.H. (2010). Educational leadership and globalization: Literacy for a glocal perspective. *Educational Policy: An Interdisciplinary Journal of Policy and Practice*, 24(1), 52–82.

REFERENCES

Abdelaziz, A. (2004). Information literacy for lifelong learning. Paper presented at the World Library and Information Congress: 70th IFLA General Conference and Council, p. 4. Available [online]: http://ifla.org/IV/ifla70/papers/116e-Abid.pdf

Afflerbach, P., & Moni, K. (1994). Legislators, reporters, and reading assessment. *Reading Research Report, 31*. National Research Center, College Park, MD.

Anderson, G. L. (1991). Cognitive politics of principals and teachers: Ideological control in an elementary school. In J. Blase (ed), *The Politics of life in schools: Power, conflict, and cooperation*, pp. 120–30. Newbury Park: Sage.

Anderson, G., & Herr. K. (1993). The micropolitics of student voices: Moving from diversity of bodies to diversity of voices in schools. In C. Marshall (ed), *The New Politics of Race and Gender*, pp. 58–68. New York: Falmer.

Anderson-Levitt, K. (2003). A world culture of schooling? In K. Anderson-Levitt (Ed.), *Local meanings, global schooling: Anthropology and world culture theory*, pp. 1–26. New York: Palgrave Macmillan.

Apple, M., Kenway, J., & Singh, M. (Eds.). (2005). *Globalizing education: Policies, pedagogies, & politics*. New York: Peter Lang.

Barro, R. (2000). *Education and economic growth*. Paris: OECD.

Barth, R. S. (2003) *Lessons learned: Shaping relationships and the culture of the workplace*. Thousand Oaks, CA: Corwin Press.

Bauman, Z. (1998) *Globalization: The human consequences*. New York: Columbia UP.

Berman, E., Marginson, S., Preston, R., McClellan, B. E., & Arnove, R. F. (2003). The political economy of education reform in Australia, England, and Wales, and the United States. In R.F. Arnove and C.A. Torres (Eds.), *Comparative education: The dialectic of the global and the local*, pp. 252–91. Lanhamn MD: Rowman & Littlefield.

Bolman, L. G. & Terrance E. D. (2003). *Reframing organizations*. 3rd ed. San Francisco: Jossey-Bass.

Bracher, P., Panoch, J. V., Piediscalzi, N., & Uphoff, J. K. (1974). *Public education religion studies: Questions and answers.* Dayton, OH: Public Education Religion Studies Center, Wright State University.

Bransford, J., Brown, A., & Cocking, R. (Eds.). (1999). *How people learn: Brain, mind, experience, and school.* Washington, DC: National Academy Press.

Briskin, L., & Priegert-Coulter, R. (1992). Introduction: Feminist pedagogy: Challenging the normative. *Canadian Journal of Education, 17*(3), 247–63.

Brooks, J. S. (2006). Tinkering toward utopia or stuck in a rut? School reform implementation at Wintervalley High. *Journal of School Leadership, 16*(3), 240–65.

Brooks, J. S., and Jean-Marie, G. (2007). Black leadership, White leadership: Race and race relations in an urban high school. *Journal of Educational Administration, 45*(6), 756–68.

Brooks, J. S., & Miles, M. T. (2008). From scientific management to social justice . . . and back again? Pedagogical shifts in educational leadership. In A. H. Normore, (Ed.), *Leadership for social justice: Promoting equity and excellence through inquiry and reflective practice,* pp. 99–114. Charlotte, NC: Information Age Publishing.

Brydon, D. (2004, fall). Cross-talk, postcolonial pedagogy, and transnational literacy. *Situation Analysis, 4,* 70–87.

Burbules, N., & Torres, C. (2000). *Globalization and education: Critical perspectives.* New York: Routledge.

Burkhardt, J. M., MacDonald, M. C., & Rathemacher, A. J. (2005) *Creating a comprehensive information literacy plan: a how-to-do-it manual and CD-ROM for librarians.* New York, NY: Neal-Schuman Publishers.

Campbell, R. F., Fleming, T., Newell, L. J., & Bennion, J. W. (1987). *A history of thought and practice in educational administration.* New York: Teachers College Press.

Capra, F. (1996). *The web of life: A new scientific understanding of living systems.* New York: Anchor Books.

Carnoy, M., & Rhoten, D. (2002). What does globalization mean for education change? A comparative approach. *Comparative Education,46*(1), 1–9.

Carvin, A. (2006, March). The gap: The digital divide network. *Reed Business Information,* p. 70.

Christians, C. (2003). The media and moral literacy. *Ethical Space, The International Journal of Communications Ethics,* 1(1), 1–17.

Christians, C., Ferre, J., & Fackler, M. (1993). *Good News: Social Ethics and the Press.* New York, NY: Oxford university Press.

Clark, T. (2007). *EPIC change: How to lead change in the global age.* San Francisco, CA: Jossey-Bass.

Collins, J. C. (2001). *Good to great: Why some companies make the leap . . . and others don't.* New York, NY: Harper Business.

Correia, A. (2002). Information Literacy for an active and effective citizenship. White paper prepared for UNESCO, the U.S. National Commission on Libraries and Information Science, and the National Forum on Information Literacy, for use at the Information Literacy Meeting of Experts, Prague, The Czech Republic.

Courchene, T. J. (1995). Glocalization: The regional/international interface. *Canadian Journal of Regional Science, 18*(1): 1–20.

Cunningham, W. G., & Gresso, D. W. (1993). *Cultural leadership: The culture of excellence in education.* Needham Heights, MA: Allyn & Bacon.

Dantley, M. E. (2005). African American spirituality and Cornel West's notions of prophetic pragmatism: Restructuring educational leadership in American urban schools. *Educational Administration Quarterly, 41*(4), 651–64.

Deal, T. E., & Peterson, K. D. (1991). *The principal's role in shaping school culture.* Washington, DC: United States Department of Education.

Deal, T. E., & Peterson, K. D. (1999). *Shaping school culture: The heart of leadership.* San Francisco, CA: Jossey-Bass.

del Val, R. E., & Normore, A. H. (2008). Leadership for social justice: Bridging the digital divide. *University Council for Educational Administration (UCEA, International Journal of Urban Educational Leadership, 2,* 1–15. Available [Online]: http://uc.edu/urbanleadership/current_issues.htm

Earle, J., & Kruse, S. (1999). *Organizational literacy for education: Topic in educational leadership.* Lawrence Erlbaum Associates, Inc., 10 Industrial Avenue, Mahwah, NJ.

English, F. W. (2002). The point of scientificity, the fall of the epistemological dominos, and the end of the field of educational administration. *Studies in Philosophy and Education, 21*(2), 109–36.

English, F. W. (2003a). Cookie-cutter leaders for cookie-cutter schools: The teleology of standardization and the de-legitimization of the university in educational leadership preparation. *Leadership and Policy in Schools, 2*(1), 27–46.

English, F. W. (2003b). *The postmodern challenge to the theory and practice of educational administration.* Springfield, IL: Chalres C. Thomas Publishers.

English, F. W. (2006). The unintended consequences of a standardized knowledge base in advancing educational leadership programs. *Educational Administration Quarterly, 42*(3), 461–72.

Fairclough, N. (1995). *Media discourse.* London, UK: Arnold.

Fairholm, G. (1997). *Capturing the heart of leadership: Spirituality and community in the new American workplace.* Westport: Praeger.

Freebody, P., & Luke, A. (2003). Literacy as engaging with new forms of life: The 'four roles' model. In G. Bull and M. Anstey (eds.), *The literacy lexicon,* 2nd ed. pp. 52–7. Sydney, AUS: Prentice Hall.

Friedman, T. L. (2005). *The world is flat: A brief history of the twenty-first century.* New York: Farrar, Sraus and Giroux.

Friedman, T. L. (1999). *The Lexus and the olive tree: Understanding globalization.* New York: Anchor.

Fullan, M. (2001). *Leading in a culture of change.* San Francisco, CA: Jossey-Bass.

Fyfe, I. (2007). Hidden in the curriculum: political literacy and education for citizenship in Australia. *Melbourne Journal of Politics.* Retrieved on January 23, 2009 from http://find books.com/p/books/

Gaudelli, W. (2003). *World class: Teaching and learning in global times.* Mahwah, NJ: Lawrence Erlbaum.

Gee, J. P. (1991). The legacies of literacy: From Plato to Freire through Harvey Graff: Literacy, discourse, and linguistics. *Harvard Educational Review, 58*(2), 195–212.

Giroux, H. A. (2002). Democracy, freedom, and justice after September 11th: Rethinking the role of educators and the politics of schooling. *Teachers College Record, 104*(6) 1138–62.

Green, A. (1997). Education, globalization and the nation state. New York: Macmillan.

Harvey, T. R., & Drolet, B. (2004). *Building teams-building people: Expanding the fifth resource.* 2nd ed. ScarecrowEducation.

Hoban, G. (2002). *Teacher learning for educational change: A systems thinking approach.* Buckingham, UK: Open University Press.

Hage, M. (2005, November). *The digital divide continues to hinder development in rural areas.* Food and Agriculture Organization in the United Nations: Second World Summit on the Information Society. Available [online]: http://fao.org

Hall, E. T. (1959). *The silent language.* New York: Doubleday Publishing Group, Inc.

Hess, F. M. (1999). *Spinning wheels: The politics of urban school reform.* Washington, DC: Brookings Institute.

Jungck, S., & Kajornsin, B. (2003). "Thai wisdom" and globalization: Negotiating the global and local in Thailand's national education reform. In K. Anderson-Levitt (Ed.), *Local meanings, global schooling: Anthropology and world culture theory*, pp. 27–49. New York: Palgrave Macmillan.

Kapur, D., & McHale, J. (2005). *Give us your best and brightest: The global hunt for talent and its impact on the developing world.* Washington, DC: Center for Global Development.

Kaufman, R., & Herman, J. (1991). *Strategic planning in education: Rethinking, restructuring, revitalizing.* Lancaster, PA: Technomic Publishing.

Klenke, K. (2006). The "S" factor in leadership: education, practice and research. *Journal of Education for Business 79*(1), 56–60.

Kohn, A. (1997, February). How not to teach values: A critical look at character education. *Phi Delta Kappan*, 429–39.

Ladson-Billings, G. J. (1995a). Toward a theory of culturally relevant pedagogy. *American Education Research Journal, 35*, 465–91.

Ladson-Billings, G. (1995b). But that's just good teaching! The case for culturally relevant pedagogy. *Theory into Practice, 34* (3), 159–65.

Lechner, F., & Boli, J. (2005). *World culture: Origins and consequences.* Malden, MA: Blackwell.

Ludwig, C., & Herschell, P. (1998). The power of pedagogy: Routines, school literacy practices and outcomes. *Australian Journal of Language and Literacy, 21.*

Maclellan, E. (2008). Pedagogical literate: What it means and what it allows. *Teaching and Teacher Education, 24*(8), 1986–92.

Malley, J. (2005). *Ethics corner: Should we teach ethics in K-12?* Available at: http://ccamain.com/pdf/k-12.pdf

Marx, G. T. (2006a). *Sixteen trends: Their profound impact on our future.* Alexandria, VA: Educational Research Service.

Marx, G. T. (2006b). *Future-focused leadership: Preparing schools, students, and communities for tomorrow's realities.* Alexandria, VA: Association for Supervision and Curriculum Development.

Marx, G. T. (2006, Winter). Using trend data to create a successful future for our students, our schools, and our communities, *ERS Spectrum.* pp. 4–8. Alexandria, VA: Educational Research Service.

Merrill, J. C. (1990). *The imperative of freedom: A philosophy of journalistic autonomy.* Latham, MD: Freedom House.

Mintzberg, H. (1994). *The rise and fall of strategic planning.* London: Prentice Hall International.

Murphy, J., & Forsyth, P. B. (Eds.). (1999). *Educational administration: A decade of reform.* Thousand Oaks, CA: Corwin Press.

Normore, A. H. (2006). Leadership recruitment and selection in school districts: Trends and issues. *Journal of Educational Thought, 40*(1), 41–73.

Normore, A. H., & Paul Doscher, S. (2007). Using media as the basis for a social issues approach to promoting moral literacy in university teaching. *Journal of Educational Administration, 45*(4), 427–50.

Organization for Economic Cooperation and Development (2003). *Source of economic growth in OECD countries*. Paris: OECD.

Olson, D. (1994). *The world on paper*. Cambridge, UK: Cambridge University Press.

Olson, D. (2001). Literate minds; literate societies. In P. Tynjälä, K. Mason and K. Lonka (ed), *Writing as a learning tool: Integrating theory and practice*, pp. 1–5. Academic Publishers, London: Kluwer.

Olson, D. (2003). *Psychological theory and educational reform*, Cambridge University Press, Cambridge.

Paul-Doscher, S., & Normore, A. H. (2009, in press). The moral agency of the educational leader in times of national crisis and conflict. *Journal of School Leadership*, 18(1).

Piacciano, A. (2007). *Educational leadership and planning for technology*. 4th ed. Upper saddle river, NJ: Pearson Education.

Ranly, D. (1992). *The lessons of general semantics*. In D. Brentari, G. N. Larson, L.A. MacLeod (Eds.), *The Joy of Grammar*, pp. 251–67. Amsterdam, The Netherlands: John Benjamins Publishing Company.

Riaz, O., & Normore, A. H. (2008). Examining the spiritual dimension of educational leadership. *University Council for Educational Administration (UCEA), Journal of Values and Ethics in Educational Administration*, 6(4), 1–8.

Robertson, R. (1995). Glocalization: Time-space and homogeneity. In M. Featherstone, S. Lash, & R. Robertson (Eds.), *Global modernity*, pp. 25–44. Lomdon: Sage.

Rosenau, J. N. (1994). New dimensions of security: The interaction of globalizing and localizing dynamics. *Security Dialogues*, 25(3), 255–81.

Saphier, J., & King, M. (1985). Good seeds grow in strong cultures. *Educational Leadership*, 42(6), 67–74.

Sassen, S. (2006). *Territory, authority, rights: From medieval to global assemblages*. Princeton, NJ: Princeton University Press.

Schein, E. H. (1992). *Organizational culture and leadership*. San Francisco, CA: Jossey-Bass.

Sachs, J. (2005). *The end of poverty: Economic possibilities for our time*. New York: Penguin Press

Scholte, J. A. (2000). *Globalization: A critical introduction*. New York: St. Martin's Press Inc.

Selwyn, N., Gorard, S., & Williams, S. (2001). Digital divide or digital opportunity? The role of technology in overcoming social exclusion in U.S. education. *Educational Policy*, 15, 258–77.

Senge, P., Smith, P., Kruschwitz, N., Laur, J., & Schley, S. (2008). *The necessary revolution: How individuals and organizations are working together to create a sustainable world*. Cambridge, MA: Doubleday Currency.

Shafritz, J. M., & Ott, J. S. eds. (2005). *Classics of Organization Theory*. 5th ed. New York: Harcourt Brace.

Shapiro, S.H. (1989). New directions for sociology of education: Reconstructing the public discourse in education. *Education and Society*, 7(2), 21–38.

Slaughter, A. M. (2006). *A new world order*. Princeton, NJ: Princeton University Press.

Smith, P. (1999). Sex, lies and Hollywood's administrators: The (de)construction of school leadership in contemporary films. *Journal of Educational Administration*, 37(1), 50–65.

Spillane, J. P., Diamond, J. B., Burch, P., Hallett, T., Jita, L., & Zoltners, J. (2002). Managing in the middle: School leaders and the enactment of accountability policy. *Educational Policy*, 16(5), 731–62.

Spring, J. (1998). *Education and the rise of the global economy*. Mahwah, NJ: Lawrence Erlbaum.

Spring, J. (2008). Research on globalization and education. *Review of Educational Research*, 78(2), 330–63.

Stevens, P., & Weale, M. (2003). *Education and economic growth*. London: National Institute of Economic and Social Research.

Stromquist, N. (2002). *Education in a globalized world: The connectivity of economic power, technology, and knowledge*. Lanham, MD: Rowman & Littlefield.

Tansley, D. (2006, February). Mind the gap: 2006 will witness the deepening of the digital divide. London, UK: The Financial Times, *13*, p. 21.

Taylor, S. (1997). Critical policy analysis: exploring contexts, texts and consequences." *Discourse: Studies in the Cultural Politics of Education*, 18(1), 23–35.

Thomas, S. (2006). *Education policy in the media: Public discourse on education*. Teneriffe, Queensland: Post Pressed.

Thompson, S. (2004). Leading from the eye of the storm. *Educational Leadership* 61(7), 60–3.

Tuana, N. (2003). Moral literacy. *Online Research/Penn State*, 24(2), available at: http://rps.psu.edu/0305/literacy.html

Turner, B. S. (2002). Cosmopolitan virtue, globalization and patriotism. *Theory, Culture & Society* 19(1–2), 45–63.

Uphoff, J. K. (2001). Religious diversity and education. In J. Banks & C. A. M. Banks(Eds.), *Multicultural education: Issues & perspectives*, 4th ed. pp. 103–21. New York: Wiley.

Weber, E. (2007). Globalization, "glocal" development, and teachers' work: A research agenda. *Review of Educational Research*, 77(3), pp. 279–309.

Welner, K.G., & Weitzman, D. Q. (2005). The soft bigotry of low expenditures. *Equity and Excellence in Education*, 38(3), 242–8.

Wenzel, J. (2000). Grim Fairy Tales: Taking a risk. In A. Amireh & L. Suhair Maja, (eds.), *Imaginary maps, Going global: The transnational reception of Third World women writers*, pp. 229–51. New York: Garland.

Willinsky, J. (1998). *Learning to divide the world: Education at empire's end*. Minneapolis: University of Minnesota Press.

Wolcott, H. F. (1991). Propriospect and the acquisition of culture. *Anthropology and Education Quarterly*, 22(3), 251–73.

Wolcott, H. F. (2003). *Teachers versus technocrats*. Walnut Creek, CA: AltaMira Press.

CHAPTER 2

Political Leadership

It is no secret that "educational leaders and school administrators find themselves in a continually contentious arena and vie for ways of balancing, directing, controlling, manipulating, managing, and surviving their edgy environments" (Lindle & Mawhinney, 2003, p. 3). Educational leaders must develop a working understanding of politics. Educational politics is commonly characterized as "the study of power, influence, and authority in the allocation of scarce and valued resources at various levels of the education sectors" (Johnson, 2003, p. 51). Considered in glocal perspective, this suggests that a politically competent educational leader is familiar both with various formal and informal processes by which people engage local and national issues and the outcomes and consequences of said processes. Moreover, in relation to educational leaders, political leadership means developing an understanding of how to act as empowered participants in these processes that influence local, national, and international decisions and policies. Mitchell and Boyd (2001) explain this orientation by arguing that globalization "is fundamentally changing the parameters of political deliberation throughout the industrialized world, raising the stakes for education policy and changing the ground rules for its adoption and implementation" (Mitchell & Boyd, 2001, p. 60).

We begin this chapter with an introduction to *learning* in relation to politics, from the schoolhouse to houses of legislature. In doing so, we emphasize the importance of political philosophy, and point out that it is important for leaders to understand their espoused and operational philosophies. Next, we present and explain the concept of political *literacy* and also introduce and explore ideas related to micropolitics, mesopolitics and macropolitics. This segues into a consideration of the role of *leadership* in which we focus on the various ways that leadership can influence political networks through the thoughtful use of power and influence. We emphasize the importance of negotiation and coalition building and urge readers to *reflect* on their own behaviors and assumptions about politics. At the end of the chapter, we offer a set of discussion and action prompts intended to help readers think through the various ways that ideas in the chapter are helpful to everyday leadership in education. Some key concepts discussed in this chapter include the following:

- Political philosophy
- Micropolitics

- Macropolitics
- Mesopolitics
- Political and Leadership Networks
- Formal and Informal Leadership

POLITICAL PHILOSOPHY: WHAT DO SCHOOL LEADERS STAND FOR?

Every school leader has a political philosophy, whether they are aware of it or not. Political philosophies are a leader's assumptions and values about the way that resources are distributed. Basically, political philosophy is what leaders believe when they think about this question—who should get what, when and how (Laswell, 1936)?

There is a wide range of political philosophies. Some are grounded in economics, some in psychology, some in philosophy and still others on notions of merit, justice, equity and excellence. Of course, most leaders will consider several of these dynamics as they make decisions in their schools. That said, it is important for a leader to consider and constantly reconsider their espoused philosophy and their operational philosophy. Put differently, understanding political philosophy will help leaders understand who they say they are, who they are in practice and the distance between those two positions. Studying and reflecting on political philosophy also helps leaders indentify the core principles on which their leadership rests. This clarity will help them make decisions that are consistent, and that help define the moral and operational values of the school. Leaders who do not reflect on their political philosophy are likely to practice an inconsistent and unjust form of leadership that advantages some and disadvantages others in an inequitable manner (Cohen & Fermon, 1996).

In the following section, we briefly discuss several political philosophies, identifying key concepts that leaders use when making decisions from that perspective. It is likely that you will be more attracted to some than others, but it is more important that you understand that each is a political philosophy that some leaders have employed in schools. As you read, we urge you to keep an open rather than dismissive countenance and think about what a school might look like if it were grounded on each set of principles. The list is selective rather than exhaustive, and we are explaining them in fairly basic ways. Keeping that in mind, we encourage you to (a) think about what you value as a leader and which political philosophies you use to guide your thinking as a leader, and (b) explore the additional readings related to each political philosophy as a way of deepening your understanding and helping you reflect on what you and your school stand for.

Anarchism

You might be surprised to see anarchy listed as a political philosophy, but it is actually a political philosophy that many schools and leaders practice, albeit unintentionally. Anarchy is a political philosophy based on the absence of authority and order. School leadership grounded in this perspective is characterized by a lack of direction, control, accountability and random acts of individual and collective improvement. Such schools lack a clear direction and are typically rife with insurrection, miscommunication, low trust, corruption and an open disdain for collegiality and social cohesion. On the other hand, anarchy may also promote creativity, offer a great deal of personal freedom and allow for exploration and discovery. While it is hard to imagine a school leader intentionally practicing anarchy as a political philosophy, there is certainly a great deal of research describing schools and organizational units within schools that operate this way (Blase & Blase, 2003; Brooks, 2006; Tscahannen-Moran, 2014).

Capitalism

Capitalist school leaders base their decisions on economic principles, such as marketization, supply and demand, competition, privatization, and equilibrium (McLaren, 2015). While there is a case to be made that in some ways schools are a business, it is important that such a way of thinking about education is tempered by a recognition that the two core aspects of schooling—teaching and learning—are not commodities. That is to say that making educational decisions based on capitalist notions is a dangerous practice that could compromise students' and teachers' experiences. Certainly, economic resources constrain any school leader's decisions—the amount of funding available in many ways dictates the quality and quantity of educational resources, technology, professional development, staff and space that leaders can provide for the school—but making decisions for economic rather than pedagogical and andragogical reasons is inappropriate and unethical in an educational organization (Gelberg, 1997).

Communism and Communitarianism

Communism and communitarianism are seemingly similar political philosophies that share a great deal but that differ in at least one key characteristic. In communism, all property is owned by the community and is distributed in an equitable manner based on needs and talents. The core tenet of communism is collectivism, and, in theory, it is a political philosophy that the group is greater than the individual and that all resources are shared as a community resource; many schools operate from a communist ethos, and it is easy to see how leadership for the collective is an appealing approach. However, communism in practice is extremely difficult to implement in schools, especially since communism is predicated on the absence of social classes and schools are often bureaucratic and hierarchical in nature (McLaren, 2015).

Communitarianism, on the other hand, places the interactions between individual and family at the core of political life. This means a leadership based on intimate and interconnected personal relationships and organization around smaller, semi-autonomous groups nested in the overall social and educational life of the school. In many schools, this might look like an organization where smaller units such as grade-level teams, departments or professional learning communities shape the everyday work of teachers and students. In communitarian schools, leadership supports rather than guides the work of these units.

Conservatism

Conservatism is a political philosophy that values tradition, constancy and stability over anything else, and leaders in such schools tend to perpetuate and defend the status quo. These leaders do not welcome or seek out substantive change, and they tend to regard new initiatives, ideas and approaches with skepticism and hostility. Conservative leaders have a tendency to view their work as an extension of history, which they generally regard in a favorable manner. Importantly, both people and systems can be conservative, both of which have a profound impact on the distribution of resources and political climate of the school and the political.

Transactionalism

Some leaders look at the way that influence, power and resources are distributed in a school as a transaction—they will do something for a follower if the follower does something for them in return. Of course, this is typically not so overt as to be a simple payment. Instead, these transactions often involve the trade of other forms of capital: social, intellectual, and cultural, among others. Transactional leadership creates favoritism, in-groups and out-groups, and by nature creates inequity throughout an organization. Transactional leaders often promote or reward followers or other leaders for reasons that have nothing to do with the good of the organization and instead invest their capital into those who can give them something in return. These leaders are interested in creating and nurturing cronyism, nepotism and ensuring that followers feel indebted to them (Dumdum, Lowe & Avolio, 2013).

Fascism

Fascism is a political philosophy that places the collective identity in higher esteem than the individual. At first glance, this might seem to be a positive way to approach making decisions in a school, but fascism is usually implemented by force, in the form of an authoritarian and unilateral approach to leadership that has very narrow views on what is best for the collective. Fascist school leadership is characterized by a centralization of power, wherein important decisions are made by one person who may or may not consult with a few trusted advisors. In schools that operate under fascist leadership, opposition to the dominant view is not tolerated—there are few collaborative processes and the judgment of the highest ranked officials in the school is law (Cohen & Fermon, 1996).

Feminism

Feminist leadership is primarily concerned with gender equality, and with distributing power, influence and resources in a manner that is sensitive to gendered inequality in school and society. As many schools and school systems suffer from longstanding gender inequality, feminist approaches to school leadership have garnered quite a lot of interest over the second half of the twentieth century. Feminist school leadership places emphasis on supporting women's liberation, empowerment and voice. As a political philosophy, feminism employs both activist methods for moving issues of gender equity to the fore while also being grounded in an ethic of care and love (Noddings, 1984). Importantly, feminist leadership can be practiced by both women and men—the key is for leadership activity to advance gender equality throughout the school community (Blackmore, 2015).

Meritocracy

In a meritocracy, leaders distribute power, influence and resources based on excellence in achievement. In such schools, there are explicit incentives and disincentives for reaching certain performance benchmarks, for demonstrating outstanding ability, or for winning academic or other educational competitions. In a meritocracy, resources are concentrated on the support of those deemed to be highest achieving. Many schools' leadership are ostensibly predicated on meritocracy. However, there are several issues that should give you pause, should you consider adopting this political philosophy. First, it is not always clear that tests measure what they claim to measure. For example, many standardized tests that claim to measure ability or achievement are better measures of socioeconomic status than learning. Second, meritocracies are often based on performance indicators that are culturally biased. Teaching and leadership can be practiced in a way that privileges some followers over others, simply because of their culture. For example, if a teacher has a classroom with students from multiple cultural groups but only uses examples, illustrations and language appropriate to one group, they are putting all other students at a disadvantage. The same applies for leadership, if it is practiced in a way that views merit in a narrow way that is only appropriate to some in the school. A leader should be careful to ascribe merit and achievement to biased measures that privilege and disadvantage certain students, staff or community members (Berliner & Glass, 2014).

Democracy

There is quite a bit of research that advocates for teachers and leaders to adopt democracy as a political philosophy in schools and classrooms (Isaacson, 2011; Wren, 1995). Democratic schools are founded on (a) the notion that there is a plurality of perspectives in a school, and (b) establishing a process whereby ideas and initiatives are (broadly speaking) shared, debated and voted upon before being collaboratively implemented. This is a particularly compelling approach for schools, as there is so much expertise and experience that can inform leadership decisions. Central to democracy is the "marketplace of ideas" wherein ideas are debated, discussed and developed. In schools, this can take many forms, but all require (a) adequate information related to the idea under consideration, (b) historical and contextual knowledge related to the idea and (c) transparency and monitoring of the way that something moves from idea to implementation. Democratic leadership is both compelling and promising, but it is important to keep in mind two important features. First, democracy is a system that encourages conflict, not consensus. This means that democratic leaders must develop their skills in conflict resolution and that they must be comfortable with moving the institution forward despite the likely occurrence that there will be disagreement and negotiation. Second, leaders should beware of the potential for a "tyranny of the majority" to take hold wherein a voting bloc is able to advance their agenda in a manner that consistently silences or marginalizes minority perspectives (De Tocqueville, 2003; Dewey, 2004).

DEVELOPING POLITICAL LITERACY: LEADING MICROPOLITICS AND MACROPOLITICS IN THE SCHOOLHOUSE

In order to increase their literacy in relation to the political leadership, there are several concepts that people working in schools need to understand. In this section, we focus primarily on micropolitical aspects of the work, those that focus on the school level, before briefly touching on mesopolitics and macropolitics—two levels of political activity that extend beyond the immediate school community.

Developing Micropolitical Leadership Literacy: Key Concepts

Defining Micropolitics

In some ways, we can think of leadership as an inherently political activity (Ball, 2012). Developing literacy in terms of political leadership demands that we think about the work by scrutinizing how politics plays out in the day-to-day work of a school. Such school-level politics are called micropolitics, which Lindle (1999) explained as "the networks of individuals and groups within and surrounding schools, who compete for scarce resources, even power. Often referred to as the informal communications of schools and school districts" (p. 171). Understanding schools as a micropolitical environment means that we are aware of the ways that power and influence shape the interactions between people, groups, teaching and learning in the school community. Importantly, micropolitical dynamics include not only the ways that people interact with one another but also the way that resources—including teaching materials, curriculum, space in the school and time—are distributed throughout the institution. Leaders have the ability to influence many micropolitical dynamics due to their authority, agency and power. Because of this, it is critical for leaders to constantly reflect on their political philosophy and core values as educators so that their practice is intentional and just. In the following sections, we will explore some dynamics related to micropolitics and discuss some of the ways that leaders can identify them in their school.

Micropolitics Has Both Formal and Informal Dynamics

Looking at schools through a micropolitical lens, there are both the *rules of the game* (formal dynamics) and the *way the game is played* (informal dynamics). As Flessa (2009) explained, "micropolitics is sometimes understood as the study of how things really work, not how an organizational chart or a principal's action plan would like them to work" (p. 331). Citing Hoyle (1982), Flessa noted that "micropolitics is characterized more by coalitions than by departments, by strategies rather than by enacted rules, by influence rather than by power, and by knowledge rather than by status" (p. 32).

The formal dynamics of micropolitics have to do with espoused policies, processes and decision-making structures that distribute resources in a school. For example, the processes that determine who teaches what class, how finances are used to support one program instead of another program, the manner in which change is designed, implemented and communicated might all be formalized in a given school—written down, if not necessarily agreed upon. When someone (or a group) with authority makes a decision based on a formal process, they are making a political decision, but one that is sanctioned by the codified policies of the school or school district. Some schools are often replete with policies and procedures to guide a wide range of decisions, both small and large in scale. Other schools lack documented procedures and policies to guide decisions. While either type of school can function, those that take the time to formalize procedures and make decisions transparent have higher levels of trust and efficiency (Tschannen-Moran, 2014).

On the other hand, many decisions in schools are influenced by informal dynamics, including coercion, cronyism, nepotism, corruption, embezzlement, deceit, half-truths, bribes, threats, and other nefarious behind-the-scenes practices. Leaders who practice such behavior often do so in spite of formal processes being in place. They pervert, circumvent or ignore formal processes for the sake of achieving some end that is antithetical to espoused organizational values, beliefs and practices. Importantly, not all informal leadership practices are unethical or immoral. Indeed, astute leaders are able to influence decision-making processes in a positive manner by making sure that people who have been socially marginalized have their perspectives heard, and by recognizing aspects of decision making that might derail an initiative. The key difference between positive and negative informal political leadership are issues of morality and ethics—is the intended process or outcome in the best interests of the students, staff and school, or are they intended to benefit a few at the expense of the many?

Open and Closed Micropolitical Systems

It is critical for school leaders to identify when a micropolitical process is part of a closed (within the school) or open (the school is part—but not all—of the situation) system. Some micropolitical issues in a school happen solely between the people and resources in the school. For example, there may be a dispute over instructional resources such as the science department wanting to purchase some microscopes while the mathematics department is asking for graphing calculators when there is only enough funding to choose one or the other. This is a decision most likely made among staff, negotiating an outcome amenable to as many as possible. However, other decisions may include political actors from outside the school. An example of this might be a vendor raising prices for a service that the school outsources. In this case, there will be a certain amount of work within the school to decide if the service should be continued, but it will also include negotiation and resourcing with external groups. It is important for leaders to properly identify the key actors in any political situation, and to think about both relationships throughout the school and relationships between those in the school and others in the school community.

Political Actors and Networks of Influence

When thinking about schools as micropolitical entities, it is common to think of those involved as political actors rather than in their formal roles. This frees you from focusing on job responsibilities and instead places the emphasis on the political relationships and activities throughout the school and into the school community. Lindle (1999) suggests that the "actors in micropolitics of schools include teachers and principals, central office staff and school Board members, parents and students," (p. 171) but certainly everysituation is likely different to some degree and possibly adds other actors to the list. Identifying the micropolitical actors relevant to activity is important so that leaders can identify the important actors likely to influence a particular process or outcome.

Actors rarely operate on their own, and instead form coalitions and networks around similar or complementary interests. These networks, which can be established for a specific purpose or standing arrangements between those in agreement, are then mobilized to influence processes and outcomes in the school. Networks can be activated toward positive or negative means and ends, but exist to advance the values and interests of those in the network. Micropolitical policy networks in schools might include a group of like-minded teachers who work together to improve working conditions for themselves, teacher unions, parent-teacher organizations, and others. From a micropolitical perspective, such networks are transactional, and their relative strength or weakness depends on the individual bonds between members, and the quality of their transactions. Such transactions might not always involve immediate material benefit, and can be based on social, cultural, political or, indeed, economic transactions.

Policy networks can be centralized, decentralized or distributed (Baran, 1964; Spillane, 2006). As illustrated in Figure 2.1, in a centralized political network, the leader (or the leader and a small group of trusted colleagues) is at the center of all activity—they are the school's gatekeeper, sanctioning or prohibiting everything from the most insignificant to the most important decisions (Ball, 2012). Many schools operate as a decentralized political network (see Figure 2.2), wherein smaller networks conduct much of the day-to-day work of the school and the leader plays more of an oversight role, rather than as a singular decision maker. More recent studies suggest that a distributed network (Figure 2.3) is perhaps the most appropriate structure for schools, as it allows for expertise throughout the organization to come to bear on the work of the school (Brooks, Normore, Jean-Marie & Hodgins, 2007). It is also a system fundamentally predicated on transparency, and, as such, is a way to promote equity and equality as an organizational quality.

How Leaders Use Power in Schools

Power is, in and of itself, not a necessarily positive or negative dynamic in schools. How power is used in schools matters a great deal and is fluid from situation to situation.

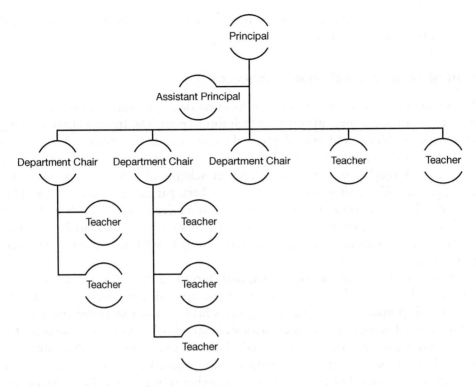

FIGURE 2.1 Centralized political network

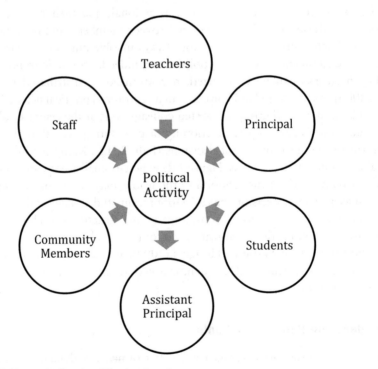

FIGURE 2.2 Decentralized political network

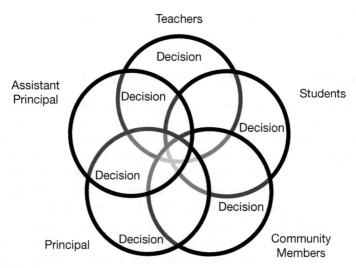

FIGURE 2.3 Distributed political network

In their classic study of principal abuse of teachers, Blase and Blase (2003) drew from May's (1972) work when identifying five types of power (p. 22):

- Exploitative Power (power over others). This is a destructive use of power used to oppress, marginalize and subjugate others. In many schools this takes the form of edicts, fiats, intimidation and professional sabotage.
- Manipulative Power (power over others). Manipulative uses of power are another way that some exercise power over others.
- Competitive Power (power against others). A situation where leaders pit members of the organization and/or their ideas against one another. This strategy has been shown to be consistently detrimental to learning and morale in schools, but may be appropriate under certain circumstances (Kohn, 1993).
- Nutrient Power (power for others). This type of power emphasizes empathy and empowerment. Transparency and trust are critical to this approach.
- Integrative Power (power with others). Integrative Power is a collaborative use of power. Leaders who use power in this manner employ consultative processes and draw on the collective expertise in the organization. The work to create the conditions for solidarity, and leaders try to flatten hierarchies for the good of individuals, groups and the school as a whole.

Again, power can be used to constructive or destructive ends. On the one hand, leaders such as Martin Luther King, Jr., Mahatma Gandhi and Wangari Mathaai used power to build peaceful and productive coalitions that created positive change in the world. On the other hand, unchecked and unethical uses of power allowed the likes of Adolph Hitler, Haji Suharto, Pol Pot, and Augusto Pinochet to wreak havoc and commit heinous atrocities. While the stakes and consequences related to the use of power for educational leaders may seem quite different than the leaders listed above, the tremendous impact of power in schools—both positive and negative—must be weighed and considered when making decisions.

Mesopolitics: School Leadership and Local Politics

While micropolitics have the most significant influence on day-to-day activity in a school, it is important to think about the school as part of the local community as well, and therefore as an integrated part of the larger political community. This means that leaders should be aware of the ways that local politics influence their work in schools, via formal structures such as school boards, parent-teacher associations, school foundations, companies and other education support providers. As with micropolitics and macropolitics, education policy comes into play at the mesopolitical level in that schools are a part of the local political economy of communities. This means that schools are often impeded and supported in their work by educational policies. In many cases these policies related to school funding, but they may also relate to community standards around a range of other concerns. Leadership at the mesopolitical level is critical, and in some ways leaders play a role as a filter, shield and conduit for political ideas and activity (Louis, 2007). It is important for school leaders to understand the mesopolitical level, as the nature and level of their engagement with local political actors may help them leverage useful educational resources or alternately leave them at the mercy of external political actors. Negotiation skills, conflict resolution and effective communication are key skills for success at the mesopolitical level.

Macropolitics: School Leadership, National Politics and Global Politics

Many leaders are only vaguely aware of the ways that national and global politics—macropolitics—influences their work in schools. They are likewise often unaware of their agency to influence such political forces. In many ways, the larger the policy, the less influence a school leader will have to directly influence it, but, nonetheless, they can play an important role in national and global macropolitics through personal means as site-level interpreters and by creating and joining political networks. Many school-level initiatives are driven by global educational policies such as UNESCO's Education 2030 (also known as the Incheon Declaration) and national education policies such as the United States' Elementary and Secondary Education Act or Australia's National Early Childhood Development Strategy. In many countries, education policy is part of constitutional or legal imperatives (Manna, 2006; Spring, 2011).

PRACTICING POLITICAL LEADERSHIP: SAVVY, SKILLS AND STRATEGIES

There are several ways to practice political leadership. In this section, we briefly touch on certain approaches leaders can use to influence political dynamics in the schools and communities, but it is important to note that every leader and every situation will be different. While we list some issues here, some will find the list to be incomplete, and all will want to think carefully about the context and how the skills and strategies we mention might be helpful, complicated and even dangerous. That said, we offer several categories that leaders will want to practice and develop in their schools.

Reflect on Your Espoused and Operational Political Philosophy

At the beginning of this chapter, we briefly described several political philosophies and urged you to reflect on your values as a way to develop a core set of principles that might help you make decisions. In addition to this reflection, it is important to constantly reflect on these principles as new issues arise and it is perhaps even more critical to do everything possible to understand the distance between espoused philosophy and philosophy in practice. Sadly, there is a long history in school leadership of administrators saying that they stand for one thing but embodying and practicing a completely different set of principles. It is important that leaders seek constant feedback throughout their school community to learn about ways that their work and the work of others throughout the organization might not be in-line with the political philosophy of the leader and the school.

Develop Your Political Savvy

Political savvy has to do with both a leader's ability to recognize the political dynamics of a situation and also to decide on and implement the most astute course of action given the circumstances. This will mean asking 10 questions about any issue:

1. Who is shaping the way that the situation is being talked about?
2. What data and viewpoints are being included and excluded?
3. What voices are included and excluded from the decision-making process?
4. Is there an extant educational policy that could guide decision making on the issue?
5. What is the history of this issue at the micropolitical, mesopolitical and macropolitical levels?
6. Who stands to gain and lose from the decision?
7. Is the decision best made through an open or closed process?
8. What are the potential intended and unintended consequences of the decision?
9. What are the short- and long-term consequences of the decision?
10. How will the decision be supported and monitored moving forward?

Again, while this is not an exhaustive list, our hope is that it helps leaders think through decisions from a political perspective. Importantly, leaders can ask that other people throughout the organization use these questions as a preliminary step of the policy-making process.

Crafting Policies That Work: Structures and Processes for Making Decisions

In addition to becoming more savvy, it is important for leaders to create and practice deliberate structures and processes for making decisions, so that all members have a heightened sense of fairness and justice when decisions are made. For example, leaders might make it clear that they make decisions in three categories:

Category 1 Decisions: These are decisions made collaboratively and democratically, with full transparency, debate and negotiation involving all members of the school. Generally, these will be related to whole-school initiatives or major expenditures.

Category 2 Decision: These are decisions that leaders make in consultation with people in the school.

Category 3 Decision: This is a decision that the leader must make without con-sultation. For example, someone might make a Category 3 decision in relation to an issue where the leader has sensitive personnel information that cannot be shared.

In the broadest possible sense, every decision falls into one of these categories. The frequency with which leaders make decisions in each goes a long way to operationalizing their political philosophy. That is, a democratic leader will have the majority of their decisions fall into Categories 1 and 2 while a Fascist or Conservative leader might have more in Category 3. Importantly, practicing transparency means being ready to explain when a decision falls into a certain category.

Transparency and Communication

Transparency and communication are key to the practice of political leadership. Making sure that decision-making rationales, processes and outcomes are effectively communicated to people in the organization will go a long way toward helping create equitable policies, helping people to be vested in school processes and distributing the work of the school in an authentic manner. Importantly, communication involves both output and intake—meaning that it is not communication to share decisions after the fact. Effective communication is about creating meaningful feedback loops, not just crafting messages (Ärlestig, 2008). Moreover, practiced properly, political leadership can enhance collaboration and diminish an emphasis on punitive compliance.

Negotiation and Conflict Resolution

Two of the most important political skills that leaders will develop have to do with negotiation and conflict resolution. It is important for leaders to understand that, in most cases, the political nature of schools will create rather than diminish the possibility for conflict. The important thing is to provide a productive space for conflict that allows for meaningful recognition of opposing viewpoints wherein all parties are heard and understand that their views need to be offered in the spirit of negotiation rather than as a make-or-break proposition. Negotiation and conflict resolution happen for both individuals and groups throughout a school community, and leaders would do well to both hone their skills and develop protocols and policies to help facilitate these and make them transparent. For example, a negotiation process might include:

1. Identifying all relevant actors and agreeing to the nature of their involvement in the process.
2. A series of conversations about the nature of the disagreement with individuals and/or groups involved.
3. A meeting of all parties to establish agreements and disagreements about issues, and to agree on a resolution process. It is important for the leader to consider and establish their role in relation to negotiations at this meeting. At the least, they will want to present the disagreement and facilitate a conversation about possible resolutions.
4. Establish, support and monitor an outcome or procedure to work toward resolution. This should include a final meeting for the individuals and/or groups to reflect on the process and assess outcomes.

POLITICAL LEADERSHIP: A CONCLUSION

In sum, nearly every decision made in a school is political, and leadership plays a prominent role in shaping the nature of political life in the organization. Transparency, communication and equity are essential for leaders to consider if they are to practice the political philosophy they espouse. Finally, it is important to remember that, if we accept the premise that work in schools is political, we must be ready to shape processes of negotiation that resolve conflicts in a constructive manner.

DISCUSSION

1. Do you believe that leadership and politics are one and the same? Discuss and support your answer.
2. Political leadership encompasses both formal and informal dynamics. Do you have a good understanding of these in your school and community? Do you have the skills to influence them in school and community?
3. Examine textbooks in your school. Do they suggest a particular ideology or political stance? What political perspectives are present or absent?
4. Many schools post an organizational chart to illustrate the flow of authority and decision making in the organization. Can you create an organizational chart that shows how decisions *really* get made in the school? Remember that it is probably not linear.

REFERENCES

Ärlestig, H. (2008). *Communication between principals and teachers in successful schools.* Doctoral dissertation, Pedagogik.

Ball, S. J. (2012). *Politics and policy making in education: Explorations in sociology.* Routledge.

Baran, P. (1964). "Introduction to Distributed Communications Networks, RM-3420-PR." August 1964, http://rand.org/publications/RM/baran.list.html

Berliner, D. C., & Glass, G. V. (Eds.). (2014). *50 myths and lies that threaten America's public schools: The real crisis in education*. Teachers College Press.

Blackmore, J. (2013). A feminist critical perspective on educational leadership. *International Journal of Leadership in Education, 16*(2), 139–54.

Blase, J., & Blase, J. (2003). *Breaking the silence: Overcoming the problem of principal mistreatment of teachers*. Thousand Oaks, CA: Corwin Press.

Brooks, J. S. (2006). Tinkering toward utopia or stuck in a rut? School reform implementation at Wintervalley High. *Journal of School Leadership, 16*, 240–65.

Brooks, J. S., Normore, A. H., Jean-Marie, G., & Hodgins, D. (2007). Distributed leadership for social justice: Influence and equity in an urban high school. *Journal of School Leadership, 17*(4), 378–408.

Cohen, M., & Fermon, N. (1996). *Princeton readings in political thought: Essential texts since Plato*. Princeton, New Jersey: Princeton University Press.

De Tocqueville, A. (2003). *Democracy in America*. Vol. 10. Regnery Publishing.

Dewey, J. (2004). *Democracy and education*. Courier Corporation.

Dumdum, U. R., Lowe, K. B., & Avolio, B. J. (2013). A meta-analysis of transformational and transactional leadership correlates of effectiveness and satisfaction: An update and extension. In *Transformational and Charismatic Leadership: The Road Ahead 10th Anniversary Edition*, pp. 39–70. Emerald Group Publishing Limited.

Flessa, J. (2009). Educational micropolitics and distributed leadership. *Peabody Journal of Education, 84*(3), 331–49.

Gelberg, D. (1997). *The "business" of reforming American schools*. Albany, NY: SUNY Press.

Hoyle, E. (1982). Micro-politics of educational organizations. *Educational Management and Administration, 10*, 87–98.

Isaacson, W. (2011). *Profiles in leadership: Historians on the elusive quality of greatness*. New York: W. W. Norton & Company.

Johnson, B. L. (2003). Those nagging headaches: Perennial issues and tensions in the politics of education field. *Educational Administration Quarterly, 39*(1), 41–67.

Kohn, A. (1993). *Punished by Rewards: The Trouble with Gold Stars, Incentive Plans, A's, Praise, and Other Bribes*. Boston: Houghton Mifflin.

Laswell, H. (1936). *Politics: Who gets what, when, how*. New York: McGraw-Hill.

Lindle, J. C., & Mawhinney, H. B. (2003). Introduction: School leadership and the politics of education. *Educational Administration Quarterly, 39*(1), 3–9.

Lindle, J. C. (1999) What can the Study of Micropolitics Contribute to the Practice of Leadership in Reforming Schools?. *School Leadership & Management, 19*(2), 171–8, doi: 10.1080/13632439969177

Louis, K. S. (2007). Managing complex change: Bringing meso-politics back in. *Managing change in the public services, 97*–115.

Manna, P. (2006). *School's in: Federalism and the national education agenda*. Georgetown University Press.

May, R. (1972). *Power and innocence*. New York: Norton.

McLaren, P. (2015). *Life in schools: An introduction to critical pedagogy in the foundations of education*. Routledge.

Mitchell, D. E., & Boyd, W. L. (2001). Curriculum politics in global perspective. *Educational Policy, 15*(1), 58–75.

Noddings, N. (1984). *Caring: A Feminine Approach to Ethics and Moral Education*. Berkeley: University of California Press.

Spillane, J. P. (2006). *Distributed leadership*. San Francisco: John Wiley & Sons, Inc.

Spring, J. (2011). *The politics of American education*. Routledge.

Tschannen-Moran, M. (2014). *Trust matters: Leadership for successful schools*. John Wiley & Sons.

Wren, J. T. (1995). *The leader's companion: Insights on leadership through the ages*. New York: Simon & Schuster.

CHAPTER **3**

Economic Leadership

For many educational leaders, the extent of their preparation with regard to economics has to do with balancing a school budget. However, educational leaders should also understand the economic realities of schools in relation to larger local and global trends. Schools are intended to educate and prepare students to enter into and thrive in a global economy (Spring, 1998). The literature is replete with commentary that education and education reform initiatives are driven by the global economy (e.g., Barro, 2000; OECD, 2003; Sachs, 2005; Stevens & Weale, 2003). Much of the educational discourse around economic leadership has centered on the need for educators to focus on a "renewed attention to the technical importance of reading and math skills. The new economic environment can only be accessed successfully by individuals who can read fluently, compute efficiently, and do both with understanding" (Mitchell & Boyd, 2001, p. 73). These skills, in particular, are emphasized as a broader recognition of the need for students to participate in a knowledge-based economy that demands increasingly sophisticated and specialized capabilities (Stromquist, 2002). At the very least, educational leaders must have a basic understanding of microeconomics and macroeconomics, which would include competency in the area of global economics. As Johnson (2003) explains in this distinction: "macroeconomics focuses on the economy as a whole: gross production, overall employment, and general price levels (Heilbroner & Galbraith, 1990; Heilbroner & Thurow, 1994). Microeconomics is concerned with the activities of individual consumers and producers" (p. 51). Additionally, Spring (2008) notes that "government and business groups talk about the necessity of schools meeting the needs of the global economy" (p. 331).

Yet Spring (1998) also cautions against a single-minded focus on global economics as the driver education as such an orientation reduces "citizens to good workers and consumers" (p. xi). Further, emphasizing global economic viability in education may exacerbate global inequities, including: (a) transnational brain drain/brain gain dynamics that would concentrate an inordinate amount of technical and conceptual expertise in a few affluent centers (Friedman, 2005; Spring, 1998), and (b) a potentially negative impact on human and educational rights, due to extreme inequality with respect to access of quality educational materials and educators (Spring, 1998; Willinsky, 1998). Economic leadership, then, extends beyond technical expertise with budgets and encompasses an understanding of the opportunities and challenges provided by a rapidly globalizing economy.

In this chapter, we begin by *learning* about issues related to economic *literacy*, and then transition to a more focused consideration of the ways that microeconomics and macroeconomics influence the practice of school *leadership*. We will cover concepts such as supply and demand, cost-benefit analysis, budget management, facilities, expenditures, outsourcing and the knowledge industry. At the conclusion of the chapter, we encourage the reader to *reflect* on educational leaders' ability to influence the economic dynamics of a school through formal and informal means. In doing so, we emphasize skills related to fund raising, fiscal austerity, how and when to share budget information, allocating resources for equity and excellence. Some key concepts discussed in this chapter include the following:

- Innovation Economics
- Microeconomics of Education
- Macroeconomics of Education
- Return on Investment
- Poverty.

INNOVATION ECONOMICS, CHANGE AND SCHOOL LEADERSHIP

Stories of success and failure from interwoven and reciprocally connected political, economic and cultural systems, coupled with an emergence of global conglomerates, monopolies and multinational corporations, has led to worldwide acceptance that globalization is critical in contemporary economic life (Friedman, 1999, 2005; Jungck & Kajornsin, 2003; Spring, 2008). General interest about globalization has expanded in the last several years and numerous media formats have surfaced as discussions, debates and research begin to emerge. Still, the under-examination of globalization and the knowledge economy is especially evident in the field of educational leadership.

A greater understanding of innovation economy is crucial to the development of contemporary educational leaders. Theoretical in nature, we focus part of our argument on six of the several distinct global "competencies"—identified in earlier work by the authors within the context of innovation economy. We believe that educational leaders must be globally competent in order to create and sustain meaningful educational experiences for students. Other parts of our argument are drawn from research by Marx (2006a, 2006b) who proposed a continued conversation about globalization and its relation to competent educational leadership while other researchers (e.g. Clark, 2007; Spring, 2008) proposed ongoing discourse for innovation economics and change in a global and innovation economy. The possible benefits of an innovation economy can be embraced through conscious, thoughtful policy decisions that help direct innovation toward widely-held human values or whether it will evolve purely through changes in economic markets. Either impetus will lead to radical changes in education away from physical infrastructure and toward networks of learning systems. Marx (2006a) asserts that educators and community leaders need to engage in developing a plan and to turn it into a living vision that will help leaders to think globally as they lead schools and communities into a successful future, replete with ongoing change.

Innovation Economics and Change

The very nature of education is changing because of the revolutionary nature of a knowledge economy. Industrial growth is now receding in favor of knowledge productivity. A shift from physical goods to digital goods will radically change the logic of production and, with it, the nature of education. The change comes from a shift in the way goods are produced. This shift derives from the characteristics of knowledge economics. Education no longer plays a supporting role as it moves toward a learning system that embraces all ages of peoples, all sectors and groups of people into a continuous system of learning and innovation (Cortright, 2001; Lundvall & Borras, 1997; Romer, 1998). The shape of this learning system is determined by the global forces that are moving us from industrial economies to a learning economy and on to an innovation economy.

Any major change in the way that economic value is created will cause a response in education. Parents, national leaders and world organizations will change education to fit job markets and income opportunities. Communities will use education to compete for better jobs and industries. Thus, if a major change in the way that economics works means that a different type of worker will be needed and rewarded with increased income, then the educational system will change to accommodate the economic change. Unlike industrial production, once an idea is created, it costs nearly nothing to duplicate the idea and spread it around (music, software, films, social networks) (Romer, 1998). Unlike human capital, ideas are used, distributed and value created for a large amount of people without using up a lot of natural resources. Since ideas can be duplicated and spread easily, they cross borders and have the potential for increasing the value of life for people dispersed by geography, race, nationality and class. In other words, *the knowledge resource has increased, the value it brings is cheaply and widely available and the knowledge needed for further value creation has increased, along with the desire for more knowledge products.*

The link between the innovation economy and education leadership is significant. Research has identified that educational leaders are in a unique and influential position to help shape the conceptualization and practice of education in various settings (Brooks & Normore, 2010). This assertion is based on a philosophy that leadership is about initiating and facilitating change, setting agendas, providing direction, exercising influence and mobilizing constituents to develop sophisticated skills in order to engage and interconnect in ways that achieve shared goals in the global arena.

Moving the education system out of the previous model and into the new model will require that a noncompetitive education model to be developed. New ideas thrive in an environment where people are free to try new things, experiment and spend time sharing ideas (Edmondson, 2008). The goals of education change from that of individual competition or institutional competition to a cooperative model where high standards of knowledge and learning are embedded. It means that the learning system must take advantage of the inherent characteristics of knowledge—that it grows naturally if provided the right environment. True to its essence, the learning method here is not institutional but instead it is one of cooperation, networking and innovation (Taylor, 2001) that fit as a piece of a large learning system. The learning network itself can be used to create a public dialogue about the parameters of the learning infrastructure—who ought to have access, when access is restricted, what elements are needed and how they are built and regulated. As public sophistication grows, it will adjust the value set, design new norms and imagine new ideals. So, a critical part of the new learning infrastructure ought to be a means whereby its parameters are set by an ongoing public dialogue. Such changes imply not only a very different type of learning system, but one led by leaders with a particular set of skills.

As previously noted, research on globalization continues to emerge in education albeit brief (Jungck & Kajornsin, 2003; Spring, 2008). However, this relatively small body of knowledge that connects globalization to educational leadership indicates that it is likely that school leaders are inadequately prepared or ill-equipped to confront the realities of what it means to lead schools in a global society. Certainly, it is possible that research and practitioner-focused works are in progress and have yet to make it to press. As suggested by Brooks and Normore (2009) in earlier work, this dearth of extant inquiry may also mean "that educational leaders are oblivious to the way that local and global forces interact to shape the context of the lives of those responsible for delivering quality instruction for student learning and the school and communities in which they lead" (p. 7). This possibility has profound implications for educational leadership insofar as these leaders may not have access to instructional resources or perhaps are not using the resources that could enhance the quality and relevance of educational opportunities and experiences of their students (Gaudelli, 2003). Furthermore, research has clearly indicated that an education must not focus on geographically-myopic perspectives that offer little benefit to students. A myopic education will not prepare them as they enter into a competitive shrinking world where an urgency to engage in global partnerships, institutions and economies becomes more evident (Kapur & McHale, 2005).

In order for innovators to combine their knowledge to build new ideas and create new ways of living, they must begin with an understanding of economic competence in terms of what this means for educational leadership.

Economic Competence

According to the New York State Commission on Higher Education (NYSCHE, 2007):

> Ideas have always mattered, but they matter today more than ever. We now live in a knowledge economy that transcends disciplines, organizations and borders. Ideas move effortlessly and rapidly. The new reality is a deeply interconnected globe whose currency is ideas. This is a reality that cannot be changed, or cannot be ignored, and must not be feared. Instead, it is a reality that we must join this global effort in order to respond successfully to new challenges (p. 10).

For the most part, educational leadership programs tend to primarily focus on one aspect of economic competence—ways of balancing a school budget (Brooks & Normore, 2009). Although schools are meant to educate and prepare students to be successful contributors in a global economy, these students learn minimum about the economic realities of schools and how these realities are connected to the larger and global trends of which they play a significant role. Yet, a wide body of literature is available that focuses on state education and education reform initiatives and how these initiatives are driven by the global economy (e.g., Barro, 2000; OECD, 2003; Stevens & Weale, 2003). Much of the educational discourse around economic competence has centered on the need for educators to focus on a "renewed attention to the technical importance of reading and math skills . . . that the new economic environment can only be accessed successfully by individuals who can read fluently, compute efficiently, and do both with understanding" (Mitchell & Boyd, 2001, p. 73). These skills, in particular, are emphasized as a broader recognition of the need for students to participate in a knowledge-based economy that demands increasingly sophisticated and specialized capabilities (author, 2000). Of equally significance is the literature that reiterates how important it becomes that "government and business groups talk about the necessity of schools meeting the needs of the global economy" (Spring, 2008, p. 331).

Emphasizing global economic viability in education may exacerbate global inequities, including a transnational brain drain/brain gain dynamics that would concentrate an inordinate amount of technical and conceptual expertise in a few affluent centers (Friedman, 2005; Spring, 2008), and have a potentially negative impact on human and educational rights, due to extreme inequality with respect to access of quality educational materials and educators (Spring, 2008; Willinsky, 1998). Given the scope of a rapidly growing global economy, it seems reasonable to expect that economic competency for educational leaders should extend beyond technical expertise with budgets.

The knowledge economy rests on the unique ways in which knowledge creates value and results in innovation. Ideas create value that can be shared, is difficult to own, often uses few natural resources, costs little to reproduce and adds to the resource base of communities. Ideas are best fostered in environments where experimentation, collective conversation and risk taking are encouraged. Such changes imply not only a very different type of global learning system, but one led by contemporary leaders with a particular set of skills and competencies including, but not limited to, economic competence.

MICROECONOMICS AND EDUCATIONAL LEADERSHIP

The "Business" of School Leadership

The field of educational leadership has long been influenced by business literature in general, and by leadership studies in particular. It is common for an idea seen as innovative or new in school leadership or management to have originated in business literature—and these concepts are at times research-based and at other times purely conjecture (Gelberg, 1997). While there are lessons to be learned from business, educational leadership scholars and practitioners should cast a critical eye over concepts before accepting or applying them (Brooks, 2016). This is because, in some cases, business processes are meant to maximize efficiency in a manner that does not always take into account the ethical, human, relational and developmental differences between education and business. For example, in many school systems, educators would find it unethical to expel students for poor performance, instead seeing their work as a moral calling to educate all students, regardless of ability or achievement. A bottom-line "raise-the-test-scores" approach might compel administrators to refuse admission or expel students not performing to a certain standard. That is not to say, of course, that standards should be dispensed as unethical, we are merely making the point that a single-minded focus on education as an outcome, without the recognition that education is an ongoing process where each student starts in a different place, grows at a different rate and ultimately accomplishes different things may compel administrators to make decisions based on non-educational reasons (Brooks, 2016). That is to say that while money matters, schools are not simply a business; decisions should be made with educational and economic considerations in balance.

Economic Capital, Human Capital, Cultural Capital and School Leadership

It is important for school leaders to understand that there are many economies that influence schools. Some are economic, while others are built on transactions of ideas, culture and other forms of positive exchanges. While there are many forms of capital, perhaps the three most used in schools are economic capital, human capital and cultural capital. In schools, economic capital relates to financial inputs, processes and outputs. This is the way that money and funds flow into, around and out of the school to support educational processes and outcomes. There are many sources of input: government appropriations, parental contributions, fundraising, bonds and levies (Ingle, Johnson, Ryan Givens, & Rampelt, 2013). These can be generated using a variety of school finance formulas, weighted and meted out based on local, state and national policies. Once in the school budget, leaders have the responsibility to appropriately apportion and use funds in a manner that supports students, faculty and staff in their pursuit of excellent and equitable educational processes.

Human capital has to do with the individual and collective professional capacity in a school. It is a way of recognizing that every member of a school community brings certain strengths and weaknesses to the work, and that each member contributes in a unique manner. Leaders who are sensitive to human capital understand that each member of the school community is in a different developmental stage. For example, a teacher with 30 years experience and one in his/her first year bring very different assets to the school community. That is not to say that one is necessarily a better teacher than the other or that one is of more value to the school, it is to recognize that they have different strengths and weaknesses that should be taken into account when making decisions in the school.

The third type of capital that leaders need to understand is cultural capital. Studies of culturally relevant pedagogy, multicultural education and culturally relevant leadership (Beachum & McCray, 2004; Horsford, Grosland, & Gunn, 2011) have shown that leaders must understand and respect the various cultures and subcultures in their school. This will allow them to make informed decisions that are appropriate for student, staff, faculty and community values around the purpose and practice of education. Educational leadership that is practiced in a manner that is indifferent or antagonistic to the various cultures and subcultures in the school is unlikely to be successful, no matter how many economic resources are put in place to support people and initiatives (Brooks & Jean-Marie, 2007).

Supply, Demand and School Leadership

The concepts of supply and demand are often evoked in schools, but not always in a manner that makes sense for education. In the most basic sense, supply and demand has to do with production of a product and consumption of a product being in equilibrium so that one does not outpace the other (Psacharopoulos, 2014). This concept is important in schools in that it can help a leader understand how they depend on, use and generate various resources—economic resources as well as those related to the various forms of capital explained above. Thinking beyond supply and demand in a financial sense and evolving toward a conceptualization that focuses on the supply and demand of excellence in classroom and school will help leaders identify areas of relative strength and weakness in the school.

Return on Investment, Cost Benefits and School Leadership

Thinking about various resources in the school as an investment in the education of students and school-community members will help leaders make informed decisions about whether or not the ways that capital is used in the school is producing intended and unintended results. Return on investment is often a cross-capital way of thinking about resource allocation. For example, if we spend the money on this program, will we see educational benefits? Such calculations are clearly open to some interpretation and should not be viewed as a simple input-output situation, as most changes in a school influences many other factors and dynamics. Leaders should certainly consider return on investment, they should just be cautious when interpreting results, particularly if they are trying to oversimplify complicated and inter-related dynamics. The same general caution allies to cost-benefit analyses, which, in schools, often differ from return on investment discussions as they are generally projections about intended benefits (Psacharopoulos & Patrinos, 2004).

School Finance and School Leadership

As budget systems and processes vary greatly from setting to setting, we refrain from getting into the technical aspects of budgets. That said, we do offer a few principles to broadly guide leaders working with them. First, budgets are a direct reflection of a school's values. Leaders must ask if budget appropriations are in-line with the schools espoused philosophy and pedagogical beliefs. Second, school finance is an indirect reflection on the community's values. It is important for leaders to consider if the ways that money is being generated and spent is in-line with what the community believes a good education looks like. Third, leaders must be aware that the degree of economic transparency they practice has great ramifications on their ability to establish and maintain trust. If people throughout the school community—particularly teachers and staff—do not know how funds are spent and how financial decisions are made, they are likely to be suspicious of a leader's intentions (Basker & Weiner, 2011).

MACROECONOMICS AND EDUCATIONAL LEADERSHIP

The Purposes of Education: Preparing Students for the Global Economy?

When school leaders look beyond the bounds of their school community, they typically see that economic forces from around the world influence education, both around the world and in their backyard. While this is perhaps most evident in relation to specific products or economic processes, it should also urge educators to reflect on the basic purposes of education. We need to ask questions like: is part of being an educational leader preparing students for economic realities that will confront them when they leave school? Are we preparing students to be workers in a glocal economy? Should we be teaching students personal finance? Should we teach entrepreneurialism in schools? Importantly, these basic, foundational questions are among many that we should ask and they span across all of the forms of leadership in this book. We urge school leaders to avoid taking a purely economic focus with respect to education and instead embrace a holistic perspective that crosses over the literacies and leadership domains we identify in this book. It is important to consider the economic implications of education, but that should not be the only aspect of education that drives what happens in schools.

Glocalization and Neoliberalism

Two connected economic forces are at play in nearly every school around the world: glocalization and neoliberalism. Glocalization is evident both in the way that local and global economic interests exert reciprocal influence on each other. Markets around the world are connected as never before and the rate of interconnectedness is likely to increase in coming years and decades. In schools, this has huge implications for leaders, in that glocalization potentially provides opportunities for a greater flow of diversified resources and ideas into the school. It may also offer the chance of establishing or expanding economic networks beyond the local community, again possibly benefitting the school and creating new and richer opportunities for students. However, a word of caution: glocalization also brings with it an increased possibility of economic exploitation, and specifically can create financial bonds with people and organizations who have no meaningful connection to the school other than increased profit (Spring, 2014). This dynamic is part of the problems associated with neoliberalism—the marketization and privatization of goods and services (Spring, 2014).

In education, neoliberalism has been particularly negative in the sense that it has led to economic and cultural exploitation in the name of profit. Davies and Bansel (2007) explained that:

The emergence of neoliberal states has been characterized by the transformation of the administrative state, one previously responsible for human well-being, as well as for the economy, into a state that gives power to global corporations and installs apparatuses and knowledges through which people are reconfigured as productive economic entrepreneurs of their own lives (248).

In schools, this is particularly problematic, as leaders who are not mindful may be compelled to make educational decisions based on economic reasons. Again, there is certainly nothing wrong with taking economic issues into consideration, but when money trumps pedagogical reasoning, neoliberalism has made the school take a turn for the worst.

Poverty, Affluence and School Leadership

School leaders should be aware of issues related to poverty and affluence in their schools and communities. A great body of research indicates that students from poorer communities are at a disadvantage in relation to those in more affluent conditions. As Van der Berg (2008) explains:

Poverty is not simply the absence of financial resources. According to Amartya Sen, poverty is the lack of capability to function effectively in society. Inadequate education can thus be considered a form of poverty. *Absolute poverty*—the absence of adequate resources—hampers learning in developing countries through poor nutrition, health, home circumstances (lack of books, lighting or places to do homework) and parental education. It discourages enrolment and survival to higher grades, and also reduces learning in schools. The *relative poverty* perspective emphasizes exclusion from the mainstream in rich countries, which can reduce the motivation of the relatively poor and their ability to gain full benefits from education (ii).

School leaders should be aware of the economic situations of their students and community if they are to provide effective and relevant educational opportunities. Teaching and leading schools in communities of poverty and affluence can look very different, both in terms of resources and in terms of the quality and nature of education delivered. One of the key issues is economics and equity of educational opportunity—that is, since not all students have the same economic situation, it may be necessary for school leaders to support certain students with greater resources than others to give them the same opportunity. This is not "unfair" but is rather morally just and equitable way to distribute resources (Darling-Hammond, 2015).

Employment, Unemployment and the Jobs of the Future

One of the oft-heard maxims of education is that we are educating students for jobs that don't yet exist and leading them toward a future we can't imagine. This is not entirely true, as school leaders can look to historical data and projections to understand the current situation and to predict future trends (Marx, 2006a, 2006b). Just as leaders must imagine and work toward a better future for their school, so too must they try and understand how local economies are changing in order to shape educational experiences toward a useful and exciting future. This will look different for every leader and school, but is a reminder that schools do not exist in a bubble that is disconnected from society. Rather, while employment is not the sole aim of education, it is important and should be a consideration for school leaders, educators and school systems in general. Such awareness places demands on the school leader that go far beyond the walls of their building—it means understanding and paying attention to worldwide, international, national, regional and local dynamics, and shaping education and the school's work in a manner that puts student experiences in that larger context.

PRINCIPLES FOR ECONOMIC LEADERSHIP

School finance is so vastly different from context to context that we offer a set of guiding principles rather than a list of skills in this particular domain of school leadership. We encourage school leaders to consider the ways that the dynamics we have discussed above look in their context and look for levers that will allow them to meaningfully shape the educational experiences of their students and educators.

1. **School leaders should keep in mind that there are ethical dimensions to economic leadership.** Decisions about funds are among the most important that a school leader will make. They must consider who will benefit and who may suffer from such decisions. It is important that school leaders keep in mind that equity means having a deep understanding of students' situations and distributing resources that will maximize the education and opportunities for all students.
2. **School leaders should put educational quality at the center of their economic leadership.** This may come in the form of redistributing resources in the school budget, but it should also entail a consideration of local and global resources that might improve education. Importantly, cost is a factor but it should not be the most important—quality education must be at the center of decision-making processes.
3. **School leaders should study local and global economic and educational trends to inform their school-level decisions.** It is important for school leaders to understand the history, the present and possibilities for the future in regard to education and economics. They must. It is not good enough to focus on the curriculum-as-written. It is important to also consider the short- and long-term economic implications of the work.

DISCUSSION

1. Examine a school's budget and then its mission statement and expression of values. Are these all in sync?
2. Discuss transparency in financial matters in a school. When would a leader want to be transparent and when would they want financial decisions hidden?
3. How does the curriculum of your school reflect trends and issues in the local and global economy? Are you preparing students for careers in rising or falling sectors?

4. Consider all of the material and intellectual resources in the school—which are absolutely essential for students to receive a high-quality education. Does the school and community focus their time, money and personnel on these essential resources?

REFERENCES

Barro, R. (2000). *Education and economic growth*. Paris: OECD.

Beachum, F., & McCray, C. (2004). Cultural collision in urban schools. *Current Issues in Education*, 7(4).

Brooks, J. S. (2016). Everything we know about educational leadership is wrong. In G. Lakomski, C. Evers & S. Eacott (Eds.), *Questioning leadership: New directions for educational organizations*, pp. 31–44. London: Routledge.

Brooks, J. S., & Jean-Marie, G. (2007). Black leadership, White leadership: Race and race relations in an urban high school. *Journal of Educational Administration*, 45(6), 756–68.

Brooks, J. S., & Normore, A.H. (2010). Educational leadership and globalization: Literacy for a glocal perspective. *Educational Policy: An Interdisciplinary Journal of Policy and Practice*, 24(1), 52–82.

Clark, T. (2007). *EPIC change: How to lead change in the global age*. San Francisco, CA: Jossey-Bass.

Cortright, J. (2001). *New growth theory, technology and learning: A practitioner's guide*. Portland, Oregon: Impressa Inc.

Darling-Hammond, L. (2015). *The flat world and education: How America's commitment to equity will determine our future*. Teachers College Press.

Edmondson, A. (2008). The competitive imperative of learning. *Harvard Business Review*, 86(7/8), 60–7

Friedman, T. L. (1999). *The Lexus and the olive tree: Understanding globalization*. New York: Anchor.

Friedman, T. L. (2005). *The world is flat: A brief history of the twenty-first century*. New York: Farrar, Sraus and Giroux.

Gaudelli, W. (2003). *World class: Teaching and learning in global times*. Mahwah, NJ: Lawrence Erlbaum.

Horsford, S. D., Grosland, T. J., & Gunn, K. M. (2011). Pedagogy of the personal and professional: Considering culturally relevant and antiracist pedagogy as a framework for culturally capable Leadership. *Journal of School Leadership*, 21, 582–604.

Ingle, W. K., Johnson, P. A., Ryan Givens, M., & Rampelt, J. (2013). Campaign expenditures in school levy referenda and their relationship to voter approval: Evidence from Ohio, 2007–2010. *Leadership and Policy in Schools*, 12(1), 41–76.

Jungck, S., & Kajornsin, B. (2003). "Thai wisdom" and globalization: Negotiating the global and local in Thailand's national education reform. In K. Anderson-Levitt (Ed.), *Local meanings, global schooling: Anthropology and world culture theory*, pp. 27–49. New York: Palgrave Macmillan.

Kapur, D., & McHale, J. (2005). *Give us your best and brightest: The global hunt for talent and its impact on the developing world*. Washington, DC: Center for Global Development.

Lundvall, B. A., &Borras, S. (1997). *A globalizing learning economy: implications for innovation policy*. Commission of the European Union. DG XII.

Marx, G. T. (2006a). *Sixteen trends: Their profound impact on our future.* Alexandria, VA: Educational Research Service.

Marx, G. T. (2006b). *Future-focused leadership: Preparing schools, students, and communities for tomorrow's realities.* Alexandria, VA: Association for Supervision and Curriculum Development.

Mitchell, D.E., & Boyd, W. L (2001). Curriculum in global perspective. *Educational Policy, 15*(1), 58–75.

New York State Commission on Higher Education (2007). *A preliminary report on findings and recommendations.* Albany, New York.

Psacharopoulos, G., & Patrinos, H. A. (2004). Returns to investment in education: A further update. *Education economics, 12*(2), 111–34.

Psacharopoulos, G. (Ed.). (2014). *Economics of education: Research and studies.* Elsevier.

Romer, P. M. (1998). Two strategies for economic development: using ideas and producing ideas. In D. Klein (ed.) *The Strategic Management of Intellectual Capital*, pp. 211–38. Butterworth-Heinemann: Boston, Massachusetts.

Spring, J. (2014). *Globalization of education: An introduction.* Routledge.

Spring, J. (1998). *Education and the rise of the global economy.* Mahwah, NJ: Lawrence Erlbaum.

Spring, J. (2008). Research on globalization and education. *Review of Educational Research, 78*(2), 330–63.

Stevens, P., & Weale, M. (2003). *Education and economic growth.* London: National Institute of Economic and Social Research.

Taylor, M. C. (2001). *The moment of complexity: emerging network culture.* Chicago, University of Chicago Press.Van der Berg, S. (2008). Poverty and education. *Education policy series, 10*, 28.

Willinsky, J. (1998). *Learning to divide the world: Education at empire's end.* Minneapolis: University of Minnesota Press.

CHAPTER 4

Cultural Leadership

Culture is both one of the most popular topics in leadership studies, and one of the most misunderstood. The literature is rife with articles, books, reports and tales of leaders who positively changed the culture of an organization and achieved great results. The same literature is replete with examples of leaders who created toxic cultures, alienated members of an organization, discriminated against people unfairly, destroyed careers and laid waste to entire educational systems. Most leaders operate somewhere in the middle of this spectrum of hero and villain, trying to make positive cultural contributions while also making missteps along the way. One thing is certain, leaders' agency, capital and positional authority gives them the potential to establish, maintain and shape the culture of a school. That said, it is critical that leaders embrace culture as a complex and protean phenomenon rather than a catchy slogan or set of words that look good on a poster.

In this chapter, we *learn* concepts that will help leaders be *literate* with respect to the diverse and dynamic cultures in their school. In considering the ways these translate to practice, we also suggest approaches and theories that help leaders intentionally practice their *leadership* in a culturally relevant manner and celebrate multicultural diversity as an organizational strength and source of innovation and learning. The chapter ends with prompts and questions to help readers *reflect* on their experiences with culture and think through the ways that it facilitates and constrains their leadership behavior. Some key concepts discussed in this chapter include the following:

- School Culture
- Layers of Culture
- Healthy and Toxic Cultures
- Culturally Relevant Leadership.

LEADERSHIP AND CULTURE: THEIR RECIPROCAL INFLUENCE IN ORGANIZATIONS AND SCHOOLS

Edgar Schein's (1992) influential work is an excellent place to begin a journey toward understanding culture and leadership. Schein contended that leadership is closely associated with the creation and management of culture. In fact, he goes so far as to proclaim that "the only thing of real importance that leaders do is to create and manage culture and that the unique talent of leaders is their ability to understand and work with culture" (p. 5). After acknowledging that there are a great many definitions of culture in the organizational studies literature, Schein provided a synthetic definition of organizational culture:

> "A pattern of shared basic assumptions that the group learned as it solved its problems of external adaptation and internal integration, that has worked well enough to be considered valid and, therefore, to be taught to new members as the correct way to perceive, think and feel in relation to those problems" (p. 12).

To Schein (1992), culture is comprised of three inter-related components: artifacts, espoused values and basic underlying assumptions. *Artifacts* may include the physical environment, language, technology, products and style of clothing, as well as the visible behavior of organizational members and organizational processes. Put differently, cultural artifacts are anything that people use or create—including both tangible artifacts created as people work together and intangible artifacts that people create as they develop relationships and working norms on a day-to-day basis. *Espoused values* are the set of values that become an essential part of organizational philosophy and serve as a guide in dealing with a variety of situations. These are the visions, missions and goals that people co-create in a school as guiding statements of value and intent. *Basic underlying assumptions* are often taken for granted and are seldom considered, confronted or debated. In a sense, these are the silent language of the organization— the assumptions about the work and human nature that we seldom pause to think about. As a result, these assumptions are very difficult to change and are usually only apparent upon deep reflection and analysis.

Culture is a pervasive organizational phenomenon that encompasses organizational members' concerns and their approaches to dealing with those concerns. Thus, cultural assumptions develop as a result of both routine and exceptional interactions between organizational members and their environment. To perform effectively, organizational members must either achieve consensus or have shared understandings about plurality, meaning that they understand and acknowledge the distributed or differential nature of the organization's work. Culture provides stability, predictability, meaning and a way to make sense of diversity in a potentially uncertain environment. It is simultaneously shaped by (i) organizational decisions in the past, (ii) current people and the nature of their contextualized interactions and (iii) individual and collective visions of the future.

Culture is an abstract concept. As organizations evolve, they inevitably develop shared assumptions of more abstract organizational issues (Schein, 2010). Organizational members develop shared basic assumptions about the nature of reality and truth, time, space, human nature, human activity and human relationships. As a result, leaders must learn to decipher a variety of cultural clues to maintain constructive relationships within the organization, to ensure organizational productivity and to monitor whether espoused organizational values are in keeping with the way things work on a daily basis (Schwein, 2010). Leaders must also acknowledge the complexity of organizational culture as well as the special power, authority and agency they possess to create, influence and shape culture.

Schein (1992) alleges that the difference between management and leadership is the leader's concern with culture. An organization's positional leader is likely to have a profound impact on the development of the organization's culture as a result of their strong (or weak) assumptions, self-confidence and determination. Because of the leader's unique position within the organizational structure, he/she will exert great influence in organizational decision-making processes and the frequency and quality of interactions between organizational members.

Leaders utilize various formal and informal mechanisms to shape culture in the organization (Fullan, 2001). The issues that leaders pay attention to, measure and control send a powerful message to other organizational members. The way in which a leader reacts during an organizational crisis may establish new norms or values and communicate other underlying assumptions. Leaders also shape culture through the budgetary process and allocation of fiscal, human and other organizational resources. Leaders serve as role models, teachers and coaches to communicate values and assumptions to other organizational members. Organizational members learn what type of behavior the organization values through the allocation of sanctions, rewards and status. A subtle way in which leaders within the organization maintain culture is to recruit, select and promote individuals with similar values and beliefs (Normore & Paul Doscher, 2007). Organizational design and structure, systems and procedures, rites and rituals, physical space, stories about important events and people, and formal statements of organizational philosophy, mission and vision may also establish and nurture culture. While it is important to have a basic understanding of how these issues play out across organizations, it is essential that we understand how they are manifested in schools.

School Culture and Leadership

There are many definitions of school culture, and we will explore several in this section. None of them is "right," and each emphasizes different aspects of somewhat similar concepts that may help a leader understand culture in a deeper or more powerful way. Sarason (1966) defined school culture as "those aspects of the setting which are viewed by school personnel as 'givens' or essential features, which would be defended strenuously against elimination or marked change, and which reflect psychological concepts and value judgments" (p. 3). Stolp and Smith's definition of school culture (as cited in Stolp, 1994) is "the historically-transmitted patterns of meaning that include the norms, values, beliefs, ceremonies, rituals, traditions and myths understood, maybe in varying degrees, by members of the school community" (p. 1).

School culture affects every facet of work in a school, and it touches every member of the school community in potentially positive and negative ways. For example, the degree to which a school culture is collaborative or individualistic has an impact on several aspects of the school. A school focused on effectiveness and productivity pro- vides teachers with opportunities for success within a narrowly-defined notion of the term success. A collegial and transparent culture is typically characterized by frequent and high-quality communication among stakeholders, and is therefore more likely to have distributed and democratic problem-solving processes. A school culture may promote successful change and improvement efforts, but it can also hold schools back from reaching their potential. A supportive, caring school environment may increase the energy and motivation of faculty, staff, students and administrators. Finally, a purposeful culture allows organizational stakeholders to focus upon key values and behaviors and what is important (Deal & Peterson, 1999).

School improvement occurs when teachers strengthen their teaching skills, the curriculum is renovated, the organization improves, and parents and citizens are involved in a partnership with the school (Saphier & King, 1985). The school culture may enhance these efforts or undermine them. According to Saphier and King, the 12 norms of school culture that affect school improvement are: (a) collegiality; (b) experimentation; (c) high expectations; (d) trust and confidence; (e) tangible support; (f) reaching out to the knowledge bases; (g) appreciation and recognition; (h) caring, celebration and humor; (i) involvement in decision making; (j) protection of what's important; (k) traditions and (l) honest, open communication. Leadership plays a role in the development of these norms. Without quality leadership, school culture will not develop nor endure over time. Whenever these norms are present within a school, principals, teachers, students and other stakeholders reflect them in the discussion of values and in their behavior.

Leaders may play a valuable role in shaping school culture. Norris (1994) suggests that shaping the school culture requires understanding, patience, and human relations and communication skills on the part of the principal. In addition, the principal must learn the existing culture by studying heroes, rituals, ceremonies and cultural networks. Establishing communication linkages allows the principal to understand facets of the school culture. The principal must also meet the social and psychological needs of teachers by documenting accomplishments and providing encouragement and resources necessary for teaching and learning to occur. The principal must create opportunities for individual teacher growth by promoting professional development and challenging teachers to expand their learning. The principal must be open to self-examination and reflection, model desired behaviors, and hire new teachers who share the same educational philosophy as the school. The principal, as a shaper of culture, communicates compelling ideas and the meaning of those ideas for organizational members (Sergiovanni, 1994).

The leader's principles, values and beliefs and how they are communicated to organizational members are extremely important. As the chief enculturation agent, the principal is the individual ultimately responsible for school culture and must establish the link between mission and practice, focus on solutions, be creative, acknowledge the needs of others, promote staff development, create learning networks and focus on student achievement as the primary goal of schooling (Krajewski, 1996). Cultural leadership on the part of the principal requires the principal to stir human consciousness, interpret meanings, articulate key cultural strands and link organizational members to them (Sergiovanni, 1984). The principal's long-range vision is also a key factor in the building of culture (Sashkin & Sashkin, 1993).

Fullan (1992) contends that the principal should enable other organizational members to become problem solvers. In facilitating the development of teachers as problem solvers, the principal creates a collaborative school culture. To realize the development of the collaborative school culture, the principal should foster vision building, create norms of collegiality while respecting individuality, develop problem-solving skills and conflict resolution strategies, promote lifelong teacher professional development that encourages teachers to be inquiring, reflective, and collaborative, and to support school improvement initiatives.

Within the context of constant pressures for school reform, Deal and Peterson (1991) link successful school reform to a productive school culture and the principal as a symbolic leader. The cultural approach to principal leadership is intimately connected to the human resource approach with a focus on individual skills and needs, the structural approach with a focus on goals and coordination, the political approach with a focus on power, conflict and interest groups within the organization, and the free market economic approach with a focus upon competition between schools for student enrollment. The cultural approach focuses upon behavioral patterns and the norms, values and beliefs that sustain these patterns over time.

School culture refers to "the character of a school as it reflects deep patterns of values, beliefs and traditions that have been formed over the course of its history" (Deal & Peterson, 1991, p. 7). A positive school culture may improve school productivity. Several studies suggest that an organization that possesses a strong identity, adapts to the changing environment and responds to the needs of its members will be more productive (Deal & Kennedy, 1982; Ouchi, 1982; Peters & Waterman, 1982). Successful schools share similar cultural characteristics; they have organizational members that share strong values promoting safety and the primacy of learning, establish high expectations for students and teachers, believe in the importance of basic skills instruction, develop performance standards and feedback procedures, and value strong leadership (Deal & Peterson, 1991).

Principals, as the shapers of school culture, must continually seek to refine the symbols and symbolic activity that provide meaning to organizational members. Principals must analyze the existing school culture and utilize the history of the school to provide a transition to the future. Once the principal has analyzed the school culture, he/she may begin to shape the culture by serving as a symbol, potter, poet, actor and healer. As a symbol, the principal affirms the values of the organization through behavior and attention to certain issues. As a potter, the principal interacts with the school's heroes, rituals, ceremonies and symbols. As a poet, the principal reinforces the school's values by using certain language to promote an ideal image. As an actor, the principal plays a role in the daily drama of school. As a healer, the principal provides stability in the presence of various transitions and the ever-changing school environment (Deal & Peterson, 1991).

Maehr and Midgley (1996) contend that two reasons exist for examining school culture. First, school culture makes a difference in the motivation and learning of students. When students sense and understand the mission of the school and recognize the salient elements of a collaborative school culture, student motivation and learning increases. Second, school culture is a manageable variable. Managing the culture, the principal may enhance the investment teachers and students make in their educational endeavors.

UNDERSTANDING CULTURE AND LEADERSHIP IN YOUR SCHOOL

In this section, we offer several ways of thinking about leadership in your school. First, we describe four continua that characterize leadership and school cultures and, in a second section, we explore the implications of the idea that everyone interprets culture in their own way. Indeed, these two ways of thinking about leadership and culture are not exhaustive—they are meant to get you thinking and perhaps even to share with your colleagues at school as you discuss extant and potential cultural dynamics.

Understanding Your School's Culture: Examining Four Continua

We ask that you consider where your school falls on each continuum and think about the ways that leadership can move the school's culture further toward each of the poles. The continua we explain are:

Continuum One: Healthy to Toxic School culture

Purkey and Smith (1985) describe the characteristics of a **healthy school culture**. In a school with a healthy culture, faculty members are given responsibility for increasing academic performance and are involved in democratic decision-making processes. Collaborative relationships and a sense of community foster faculty involvement in these decision-making processes. Strong leadership within the school emerges to initiate and maintain school improvement efforts. Students spend a majority of their time engaged in active learning activities related to a well-articulated, coordinated curriculum. Ongoing staff development addresses the specific organizational and instructional needs of faculty and students. Parents are actively involved in the school community. Schoolwide recognition is provided to students achieving academic excellence. The district office supports the efforts of the faculty, staff and administration. The mission and vision of the school are clearly articulated leading to clear goals, high expectations, order and discipline.

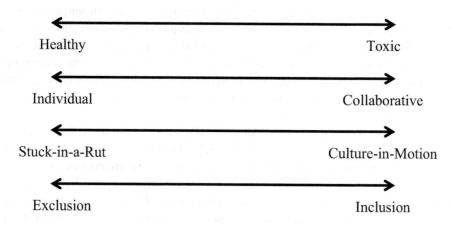

FIGURE 4.1 Continua for Understanding School Culture

Toxic school cultures, on the other hand are characterized by cultural norms such as a lack of transparency, low trust, cronyism, poor communication (or even miscommunication), lying, abusive relationships, low professionalism and career sabotage. Leadership plays just as important a role in creating, establishing and nurturing a toxic culture as they do a healthy one. Leadership in a toxic culture can either be by omission—ignoring abhorrent behavior and cultural norms—or by commission, taking part in behavior that destroys people and groups in the school community. Importantly, a toxic school culture often has the appearance of being a healthy culture. Though nasty in their day-to-day behavior, members will use the language of positivity to give outsiders the impression that all is well—only those who work and learn in the school will know if a culture is truly toxic and even within the school there will be variation. This variation is due to the fact that one person's toxic school culture may be another's healthy culture, given their perspective on how things should work and what they hope to get out of interactions with their peers and groups throughout the school community. That said, there are four fundamental differences between leadership in a toxic culture and one in which people have many different needs and wants as far as what makes a healthy culture: leaders in a healthy school culture provide all members of the organization, regardless of their varied needs, ability and dispositions, with care, support, respect and inclusion.

Continuum Two: Individualistic to Collaborative School Culture

School cultures characterized as individualistic are not necessarily bad, but they do not allow for a school to reach its potential, as efforts do not undergo critique or enhancement through interaction. Individualistic school cultures are marked by isolation, and conversations and collaboration are minimal. For some educators and students, this may be comfortable, but it is a school leader's responsibility to facilitate curriculum coherence, collaborative support of students and bring the school's collective wisdom to bear on problems and initiatives. For these reasons, it is more desirable for leaders to work toward a collaborative school culture (Brooks, 2006).

A collaborative school culture may impact the school in many ways. A collaborative school culture fosters school effectiveness and productivity. In addition, collegial and collaborative activities that foster better communication and problem-solving activities develop. This culture, in turn, promotes successful change and improvement efforts. Faculty, staff, students and administrators commit to and identify with the organization. As the culture increases the energy and motivation of faculty, staff, students, administrators and community, these stakeholders increasingly focus upon what is important and valued (Deal & Peterson, 1999).

Cunningham and Gresso (1993) offer similar suggestions for enhancing school improvement efforts through school culture. School culture may be enhanced by providing all organizational members with the opportunity to communicate about organizational issues on a regular basis. Quality information is provided to all organizational members to promote quality decision making. The development of a collective vision allows for collective action toward a common goal. Collegiality and collaboration foster cohesion between organizational members and develop common understandings. Trust and support among faculty, staff and administration is prevalent. When conflict emerges between individuals or groups, a spirit of compromise emerges. Individual empowerment and lifelong growth are promoted within the school. Finally, these processes contribute to sustained inquiry and continuous school improvement efforts.

Collaboration and collegiality are very important for school improvement efforts (Barth, 1990). Barth suggests that most teachers and principals exhibit congeniality—not collegiality. In a collegial environment, principals and teachers talk openly about best practice. Teachers observe one another in their respective classrooms, work together in planning and designing curriculum, and teach each other about new and innovative teaching practices. Collegiality results in better decisions, higher morale and trust among teachers and principals, sustained interest in adult learning, and increased motivation on the part of students. These collaborative cultures are created and maintained through structures deliberately created by individuals within the organization (Hopkins, Ainscow, & West, 1994). Most often, the principal has the greatest ability to modify these structures.

Continuum Three: Stuck-in-a-Rut to Culture-in-Motion

Each school has a unique culture and may be characterized as forward moving or stuck-in-a-rut (Rosenholtz, 1989). Forward-moving schools are characterized by an emphasis on values and beliefs that are used to guide decision-making processes. Within these schools, stakeholders collaborate extensively in meaningful ways and trust one another to individually and collectively improve the ways that organizational members work together to improve education. Teachers emphasize student learning and experiences, work together, and share instructional strategies. On the other hand, in stuck schools, teachers are isolated from one another, self-reliant, and reluctant to share or collaborate (Brooks, 2006a). Stuck schools are further characterized by teacher and administrator isolation, lack of professional dialogue, inadequate induction and professional development, and a lack of involvement in the school's decision-making processes. Fullan and Hargreaves (1996) describe stuck schools as having a fragmented culture wherein teachers are autonomous, self-reliant and unaware of the activities in other teachers' classrooms. While individualism is encouraged, collaboration is discouraged. Because teachers are content with existing teaching practices, new and innovative teaching practices are not considered. The principal is seldom available for assistance. When the principal provides assistance, teachers perceive the assistance as arrogance on the part of the principal and incompetence on the part of the teacher. Another variation is a balkanized culture, where teachers collaborate and share only with friends or groups that are like minded. These subcultures of teachers are strong and defensive, competing for position, resources and territory. Members of these subcultures create shared perceptions of learning, teaching styles, discipline and curriculum with each other—but only with each other. Conflict results when teachers attempt to collaborate outside their respective subculture. The balkanized culture is characterized by poor communication, indifference and divergent groups of teachers (Fullan & Hargreaves, 1996).

Continuum Three: Contrived Collegiality to Comfortable Collegiality

Contrived collegiality results when school leadership creates the processes or structures for collaboration, but puts people together for inauthentic purposes. This happens when school leaders attempt to force teacher collaboration by putting them into teams, committees or communities around issues where they lack expertise, interest and where trust and commitment are low. As a result, teacher interactions are regulated and imposed rather than being liberating and generative. While this culture is meant to support new and innovative approaches to teaching, it actually reduces teacher motivation to cooperate beyond normal expectations. Such a culture discourages true collegiality because it provides a credible starting point for the development of a true collaborative culture (Fullan & Hargreaves, 1996).

In a comfortably collaborative culture, teachers engage in conversations about schooling; however, these conversations do not involve critical questions about their work nor how to improve the work. The conversations result in comfortable support for one another without constructive criticism. Teachers are aware of other teachers' classroom activities and discuss strategies for dealing with problem students (Fullan & Hargreaves, 1996).

A collaborative culture exists when teacher development is facilitated through interdependence. A majority of teachers agree on educational values and are committed to change and improvement. Teachers help, support and trust one another and are aggressively curious about teaching and learning. Conversations among teachers focus upon school improvement. Teachers frequently observe other teachers in their classrooms. As a result of this observation, teachers engage in a critical analysis of teaching practices. School leaders challenge ineffective teaching practices while encouraging the professional development of individual teachers (Fullan & Hargreaves, 1996).

Continuum Four: Exclusion to Inclusion

One of the key cultural dynamics in a school is the issue of who is included and who is excluded from various aspects of the organization's work. Are leaders making use of the collective expertise in the school community or are they choosing to make decisions alone or with the input of only a few trusted advisors? Leaders have a tremendous capacity to influence the degree to which students, staff, teachers and community members have input into the school's work. They also help shape whether the involvement is symbolic or substantive. Leaders should look at both processes and outcomes to determine whether or not people are excluded from various aspects of the school's work and strive to create an inclusive rather than exclusive culture.

In many schools, participation exists on paper but not in practice. In such schools, there is talk of student voice but little or no meaningful ways of involving students in a substantive or meaningful way. There may be structures that "ensure" engagement such as Professional Learning Communities, committees, task forces and so on, but the actual influence these structures have in practice is marginal or negligible. Leadership can perpetuate such practices by giving the illusion of democratic decision making or it can make such structures a meaningful way to get input into the direction and work of the school. One dynamic that is essential for leaders to consider is the degree to which they systematically include or exclude people from the work of the school—are women, students, people of color, community members, early career educators, experienced educators or other groups routinely left out of (or included in) decisions and processes that affect their work? It is important, then, to consider not only which individuals are included and excluded, but which systems of exclusion and inclusion exist for groups of people in the school community.

UNDERSTANDING YOUR SCHOOL'S CULTURE: WE ALL EXPERIENCE CULTURE AND SCHOOL LEADERSHIP IN A UNIQUE WAY

Educational leadership literature tends to emphasize school and organizational dynamics as a means of understanding culture, yet all of you are simultaneously engaged in multiple cultures and each of us has a unique experience based on our participation in these cultures (Cunningham & Gresso, 1993; Deal & Peterson, 1991, 1999). It is important for school leaders to understand that people in a glocalized world exist in multiple cultures simultaneously, and the particular cultures of which each person is part have a profound effect on education (Spring, 2008). Although this assertion is hardly novel, a growing body of research indicates that "cultures are slowly integrating into a single global culture" (Spring, 2008, p. 334). This global culture, connected most obviously by technology and interconnected multinational economic webs, is also merging a world knowledge base that in turn influences what and how topics are taught (Lechner & Boli, 2005). However, understanding that people are connected through a developing global culture is only part of the complexity educational leaders must understand. There are at least 12 cultures in which we all take part:

1. Individual. Each person experiences culture in a unique way.
2. Dyadic. This is a culture that develops between any two people. In some ways, culture is a complex web of individual relationships we develop between single people.
3. Small Group. This is a culture that develops in any group with less than 12 members. These can be formal or informal and occur throughout most schools.
4. Large Group. Large group cultures exceed 12 members but do not include the entire school.
5. School. The formal and informal culture of the school.
6. District. The culture of the district has a tremendous influence on leadership and school culture through both formal and informal dynamics.
7. Community. All students and educators in the school are also community members. They are therefore influenced by community happenings, subcultures in the community and familial dynamics.
8. State/Province. State and province cultures typically impact the school in terms of laws and policies.

9. Regional. Many cultural dynamics like racism, sexism, ableism and ageism are regional in nature.
10. National. National culture has to do with various issues related to identity, patriotism and history.
11. International. The specific relationships that people in the school have with other nations have a tremendous influence on culture and leadership. This is particularly evident with immigrant and refugee populations in the school.
12. Global. Everyone is part of global culture, where ideas, norms, art, economics, educational practices and so on are shared (and marginalized) on a worldwide level.

As you can see, the cultures in which we participate range from extremely small to worldwide. These cultures are protean, meaning that they are always changing and each of them is influenced by changes in the others. Put differently, everything is changing and these changes have a reciprocal influence on all of the cultures in which we participate. This means that culture is infinitely complex, and that it is as important to understand the similarities that we share as it is to try and be aware of the individual differences that manifest in our experiences of culture. Educational leaders must be mindful of how their practice and decisions help create an environment where cultural differences and similarities collaborate synergistically or potentially pit people and groups in the school community in adversarial stances (Brooks & Jean-Marie, 2007).

Importantly, while culture is typically defined as something shared, our individual experiences and interpretations of culture is perhaps the single most important cultural dynamic for leaders to understand. Anthropologists have developed a useful concept to help us understand individual experiences of culture. Propriespect is the notion that each person constructs a unique cultural experience rather than necessarily adopting or assimilating group and/or organizational values and norms. Put differently, everyone has an individual culture. Wolcott (1991) suggested the concept "as a complement to the global reference to all the information aggregated within an entire cultural heritage" and recognized a "need to specify the particular information that any particular human, who must therefore be a member of a particular subset of human groups, actually knows" (p. 257). Thinking of culture in this way is very similar to the widely recognized notion that each student learns differently, and that educators and educational leaders who individualize their practice can have the most positive influence on a student. Understanding culture in terms of propriespect, an educational leader will understand and value the importance of individual histories, values and beliefs in addition to those that espoused in plenum. Indeed, leaders with this kind of literacy might be said to practice a culturally relevant leadership, similar in some ways to culturally relevant pedadgogy (Ladson-Billings, 1995a, 1995b), an approach to education centered on individual children's culture. The figure below illustrates the various cultures in which people engage—it also represents various spheres in which leaders should be aware when they lead in schools. It is powerful and illustrative for school leaders to consider both their own culture relative to this model but also the various cultures of other educators, staff and students in their school.

TOWARD CULTURALLY RELEVANT LEADERSHIP

So what does a better understanding really mean for educational leaders? How can they lead better? What are some principles they might keep in mind as they practice their work in schools? Thankfully, we can take some guidance from several decades of outstanding work from teacher educators practicing culturally relevant pedagogy and from leadership scholars working in the area of culturally relevant leadership.

Culturally relevant pedagogy is "a theoretical model that not only addresses student achievement but also helps students to accept and affirm their cultural identity while developing critical perspectives that challenge inequities in schools (and other institutions) perpetuate" (Ladson-Billings, 1995a, p. 469). Culturally relevant pedagogy has informed the development of culturally relevant leadership (Horsford, Grosland & Gunn, 2011). These approaches to education and leadership are context-specific, but emphasize several propositions that can help guide leaders in their work.

Culturally Relevant Pedagogy and Leadership Are Focused on Both Academic and Non-Academic Success

Banks and Banks (1995) suggest that "despite the current social inequities and hostile classroom environments, students must develop their academic skills. The way those skills are developed may vary, but all students need literacy, numeracy, technological, social and political skills" (p. 160). Importantly, while academic skills are at the heart of this orientation toward education, it also makes clear that these skills must be relevant inside and outside of the classroom. Success, then, is not limited to strictly classroom success, but also to success more broadly conceived as enhanced quality of life, which also includes economic, social and political prosperity. For leaders, this highlights the importance of practicing a holistic approach to the work. Simply ignoring the multiple cultures in which people participate is critical to making a positive difference in their lives. School leaders must learn about both the cultures within the school and the cultures beyond the school walls if they are to practice a culturally relevant form of leadership. Academic success and practicing a leadership that is rooted in cultural awareness are inextricably connected. Leaders who practice a one-size-fits-all, or culturally irrelevant form of leadership will not help the educators and students with whom they work, and their leadership is likely to impede their learning and development (Brooks, 2006).

Culturally Relevant Pedagogy and Leadership Demand a Critical, Deep and Ongoing Understanding of Self, Other and Context as the Foundation of Education

This means that for education to be culturally relevant, leaders, teachers and students must begin their work by reflecting on their own culture, values, knowledge and situations and by seeking to understand the culture, values, knowledge and situations of the other people with whom they will co-construct their education, and the multiple contexts in which they will learn and teach. Culturally relevant pedagogy and leadership, then, are simultaneously about learning visible curricula and unlearning hidden curricula. Leaders, students and teachers bring intentional and unintentional attitudes, dispositions, and biases to their educational practice that need reflection, discussion and, at times, change. Effective cultural leadership cannot take place without deep reflection and questioning of one's assumptions, values and behavior.

Culturally Relevant Pedagogy and Leadership Are a Constructivist Approach to Education

Culturally relevant pedagogy and leadership assumes that knowledge is co-constructed by people as they learn and lead in context. This has implications for instruction, leadership, curricula and many other aspects of education. Certain instructional approaches such as problems-based learning (Brooks, 2008) and cooperative learning (Banks & Banks, 1995) hold more promise for promoting co-construction than didactic approaches such as lectures, though these certainly have their place. Curricula should be flexible, relevant and adaptable rather than monolithic and static. There is no immutable base of knowledge for the culturally relevant educator and leader—they constantly revise their approach when they learn more about the cultures in which they take part. Further, as constructivism suggests an approach to education that prizes an assimilation of existing knowledge with extant knowledge through higher order critical thinking, it likewise demands an approach to leadership that is done with followers and not at them. Put another way, culturally relevant leaders acknowledge that there is no single knowledge base, but multiple knowledge bases that continually evolve as new information and experiences challenge and extend existing information and experiences.

Culturally Relevant Pedagogy and Leadership Stress the Importance of the Immediate and Long-Term Usefulness of Education

Since culturally relevant pedagogy and leadership are founded on prior knowledge of students and teachers, it is of immediate use in that it builds on what is already there in a manner that allows people to meaningfully and progressively enhance current perspectives and knowledge. Additionally, since culturally relevant pedagogy is grounded in a critical perspective toward the assimilation of that which is new and that which is old, it equips leaders, students and teachers alike with a set of skills and dispositions oriented toward lifelong learning.

Each of these propositions must be understood not as normative dicta, but as specifically contextualized and idiosyncratic manifestations germane ultimately to *particular* relationships, situations and contexts. While culturally relevant leadership is rooted in constructivist ontology, the propositions nonetheless acknowledge each person's discrete influence in shaping their relationships with students, and also their influence in shaping relationships with the base of knowledge that undergirds curriculum and instruction in a given course or educational situation. Culturally relevant leadership is, importantly, practiced from a critical perspective. It recognizes that status-quo educational practice—especially those practices that are culturally irrelevant—will perpetuate a deeply rooted cultural hegemony that stands only to perpetuate inequities rather than ameliorate them. In the end, culturally relevant leadership focuses on two central tenets: (a) leading *with* rather than *at* people; (b) understanding that cultural differences between and among people demands an approach that is sensitive to needs, traditions and mores of individual students, as well as cultures and subcultures within an educational setting and the ways they connect to cultures external to the school and around the world.

DISCUSSION

1. Fill out the table below and discuss with your peers. In what ways did you answer in a similar manner? How did you answer differently and why?

Discrimination	Prompts	How does this look in your school?
Ableism	Does the leadership activity formally or informally privilege, exclude or marginalize people or groups in terms of physical or mental ability?	
Adultism	Does the leadership activity privilege, exclude or marginalize children?	
Ageism	Does the leadership activity privilege, exclude or marginalize people in terms of age or experience?	
Classism	Does the leadership activity privilege, exclude or marginalize people in terms of their socio-economic status or means?	
Ethnocentrism	Does the leadership activity privilege one cultural tradition or ethnicity and exclude or marginalize others?	
Heterosexism	Does the leadership activity privilege, exclude or marginalize people based on their sexual orientation?	
Racism	Does the leadership activity privilege, exclude or marginalize people based on their race or ethnicity?	
Religious imperialism	Does the leadership activity privilege, exclude or marginalize people in terms of their spirituality or religion?	
Sexism	Does the leadership activity privilege, exclude or marginalize people based on their gender?	

2. How many languages are spoken among faculty, staff and students at your school? How do you know this and what does this diversity suggest about the forms of leadership you should practice?
3. What cultural values does your school espouse? Are these philosophical beliefs different from beliefs in practice?

4. Ask people throughout a school or classroom to name the three words that mean the most to them and that they feel define their character. How many words are similar or different? Discuss the variety of words.

REFERENCES

Abdelaziz, A. (2004). Information literacy for lifelong learning. Paper presented at the World Library and Information Congress: 70th IFLA General Conference and Council, p. 4. Available[online]: http://ifla.org/IV/ifla70/papers/116e-Abid.pdf

Barth, R. S. (1990). *Improving schools from within: Teachers, parents, and principals can make the difference.* San Francisco, CA: Jossey-Bass Publishers.

Bates, R. J. (1984). Toward a critical practice of educational administration. In T. J. Sergiovanni & J. E. Corbally (Eds.), *Leadership and organizational culture: New perspectives on administrative theory and practice*, pp. 260–74. Urbana: University of Illinois Press.

Bogotch, I., Beachum, F. Blount, J., Brooks, J. S. & English, F. W. (2008). *Radicalizing educational leadership: Toward a theory of social justice.* Sense Publishers, Netherlands.

Bolman, L. G., & Deal, T. E. (1997). *Reframing organizations: Artistry, choice, and leadership.* 2nd ed. San Francisco, CA: Jossey-Bass Publishers.

Brooks, J. S. (in press b). The miseducation of a professor of educational administration: Learning and unlearning culturally (ir)relevant leadership. In A. K. Tooms & C. Boske (Eds.), *Educational leadership as International social justice discourse: Navigating collaborations, careers, and challenges in a global context.* Charlotte, NC: Information Age Publishing.

Brooks, J. S. (2006a). Tinkering toward utopia or stuck-in-a-rut? School reform implementation at Wintervalley High. *Journal of School Leadership*, 16(3), 240–65.

Brooks, J. S. (2006b). *The dark side of school reform: Teaching in the space between reality and utopia.* Rowman & Littlefield Education: Lanham, MD.

Brooks, J. S., Hughes, R., & Brooks, M. C. (2008). Fear and trembling in the American high school: Educational reform and teacher alienation. *Educational Policy*, 22(1), 45–62.

Brooks, J. S., & Jean-Marie, G. (2007). Black leadership, white leadership: Race and race relations in an urban high school. *Journal of Educational Administration*, 45(6), 756–68.

Brooks, J. S., & Miles, M. T. (2008). From scientific management to social justice . . . and back again? Pedagogical shifts in educational leadership. In A. H. Normore, (Ed.), *Leadership for social justice: Promoting equity and excellence through inquiry and reflective practice*, pp. 99–114. Charlotte, NC: Information Age Publishing.

Brooks, J. S., Normore, A. H., Jean-Marie, G., & Hodgins, D. (2007). Distributed leadership for social justice: Influence and equity in an urban high school. *Journal of School Leadership* 17(4).

Brooks, J. S., Scribner, J. P., & Eferakorho, J. (2004). Teacher leadership in the context of whole school reform. *Journal of School Leadership*, 14(3), 242–65.

Capra, F. (1996). *The web of life: A new scientific understanding of living systems.* New York: Anchor Books.

Cassel, C. A., & Lo, C. C. (1997). Theories of political literacy. *Political Behavior, 19*, 317–35.

Courchene, T. J. (1995). Glocalization: The regional/international interface. *Canadian Journal of Regional Science, 18*(1): 1–20.

Cunningham, W. G., & Gresso, D. W. (1993). *Cultural leadership: The culture of excellence in education.* Needham Heights, MA: Allyn & Bacon.

Dantley, M. E. (2005). African American spirituality and Cornel West's notions of prophetic pragmatism: Restructuring educational leadership in American urban schools. *Educational Administration Quarterly*, 41(4), 651–74.

Deal, T. E., & Kennedy, A. A. (1982). *Corporate cultures: The rites and rituals of corporate life.* Reading, MA: Addison-Wesley.

Deal, T. E., & Peterson, K. D. (1991). *The principal's role in shaping school culture.* Washington, DC: United States Department of Education.

Deal, T. E., & Peterson, K. D. (1999). *Shaping school culture: The heart of leadership.* San Francisco, CA: Jossey-Bass.

Earle, J., and Kruse, S. (1999). *Organizational literacy for education: Topic in educational leadership.* Mahwah, NJ: Lawrence Erlbaum Associates.

Fullan, M. (2001). *Leading in a culture of change.* San Francisco, CA: Jossey-Bass.

Fullan, M. G. (1992). Visions that blind. *Educational Leadership*, 49(5), 19–22.

Fullan, M., & Hargreaves, A. (1996). *What's worth fighting for in your school?* New York, NY: Teachers College Press.

Gelberg, D. (1997). *The "business" of reforming American schools.* Albany: State University of New York Press.

Glickman, C. D., Gordon, S. P., Ross-Gordon, J. M. (2001). *Supervision and instructional leadership: A developmental approach.* Needham Heights, MA: Allyn & Bacon.

Greenfield, T. B. (1988). The decline and fall of science in educational administration. In D. E. Griffith, R. T. Stout, & P. B Forsyth (Eds.), *Leaders for America's schools*, pp. 131–59. Berkeley, CA: McCutchan.

Griffiths, D. E. (1995). Theoretical pluralism in educational administration. In R. Donmoyer, M. Imber, & J. J. Scheurich (Eds.), *The knowledge base in educational administration: Multiple perspectives*, pp. 300–9. Albany: State University of New York Press.

Griffiths, D. E. (1997). The case for theoretical pluralism. *Educational Management & Administration*, 25, 371–80.

Hopkins, D., Ainscow, M., & West, M. (1994). *School improvement in an era of change.* New York, NY: Teachers College Press.

Horsford, S. D., Grosland, T. J., & Gunn, K. M. (2011). Pedagogy of the personal and professional: Considering culturally relevant and antiracist pedagogy as a framework for culturally capable Leadership. *Journal of School Leadership*, 21, 582–604.

Kilman, R. H., Saxton, M. J., & Serpa, R. (1986). Issues in understanding and changing culture. *California Management Review*, 28(2), 87–94.

Krajewski, R. J. (1996). Enculturating the school: The principal's principles. *NASSP Bulletin*, 80(1), 3–8.

Ladson-Billings, G. J. (1998). Teaching in dangerous times: Culturally relevant approaches to teacher assessment. *The Journal of Negro Education*, 67(3), 255–67.

Ladson-Billings, G. J. (1997). *The dreamkeepers: Successful teachers of African-American children.* San Francisco, CA: Jossey-Bass.

Ladson-Billings, G. J. (1995a). Toward a theory of culturally relevant pedagogy. *American Education Research Journal*, 35, 465–91.

Ladson-Billings, G. J. (1995b). Toward A critical race theory of education. *Teachers College Record*, 97, 47–68.

Ladson-Billings, G. (1995c). But that's just good teaching! The case for culturally relevant pedagogy. *Theory into Practice*, 34(3), 159–65.

Ladson-Billings, G. (1992). Liberatory consequences of literacy: A case of culturally relevant instruction for African American students. *The Journal of Negro Education*, 61(3), 378–91.

Larson, C. L., & Murtadha, K. (2002). Leadership for social justice. *Yearbook of the National Society for the Study of Education*, 101(1), 134–61.

Lechner, F., & Boli, J. (2005). *World culture: Origins and consequences*. Malden, MA: Blackwell.

Liable, J. (2000). A loving epistemology: What I hold critical in my life, faith, and profession. *International Journal of Qualitative Studies in Education*, 13(6), 683–92.

Lortie, D. C. (1975). *Schoolteacher: A sociological study*. Chicago: University of Chicago Press.

Maclellan, E. (2008). Pedagogical literate: What it means and what it allows. *Teaching and Teacher Education*, 24 (8), 1986–92.

MacKenzie, D. E. (1983). Research for school improvement: An appraisal of some recent trends. *Educational Researcher*, 12(4), 5–17.

Maehr, M. L., & Midgley, C. (1996). *Transforming school cultures*. Boulder, CO: Westview Press.

Marcoulides, G. A., & Heck, R. H. (1993). Organizational culture and performance: Proposing and testing a model. *Organization Science*, 4(2), 209–25.

Marx, G. T. (2006). *Future-focused leadership: Preparing schools, students, and communities for tomorrow's realities*. Alexandria, VA: Association for Supervision and Curriculum Development.

Mintzberg, H. (1993). *The rise and fall of strategic planning: Reconceiving roles for planning, plans, planners*. New York: Simon & Schuster.

Morgan, G. (1997). *Images of organization*. Thousand Oaks, CA: Sage Publications.

Normore, A.H., & Paul Doscher, S. (2007). Using media as the basis for a social issues approach to promoting moral literacy in university teaching. *Journal of Educational Administration*, 45(4), 427–50.

Norris, J. H. (1994). What leaders need to know about school culture. *Journal of Staff Development*, 15(2), 2–5.

Ouchi, W. G. (1982). *Theory Z*. Reading, MA: Addison-Wesley.

Peters, T. J., & Waterman, R. H., Jr. (1982). *In search of excellence: Lessons from America's best-run companies*. New York, NY: Harper and Row.

Purkey, S. C., & Smith, M. S. (1985). School reform: The district policy implications of the effective schools literature. *The Elementary School Journal*, 85(3), 353–89.

Rafaeli, A., & Worline, M. (2000). Symbols in organizational culture. In N. M. Ashkanasy, C. P. M. Wilderom, & M. F. Peterson (Eds.), *Handbook of organizational culture and climate*, pp. 71–84. Thousand Oaks, CA: Sage Publications.

Rosenholtz, S. J. (1989). *Teacher's workplace: The social organization of schools*. White Plains, NY: Longman.

Saphier, J., & King, M. (1985). Good seeds grow in strong cultures. *Educational Leadership*, 42(6), 67–74.

Sarason, S. (1966). *The school culture and processes of change*. College Park, MD: University of Maryland.

Sashkin, M., & Sashkin, M. G. (1993). Principals and their school cultures: Understanding from quantitative and qualitative research. In M. Sashkin & H. J. Walberg (Eds.), *Educational leadership and school culture*, pp. 100–23. Berkeley, CA: McCutchan Publishing.

Schein, E. H. (2010). *Organizational culture and leadership*. 2nd ed. San Francisco, CA: Jossey-Bass.

Sergiovanni, T. J. (1984). Cultural and competing perspectives in administrative theory and practice. In T. J. Sergiovanni & J. E. Corbally (Eds.), *Leadership and organizational culture*:

New perspectives on administrative theory and practice, pp. 1–17. Urbana, IL: University of Illinois Press.

Sergiovanni, T. J. (1994). *Building community in schools*. San Francisco, CA: Jossey-Bass.

Siegrist, G. (1999). Educational leadership must move beyond management training to visionary and moral transformational leaders. *Education, 120*(2), 297–303

Spring, J. (2008). Research on globalization and education. *Review of Educational Research, 78*(2), 330–63.

Spring, J. (1998). *Education and the rise of the global economy*. Mahwah, NJ: Lawrence Erlbaum.

Stolp, S. (1994). Leadership for school culture. *ERIC Digest #91*. Eugene, OR: ERIC Clearinghouse on Educational Management.

Trice, H. M., & Beyer, J. M. (1993). *The culture of work organizations*. Englewood Cliffs, NJ: Prentice Hall.

Weber, E. (2007). Globalization, "glocal" development, and teachers' work: A research agenda. *Review of Educational Research, 77*(3), 279–309.

Stevens, P., & Weale, M. (2003). *Education and economic growth*. London: National Institute of Economic and Social Research.

Westheimer, J. (1998). *Among school teachers: Community, autonomy, and ideology in teachers' work*. New York: Teachers College Press.

Wolcott, H. F. (1970). An ethnographic approach to the study of school administrators. *Human Organization, 29*(2), 115–22.

Wolcott, H. F. (1991). Propriospect and the acquisition of culture. *Anthropology and Education Quarterly, 22*(3), 251–73.

Brooks, J. S. & Miles, M. T. (2010). The social and cultural dynamics of school leadership: Classic concepts and cutting-edge possibilities. In S. D. Horsford (Ed.), *New perspectives in educational leadership: Exploring social, political, and community contexts and meaning* (pp. 7–28). New York, NY: Peter Lang Publishing.

CHAPTER 5

Moral Leadership

In this chapter, we argue that use of a moral literacy approach to analyzing and interpreting social events, equity and equality builds amity, harmony and trust among stakeholders, positioning educational leaders to make risky, yet transformational and ethically responsible decisions for the benefit of morally competent school communities, morally competent nations and a morally competent world (Paul-Doscher & Normore, 2008). Since public life is interwoven by social values, opportunities to engage in moral leadership interpretations enable the public to come to grips with the common good for the greater society.

Moral leadership promotes development of knowledge and moral virtues in students, and helps to develop skills for moral reasoning. To become moral agents, educators need to acknowledge and honor the importance of assuming responsibility to be informed before making moral judgments—whether locally, nationally or globally. Tuana (2003, p.8) asserts that social imperatives must be taken into account. She states, "Our sense of ourselves, as well as what others think of us, often rests on the extent to which we live up to these virtues" (p. 8). Consequently, developing skills for moral reasoning is necessary, whereby students and those who teach them develop the skills and dispositions to identify the critical values at play. While some cultures do not seem to have the same definitions of "fairness" or "respect" (e.g., in fundamentalist Islamic cultures as compared to European definitions, or adhering to the Geneva conventions as guidelines for "civilized war"), other moral virtues are shared across many cultures (Normore & Paul-Dosher, 2007). These include honesty, fairness, respect, responsibility and caring (Christians, 2003; Tuana, 2003). By engaging education leaders in such a discourse, analysis can harness understanding of responsible leadership and learn the reflective practices that can filter throughout school systems and connect to morally competent citizenship (Tuana, 2003; Widdowson, 1995).

For the remainder of this chapter, we present ideas and concepts focused around Starratt's notion of responsible leadership (Starratt, 2005), and show how media can stimulate discourse around social, cultural, economic, and political issues. The emotional "ups and downs" generated by the media can provide a grand array of opportunities and teachable moments that educators can employ to empower students to become responsible, morally literate, and transformational leaders. Regional, national, and international social issues are regularly reported on the internet, in the local, regional, and international media. These issues are complex and often unique, defying quick moral interpretations. Consequently, the argument is made that moral literacy ought to be a component of the formal educational leadership experience throughout the formative schooling and university teaching and learning.

Starratt (2005) posed a framework consisting of five domains of moral responsibility for educational leaders. These serve as key concepts of this chapter and include:

- Moral responsibility as human being
- Moral responsibility as citizen and public servant
- Moral responsibility as an educator
- Moral responsibility as an educational administrator
- Moral responsibility as an educational leader.

Other key concepts include:

- Moral literacy
- Moral agency.

The application of each domain to the ethical analysis of dilemmas brought forth by current national and international crises and conflicts reveals archetypal behaviors of educational leaders as proactive morally literate agents. We contend that Starratt's framework represents a process that can be integrated into teaching and learning experiences for aspiring and practicing school leaders when responding to controversial issues through the use of moral and transformational means of problem solving.

We begin with an introduction to the *learning* about educational leadership concepts such as ethics, social justice, fairness, equity, equality, and morality. Next, we will demonstrate how moral *literacy* is analyzed through the use of school teaching and university teaching. We refer to various media venues from the last 10 years (2005–2015) to illustrate the point. This is intended to help readers identify and analyze the way that various concepts are practiced in their schools, local communities and throughout the world. Then, we focus on an educational *leaders'* ability to influence the cultural dynamics of a school through formal and informal means. It emphasizes skills that include open-mindedness, careful attention to others' views, considering ethical implications of decisions, learning how to evaluate strengths and weakness of our own and others' positions, taking responsibility for our actions and beliefs, and exercising fairness and respect for social and cultural differences. Finally, we offer a series of *reflective* questions to help decipher how moral literacy is practiced on a daily basis for educational leaders.

Many educational leaders are motivated by a sense of duty to leave the world a better place than it was before they arrived. An internal moral compass directs them to take on tasks, assume styles, and behaviors commensurate with their beliefs regarding right and wrong, virtue and vice, and social responsibility. Much as a ship must have a compass and rudder to reach its destination on a stormy sea, an educator must likewise be guided by personal, thoughtful, considered action to attain personal and organizational goals (Begley et al., 2006; Brooks & Normore, 2005). Leadership in any endeavor is a moral task, but even more so for educational leaders. While educational leaders are responsible for the success of their particular institution, their work also impacts other institutions both now and in the future, for those who are taught are the future leaders of tomorrow. According to Berreth and Berman (1997), adults need to demonstrate by role modeling to youth that it is possible to live one's values and advocate for a more just and responsible society. Educational leaders must constantly monitor and reflect upon their actions as they speak volumes about the values these leaders support. Proactive stands taken by educational leaders are commentaries on how things should be done—the definition of moral action—viewed by everyone, especially students.

Moral literacy. Moral literacy ensures that students are knowledgeable, hold moral virtues, and develop skills for moral reasoning. To become moral agents, students must be taught the importance of assuming responsibility to be informed before making moral judgments. Tuana (2003, p.8) asserts that social imperatives must be taken into account. She argues, for example, that "the news media . . . in striving to provide interesting sound bites about human cloning has often been ethically irresponsible in failing to adequately explain the science of cloning" and "politicians debating cloning legislation often do not acknowledge the full range of scientific options that are available." However, Marginson (1987, p.16) asserted that "media is there for educators to understand and use, to use more effectively than we have done up to now." Media knowledge as communication is always a form of social practice (Giroux, 2002).

While some cultures do not seem to have the same definitions of "fairness" or "respect" (e.g., in fundamentalist Islamic cultures as compared to European definitions, or adhering to the Geneva conventions as guidelines for "civilized war"), other moral virtues are shared across many cultures. These include honesty, fairness, respect, responsibility, and caring (Christians, 1995, 2003; Tuana, 2003). As Tuana (p.8) states, "Our sense of ourselves, as well as what others think of us, often rests on the extent to which we live up to these virtues." Consequently, developing skills for moral reasoning is necessary, whereby we develop the skills and dispositions to identify the critical values at play in moral situations. Skills such as open-mindedness, careful listening to others' views, considering ethical implications of decisions, learning how to evaluate strengths and weakness of our own and others' positions, and taking responsibility for our actions and beliefs have been articulated by Tuana. By engaging school leaders—aspiring and practicing—in such a discourse analysis, these leaders can harness understanding of responsible leadership and learn the reflective practices that can filter throughout school system and connect to local, national, and global awareness (Tuana, 2003; Widdowson, 1995).

RESPONSIBLE LEADERSHIP

Whether identifying geographic locations, discussing political ideology, culture or day-to-day life, most American students do not know how people in other countries live. This is a critical disadvantage to students who will join a job market heavily influenced by international economics and politics. In a 2005 speech given in Seattle for the National Association for Independent Schools, Fareed Zakaria, Editor of *Newsweek*, indicated that schools have a responsibility to equip students to live in the global community. According to MindWare Publishing (2006, p.3) a Seattle-based developer of creative training solutions to help educational institutions teach students global awareness about the social, political, and cultural issues facing people, Zakaria stated:

> The most important thing that schools can do is to make people aware that understanding the world is very much part of the requirement of being an educated person . . . If you look at what's happening in India, China and Brazil, you are seeing the rise of a new world, where these countries see themselves as equals . . . But we're a country where very few people . . . know much about the world.

Schools with an established culture of cross-curricular connections and considered academic discourse have been able to successfully subsume current events into regular curriculum content (Diem, 2002). For example, school leaders who had taken a proactive approach to students' social and emotional learning prior to the September 11th crisis were found to be better prepared to assist children in coping and returning to business as usual than those who did not (Lantieri, 2002).

To return to the five domains of ethical responsibility outlined by Starratt (2005), educational leaders have a duty to gather school resources, structures, and processes in support of this kind of constructivist teaching and learning. Starratt poses a framework to assist educational leaders in fulfilling this obligation, identifying five domains of ethical responsibility. He encourages leaders to investigate issues from multiple perspectives, identify best practices, and confront ethical concerns through a scaffold moral approach. Together the domains represent an integrated moral system; the implementation of each successive domain incorporates those previous and encourages broader and deeper reflection-in-action. Starratt's framework invites leaders to move beyond transactional ethical decision making into the realm of transformational leadership practice. Analysis of the application of each domain to particularly complex educational dilemmas—those resulting from recent national and international crises and conflicts as highlighted in the media—reveals the constructive potential of Starratt's framework when using media as a social issues approach to promoting moral literacy in university teaching.

Responsibility as a Human Being

Starratt (2005, p. 125) writes that in this domain "an educational leader considers the humanly ethical thing to do, taking into account the intrinsic dignity and inviolability of the other person." Morality is based on respect, compassion, and dignity. Starratt concludes that people must act with delicacy and diplomacy toward one another, for a denial of respect and dignity is a denial of others' humanity—an ethical violation.

Intrinsic to this domain is the ethic of care in which practitioners grapple with issues of loyalty and trust (Shapiro & Stefkovich, 2005). In the days following the September 11 attacks and the instigation of the war in Iraq, pundits and educators alike recommended stepped-up curricular attention to international education (Argetsinger & Strauss, 2002; Casey, 2003; Levy, 2002; Sanders & Stewart, 2004). More recently, headlines in the media have been cause for discourse on the ethical responsibilities of human beings. Multiculturalists perceived the controversies associated with September 11 and the Iraq War as teachable moments for peace and opportunities to break down the distrust, fear, ignorance, and misunderstandings that had engendered such crises. Similar to what Fairclough (1995) suggested, graduate students in the same ethics class engaged in group discussions about theorizing "news" as discourse when presented with these media headline. These students highlighted the discursive nature of media power and its influence on knowledge, beliefs, values, social relations, and social identities through particular ways of representing the world, its particular constructions of social identities and its particular constructions of social relations.

Starratt urges leaders who want to rise to the level of moral agents to steer clear of both polarized positions. According to Starratt's concept of human responsibility, leaders should exercise the ethic of care, not so much on the subject of study but upon its object, the free flow of objective, constructive information between and among teachers and students. The first responsibility of school leaders is to bridge the knowledge gap that exists within their schools. They felt the need to cultivate respect for the dignity of learning and analysis; they cannot do so if they have adopted a predisposition toward the interpretation of knowledge or its wider political purpose. Educators are responsible to maintain objectivity, neutrality, and independence regarding teaching and learning. Impartiality enables delicacy and diplomacy in the treatment of controversial topics. Human beings' tendency toward cultural relativism makes learning to understand one another a controversial act; educators are positively responsible to maximize students' clarity of thought and mitigate distortion caused by personal biases (Paul-Dosher & Normore, 2006).

Responsibility as a Citizen and Public Servant

In this domain, Starratt (2005) obliges educational leaders to respect the rights of other citizens and the public order. Moral leaders' ethic of citizenship leads them to work primarily for the common good; as public servants, they provide valuable services to the community. Starratt sees educational leaders as the state-in-action. Their responsibility is to enhance the scope and functioning of democracy while upholding the law and maintaining the public trust. Civil liberties are often the subject of controversy in times of national crisis and conflict. A teacher who had compared the foreign policy speeches of George Bush to those of Adolph Hitler was recently reinstated to an Aurora, Colorado high school after being placed on leave for his classroom remarks (Rouse, Bentley & Nicholson, 2006). A little known provision of the No Child Left Behind Act, requiring all public high schools to provide military recruiters unhindered access to student information pending loss of federal aid, has been challenged by those advocating students' right to privacy (Goodman, 2004).

Recent events have also placed educators in the crossfire between the competing needs of the community vs. the nation. All three headlines reignited the debate over poverty and equity and moral responsibility. The reports provided an opportunity for graduate students to engage in discussion about the responsibility of an educational leader as a citizen and a public servant. Students reacted to the headlines by commenting on a recent plan posed by a conservative US Congressman to pay for the anticipated $263 billion bill to restore the Gulf Coast includes cuts to Medicaid and food stamps and economy-spurring tax cuts for the wealthy, thus equally distributing the costs to the nation's senior citizens (who are often on the edge of poverty) and the nation's wealthy citizens. A response engendered by students about their roles as citizens of the United States focused on the Gulf Coast region's public schools. They felt that public schools, segregated more than ever by race and class, are required to compete for scanty federal and local funds with burgeoning private and charter school programs. One student made reference to Robert Greenstein, director of the Center on Budget and Policy Priorities. According to Hardy (2006, pp. 29–30), Greenstein stated "We've gone from a situation in which we might have a long-overdue debate on deep poverty to the possibility, perhaps even the likelihood, that low-income people will be asked to bear the costs."

In another article—one that was highlighted in the *Michigan Citizen*—Lee-Boggs (2007) asserts that education is not only information, it is tied up with self-esteem and knowing that one is worthwhile. Graduate students felt that education is not confined to classrooms, instead it is all over the place—that it comes from everywhere, from all directions. Lee-Boggs further states (p. 13):

> The kids themselves have to decide which way they are going to go. We can help them decide by encouraging and helping them to become more introspective, to keep asking themselves, "Who am I? What is my purpose in life?" We can help them develop their self-esteem by learning how to communicate better and by providing opportunities for them to connect with people and groups in the community who are doing positive work. We have to find ways in our schools to discuss divisive issues like light and dark skin and hair, which we still have in our community. So much damage has also been done to our kids by TV and radio. Having conversations about these things in our schools can lead to understanding rather than conflict. We need dialogue about these questions as much as we need dialogue about military recruitment. Once you make a child feel bad about herself, her color, her hair, education stops. We have to protect a child's self-esteem. We have to lift children up and keep them whole, just as we have to look at education holistically.

There are different kinds of education, and educational leaders must embrace all forms. There is academic education, and there is education for life. Life is problem solving. Often, education is talked about as if it exists in one form only. However, according to Lee-Boggs (2007, p.2):

> All the disruptions that happen every day in school are challenges we have to face in life and our students have to figure these out and still come out OK. From that point of view, students are getting a social education in our schools which some people never get. The school is not divorced from the community. The community is in the school. Our schools are a reflection of our society and we have not fixed our society. We have to address issues that have nothing to do with academic education.

One of the hottest curriculum trends in the United States is homeland security education. National security issues press educators in times of conflict. Community colleges around the nation are retooling and renaming existing public safety and emergency response training programs in order to take advantage of billions of dollars in federal homeland security funds (Barr, 2001; Seyfer, 2003). To prepare students for popular homeland security degrees, secondary school districts are creating specialized vocational programs (Cavanaugh, 2004) and adopting new curriculum strands in terrorism and Middle Eastern area studies (Argentsinger & Strauss, 2002). Foreign language study is once again being called a national security priority. President George Bush pledged $114 million for the National Security Language Initiative; the Department of Defense announced it would spend $750 million over the subsequent 5 years to increase personnel with abilities in Arabic, Chinese, Russian, Hindi, Farsi and other critical languages (US Department of State, 2006). Students reflected on the potential impact of the initiative amid concerns about academic freedom and covert recruitment policies. One student presented his thoughts about how government security projects and campuses can be uneasy bedfellows. Another student cited research that reiterated how community colleges and public school foreign language programs, already squeezed for funds, feel forced to accept homeland security aid as their only means of survival (Hines, 2003). Young, poor people of color may be disproportionately targeted for postgraduation homeland security or defense employment due to their greater need for higher education scholarships. Language experts likewise bemoan the fork in the road which they tread (Hines, 2003, p. 21): "languages for intellect and illumination in one direction, languages as tools in the conduct of business, diplomacy and intelligence activity in the other direction."

Some educational leaders are responding to the challenge of educating the citizenry. Nelson (2002, p. 155), writes of the democratic agency of the moral leader:

> I believe that we need to make ourselves available for public foray, for gatherings of citizens who come together to wrestle with the confusing and catastrophic issues our country now faces . . . whatever the arena, we need to be in the forefront of it. This does not mean that we know more of the "right" answers, but it does recognize the various special abilities that we have as social educators; recognizing and explicating a variety of viewpoints, supporting or clarifying potentially unpopular views, helping to separate "noise" from actual information, and helping to provide some historical or cultural foundation for the issues at hand.

In short, educators as citizens and public servants must incorporate their objective and neutral responsibilities as human beings into their duty to facilitate and participate in democratic discourse. Nelson (2002, p.156) also writes of the educator's ability to view issues holistically and to assist in "separating the grams of knowledge from the tons of available information." He urges leaders to break out of internal educational debates and respond to parents and citizens' critical questions in times of crisis, serving as resources, brokering academic views, and promoting discussion. This approach is aligned with both Starratt's ethic of public citizenship and the ethic of critique as embodied in democratic patriotism, which engenders civic virtue through reflection, inclusiveness, and pluralism (Casey, 2003; Shapiro & Stefkovich, 2005).

Responsibility as an Educator

At this third level of responsibility, educators are charged with knowing (Starratt, 2005, pp. 126–27) "curriculum material in sufficient depth to understand the multiple applications and uses that knowledge provides to the community." This includes staying abreast of current research, expunging inaccurate or misleading information from the curriculum, and scaffolding learning activities to make learning accessible at all levels. Starratt (2005, p. 128) insists that educators recognize the validity of others' interpretation of knowledge and ensure, through their hiring, evaluation, and professional development programs, that teachers will:

• know the curriculum they are expected to teach and the academic disciplines that stand behind the curriculum;
• know how to communicate that curriculum in ways that enable youngsters to comprehend and appreciate the many facets of what they are studying;
• insist that students take away from their learning important life lessons that will shape how they look upon the natural, cultural, and social worlds, and appreciate the human adventure more deeply because of their studies; and
• know their students well, enabling them to craft learning tasks to respond to the background, interests, and prior experience of their students—in short, to respond to their moral quest for and ownership of their authentic identity.

Educational organizations have been sharply criticized for this kind of professional activity. As indicated by Paul-Dosher and Normore (2006), a high-profile public controversy raged over the National Education Association's Remember 9/11 website that was intended to assist teachers in lesson planning to commemorate the tragedy's first anniversary. When asked to comment about the controversy, students indicated that pundits disparaged the site for failing to identify the tenets of Islam as the cause of the terrorist attacks and for adopting the *blame America* approach. The National Education Association was censured for its lack of political savvy in publishing educational links that left the organization vulnerable to opponents' criticism. Analysts criticized the long-term significance of post-9/11 curricular changes and called attention to the haphazard ways in which educators made them. Teachers were warned of the risk of "adopting a curriculum of crisis" in their attempt to capitalize on student interest by incorporating current events (Levy, 2002, p. 2).

The morality of this domain dictates that educators actively engage in professionally ethical behaviors. Starratt (2005, p. 127) writes, "the ethic of educating is connected to the ethic intrinsic in learning itself. Learning always should be an activity of coming to know and understand something, because knowledge and understanding are always incomplete." In support of Starratt (2005), the aspiring and practicing school leaders in the ethics and educational leadership class emphasized that leaders must protect the integrity of the pursuit of knowledge and scholarship by protecting the activity itself, for example, eschewing preconceived notions of subject matter that obstructs acceptance of what one is striving to know. They further added that moral agents should therefore invite public scrutiny of their presentation of information as well as their sources. This may require that leaders, students, and citizens learn the different levels of "proof" as well as the different criteria for what constitutes reliable measures or indicators—in short, rules for deciding "good information" from questionable or even reliable sources. They should respond to critics by continuously striving to learn more and involve others in their learning (Christians, 1995). Furthermore, educators should refrain from admonishing others for their earnest, though less than thorough, understanding of subject matter, and reprove of those who purposefully misrepresent the facts or represent themselves as all-knowing (Marsch, 2006; Thomas, 2006).

Responsibility as an Educational Administrator

The moral administrator in this domain bears a special responsibility to promote the integrity of the learning process through school structures and policies. Here the ethic of justice comes into play; Starratt (2005, p. 128) explains that administrative mechanisms are not neutral, they either support the school's "core work—authentic learning—or they curtail or block" it. He proclaims that administration often does both simultaneously, to the advantage of the traditionally advantaged and the disadvantage of others. The one-size-fits-all approach to learning schedules, instructional style, textbooks, and assessments leaves low-performing students behind. The same approach to teacher evaluation frustrates some and intimidates others. Negative student labeling, biased student tracking, and preferred teacher assignments—administrators could reform all of these in order to raise student achievement.

Some have spoken of Hurricane Katrina's silver lining as being the ability to start with a blank slate in the rebuilding of the broken New Orleans school system (Hardy, 2006). The complete devastation brought on by this disaster, while resulting in a "diminished sense of security and a pervasive feeling of loss" (Sanoff, 2002, p. 30), prompts re-evaluation of traditional customs and priorities. Responses to critical incidents such as these, however, may be less determined by concepts of security and reality than by personal coping styles. Three primary strategies emerge from the literature: passive, avoidance, and active problem-focused (Franklin, 2002). Children and adults who adopt a passive style "feel paralyzed and helpless in the face of recent events . . . Some schools, for example, did nothing to process feelings about the recent terror attacks because they did not know how to respond" (Franklin, 2002, p. 4). Those tending toward avoidance are unwilling to discuss events, how they affect the world generally or themselves personally. This reluctance may be the result of a continuing sense of physical danger or fear of offending others' sensibilities. Administrators in avoidance adopt behaviors associated with their feelings of detachment, numbness, apathy or confusion (Franklin, 2002).

In contrast, Starratt's ideal moral educational administrators are problem-focused copers. They "take action and, despite feelings of anger, fear, or grief, purposefully act, or refrain from acting, to make things better" (Franklin, 2002, p. 4). Coupled with both vigilant objectivity and active pursuit of democracy and understanding in the previous domains, problem-focused leaders are more likely to be prepared to confront and create new norms resulting from national crises and conflicts. Likewise, moral administrators work to instill these capacities in others. Research indicates that problem-focused coping skills can be taught in age-appropriate ways at all levels (Franklin, 2002). Educational leaders who reach out to their community to teach problem-focused coping skills adopt an inherently moral stance. Their work is naturally practical and proactive; the trust, democratic discourse, and open-mindedness cultivated through attention to the previous domains facilitate consensus building during the problem-solving process.

In a *Maclean's* and *Time's* issue, a discourse opportunity for students became available in two similar articles that allowed them to engage in reflection-in-action, overcome reflexive emotional and behavioral reactions, and evaluate potential strategies and consequences from religious perspectives. The reports were titled, *The Da Vinci Code: The author who inspired The Da Vinci Code wages a new war over Jesus: Did he really die on the cross?* (Bethune, 2006b). A headline on the cover of *Time* carried the title, *The Opus Dei Code: The real story about the mysterious group that has a direct line to the Vatican* (Van Biema, 2006). In response to these media items, rather than center on a discussion about the media representation of whether or not Jesus died on the cross, students emphasized the importance of noting that ethics may not depend on religion, but even if religious ethics are not essentially different from secular ethics, religion can provide other benefits, such as motivation and satisfaction. Further discussion lead to an evaluation of personal and professional codes of ethics where students found themselves grappling with both. Since the class composition was diverse alon these lines (i.e., Christianity, Islam, Hinduism, and Judaism), students shared thoughts about moral relativism and an ethics of belief whereby the behaviors of one group could affect the welfare of other groups or of the world in general. Essentially, a common interest among the students focused on the need to engage in diligent efforts to better understand the commonalities among the religious beliefs found in the world, as well as secular beliefs that may provide a valid foundation for attempts to develop a "global ethic" toward which we may all aspire. Reflection of this nature enabled students to share viewpoints of various religions of the world today and think about ways they may each contribute to such an ethic.

Responsibility as an Educational Leader

At this level of moral practice, the leader "calls on students and teachers to reach beyond self-interest for a higher ideal—something heroic" (Starratt, 2005, p. 130). Here transactional leaders are invited to become transformational who exhibit a more "courageous humanity" (Starratt, p. 130) and who elicit the same from students and staff. Transformed schools are self-regulating, self-governing, and interactive with the wider world, able to change and be changed through their broad functioning. Teaching is deeply connected to students' inner life and lively pursuits in order to enlighten through learning. Starratt (p. 131) describes this as a value-added level of ethical enactment, often ignored or considered unattainable by professionals whose more immediate concerns are "preventing harm to students and teachers, guaranteeing their security and safety, supporting equitable consideration, and fulfilling contractual obligations out of a sense of justice."

Gerald Tirozzi, President of the National Association of Secondary School Principals, calls groundbreaking, transformational school programs "victory gardens"

(Sanders and Stewart, 2004, p. 201). Recent research indicates that world views and relationships are expanding in select classrooms, schools, and districts around the country. For example, the International School of the Americas in San Antonio and the Snowden International High School in Boston both offer low-income students international internships in corporations and nonprofit organizations. The Glastonbury School District in Connecticut places an emphasis on global education; 95 percent of students in the district take a foreign language (Paul-Doscher & Normore, 2006). Students in Newton Public Schools in Massachusetts learn not only from textbooks but also from the district's 20-year-long relationship with the Jingshan School in Beijing, China (Sanders & Stewart, 2004). Individual teachers, often lacking support from principals and superintendents, infuse international, cultural, and historical analysis into their lessons during teachable moments.

Few argue that schools must fulfill a basic responsibility to prepare a competent workforce and informed citizenry. But as former Governor of North Carolina in the United States, James Hunt, has said, "Our children are growing up in a whole new world, and . . . we have a responsibility to see that they understand that world" (Sanders & Stewart, 2004, p. 205). Our students live in a world transformed from the one in which school leaders were raised. How can educators who barely understand this brave new world themselves be expected to fill such a tall order? Having adapted to the Agricultural, Industrial, and Information Ages, school leaders must now adapt to the demands of the Global Age. The federal government can take a leadership role in this process through funding and legislation, but superintendents, principals, teachers, and parents must lay the groundwork and engage in the daily toil of transforming schools to address this New Order. Educational leaders bear an ethical responsibility to adjust not only school structures, but also their personal leadership style.

Although Starratt (2005, p. 131) poetically describes transformational educational leaders as players in this "drama of the human adventure", he neglects to invoke one of the aspects of participation in the spectacle—the element of risk. A core value of the transformational leader is a willingness to take personal risks in the name of a higher goal and ought to be addressed in educational leadership programs as well as by school leaders. If the risk is too high, one might argue that the educational leader is no longer privileged to exercise leadership role. Transformative leadership also concerns the process of affecting social changes over time (Aviolo & Gibbons, 1988; Burns, 1978, Leithwood et al., 1999; Tichy & DeVanna, 1990; Weber, 1947). Foster (1989) asserts that transformation encourages and supports the examination of one's life, ideas, and willingness to take risks, which in turn leads to the development of a critical framework for leadership. Self-reflective, transformational leaders who have earned the trust of their community by fulfilling their responsibilities as humans, citizens and public servants, educators, and administrators are indeed better positioned to take risks; nevertheless, at the end of the day transformational leaders are out on a limb all by themselves. Should they fall, there may or may not be someone there to catch them.

The previous four domains outlined by Starratt are primarily transactional; the ethic of justice directs leaders to adhere to explicit objective criteria when dealing with controversies engendered by media crises (Harf, 1989). Detachment and neutrality are implicit in all four of the previous domains. Transformational educational leaders, however, are those who have built up a sufficient bank of respect and goodwill to be able to break free of those constraints and risk espousing proactive, personal and subjective points of view. Dantley and Tillman (as cited in Marshall and Oliva, 2006) maintain that transformative leadership is about social change with a belief that transformation is a process that occurs over time. This kind of leadership, Starratt (2005, p. 131) writes, can be very messy, but the transformational leader "uses the messes as learning opportunities."

Four media headlines that provided opportunities to engage in such learning opportunities were reported in Maclean's: Tyrants of the Caribbean: A summit in Cuba (Petrou, 2006a); A pope unleashed: First he scolded godless Canadians. Then he took on militant Islam—Benedict XVI is just getting started (Bethune, 2006a); Russia goes to hell: Vladimir Putin is quashing freedoms, stifling opposition, bullying neighbors, encouraging Iran, promising an arms race and threatening a new Cold War (Petrou, 2006b), and The scariest man on earth: The nuke-happy, Jew-hating lunatic president of Iran (Petrou, 2006c). In response to these headlines, students discussed the concept of leadership and how there is no single set of moral concepts or ethical principles upon which to base decision making in educational leadership. They referenced Gardner's (1990) five points on what schools do not need in educational leadership: leaders who inflict punishment on followers; leaders who treat subordinates well, but encourage evil acts against others; leaders who use bigotry, hatred, revenge, or fear as motivators; leaders who make followers dependent; and leaders who destroy human dignity. As stated by noted ethicist, Alasdair MacIntyre (1966, p. 266), "Conceptual conflict is endemic in our situation because of the depth of our moral conflicts . . . each of us therefore has to choose both with whom we wish to be morally bound and by what ends, rules, and virtues we wish to be guided."

THE MORAL AGENCY OF THE EDUCATIONAL LEADER

There are leaders, and then there are Leaders. Leaders (with a lower case *l*) are those whose power is based on bureaucratic or personal authority; their transactional activities are characterized by bartering, building, and binding support from staff, students, parents, and community. Leaders (with a capital *L*) share their moral authority with stakeholders (Paul- Doscher and Normore, 2006). They are bound to the community with whom they pursue school improvement commitments through "mind, heart, and practice" (Sergiovanni, 2006, pp. 159–164). These two styles may converge in the first four domains of moral responsibility—that of the human, the citizen and public servant, the educator, and the administrator—but they diverge in the fifth, transformational educational leadership. It has been suggested that a defining characteristic of the transformational leader is a willingness to take risks for moral beliefs. This gamble is inherent to moral agency. It is also an element of the transformational leader's distinctive consciousness, which extends beyond the rational into the intuitive.

Certainly, both types of leaders are rational in that they are capable of logical, coherent thought. They are also both capable of moral consideration: the weighing of relative degrees of suffering or relief resulting from various decisions. When faced with moral dilemmas, both may choose to act as *homo economicus* by pursuing the greatest utility obtainable through available opportunities. As discussed, however, there are some dilemmas of huge proportions—national crises and conflicts—in which leaders may feel they have no choices. Having examined the situation objectively from as many points of view as possible—human, civic, educational, administrative—they may determine that the core problem is simply too big to tackle in its entirety alone. They may feel that every alternative presents so little utility it is useless to make proactive moves, leaving them in a fully reactive mode, solely composed of transactional consideration.

Transformational leaders as moral agents will not and cannot exist in a purely reactive state. They possess more than a moral compass—their moral agency is an inner intuitive engine, propelling them toward the pursuit of greater good. They may know that their acts may be a drop in the bucket toward solving problems, but they are compelled to act, nonetheless. They feel obligated to contribute their part in solving the equation; to quote an old saw, they need to be part of the solution, not part of the problem. Knowing the risks, and after having gained the trust of their community through moral fulfillment of moral responsibilities, transformational educational leaders instinctively choose to take positions and pursue programs out of their need to leave the world a better place. In doing so, they transform more than their schools and communities, they transform themselves from being victims of their circumstances into proactive moral agents. That is why it is so crucial that we rethink and transform education at all levels from kindergarten to doctoral degrees. What we urgently need are school boards, school superintendents and college presidents with the imagination and courage to introduce innovative curriculums and structures that create a much more intimate connection between intellectual development and practical activity, root students and faculty in their communities and natural habitats, and engage them in the kind of real problem solving in their localities that nurtures a love of place and provides practice in creating the sustainable economies, equality, and community that are the responsibilities of citizenship. Schools and colleges dedicated to this kind of education would look and act very differently from today's educational institutions.

Discussion

There are specific discussions from the analysis of Starratt's five domains to real-world global problems and include the following:

Case Studies of Controversy and Objectivity

1. How can educational leaders—teachers, school leaders, and parents alike—benefit from study of moral literacy and ethical case studies involving dilemmas of controversy and objectivity?
2. Pre-service and in-service professionals can prepare themselves for inevitable educational predicaments by thoroughly contemplating the application of Starratt's

five domains to real-world problems. How do educational leaders choose useful texts that focus on particular salient issues, for example, militarism, creationism or human sexuality?

3. How can educational leaders scaffold case studies in such a way as to examine the issue from multiple moral perspectives and lead the reader away from transactional thinking and toward transformational ideas?

Research

1. Qualitative and quantitative research is needed to support the efficacy of Starratt's framework. How do educational leaders conduct an applicable analysis in the following areas?

    (a) Policies and regulations functioning to support or subvert academic freedom and integrity in primary and secondary schools
    (b) Methods for scaffolding instruction of controversial subjects in order to build complex understandings over time
    (c) Mechanisms for teaching and supporting problem-focused coping skills for educational leaders and their communities
    (d) Historical analysis, from the perspective of each of Starratt's five domains, of transformational leaders' failed and successful innovations

Advocacy

1. The ability to explain professional practices to the general public will determine leaders' success or failure in adopting Starratt's philosophy of moral agency. How can educational learn to advocate for their own objective and subjective positions, as well as the rights of others to adopt the same?
2. How can professional organizations encourage and support leaders who engage in public citizenship activities—answering critical questions, brokering views, encouraging discussion, and serving as resources?
3. Should the educational leader as moral agent act not only as an arm of the state, but also as the ideal of government in action? Why of why not?

We believe every educator is a leader and has the potential to be a morally literate and authentic leader if he/she chooses "to do the right thing" and has the courage to act in a manner consistent with their convictions. As we become aware of the issues and concerns facing education and our communities, we argue that one thing is certain—responsibilities will not diminish. In fact, they will likely become more difficult. Faced with unprecedented demands to respond effectively and appropriately to escalating roles and responsibilities, education in general has an urgent need for leaders who can inspire people, help shape them ethically and morally, and spur them on to purposeful action for moral literacy.

At the end of each day, we encourage all educators to reflect on your actions of that day. Drawing from the theory and pragmatism about moral literacy, ethics, morals, values and leadership in the various branches of education (e.g., Normore, 2014), we urge you to consider the short term vs. the long-term consequences of your daily actions and use the following reflective questions to enhance your understanding of the personal, interpersonal and organizational consequences of your actions:

1. Did I exercise my virtues today?
2. Did I share and model integrity, trustworthiness, honesty and compassion?
3. How did people around me react to me today?
4. Think of the best instructor (or school teacher) you ever had and then list two characteristics of what made that person the best. Every day before you go to work reflect on these characteristics and decide whether or not this is what you want to be remembered for.
5. Did I affirm, in some way, every person I encountered today?
6. Was I more positive than negative in my attitude and behavior?
7. All human beings have the right to be treated with dignity simply because they are human. Did I treat people with dignity and respect?
8. Did I consciously try to separate personhood from behavior in each difficult situation?
9. Did I practice fairness and justice today?
10. In what ways did I benefit those around me? In what ways was I more of a hindrance?
11. On what basis did I decide what was just; that is, mission statement, code of ethics, values statement, the law?
12. How did I explain the decision? How was it accepted? What could I have done differently?
13. Did I make my organization better because I was there today?
14. Was I better because I was a part of this organization?
15. Was I able to get beyond my own interests to make the organization stronger?
16. Was I able to draw upon the strengths of the organization to help me become more human and a better professional?

On a final note, remember to affirm your self-esteem as an educator and educational leader, and disagree with immoral behaviors and unethical practices, and work at recognizing this distinction every day.

REFERENCES

Afflerbach, P., & Moni, K. (1994). *Legislators, reporters, and reading assessment reading research report No. 31*. College Park, MD: National Research Center.

Allan, M., & Ratnesar, R. (2006). The end of Cowboy diplomacy: What North Korea, Iraq, and Iran teaches us about the limits of going it alone. *Time*, July 17, 20–6.

Arenas, A., & Pedicone, J. J. (2005). Working through trauma. *Education Week, 25*(13), 36–37.

Argetsinger, A., & Strauss, V. (2002). Schools translate terror into curriculum changes. *The Washington Post*, February 8, A.01.

Avioli, B, J., & Gibbons, T. C. (1988). Developing transformational leaders: A life span Approach. In J. A. Conger, R. N. Kanungo, & Associates (Eds.), *Charismatic leadership: The elusive factor in organizational effectiveness*, pp. 276–308. San Francisco, CA: Jossey-Bass.

Barr, S. (2001). National security incentive plan has a not-so-secret weapon: Money. *The Washington Post*, December 6, B.02.

Bednar, M. (2003). Stop congressional policing of curricula in area studies. *The Arab American News*, October 31, 18.

Begley, P. T., Shapiro, J., Normore, A. H., & Leonard, P. (2006). Integrating values and ethics into teaching. Invited keynote panel presented at the 11th Annual Values and Leadership Conference, Victoria, British Columbia, October 5–7.

Bell, A. (1998). The discourse structure of news stories. In A. Bell, & P. Garrett (Eds), *Approaches to Media Discourse*, pp. 64–101. Oxford, UK: Blackwell.

Berkowitz, P., & McFaul, M. (2005). Studying Islam, strengthening the nation. *The Washington Post*, April 12, A.21.

Berreth, D., & Berman, S. (1997). The moral dimensions of schools. *Educational Leadership*, *54*(8), 24–7.

Bethune, B. (2006a). A pope unleashed: First he scolded godless Canadians. Then he took on militant Islam, Benedict XVI is just getting started. *Macleans*, October 2, 30–3.

Bethune, B. (2006b). Da Vinci Code: The author who inspired The Da Vinci Code wages a new war over Jesus: Did he really die on the cross? *Macleans*, April 3, 33–9.

Bethune, B. (2006c). It happened here—Yes, Canada had slaves too—for 200 years . . . one who fought for her freedom and burned down the central core of Montreal. *Macleans*, January 30, p. 26.

Bok, S. (1995). *Common Values*, Columbia, MO: University of Missouri Press.

Bowers, P. (2002). Charles Taylor's practical reason. In S. Bracci, & C. Christians (Eds.), *Moral engagement in public life: Theorists for contemporary ethics*, pp. 35–52. New York, NY. Peter Lang.

Boydon, J. (2006, January 9). Desperate optimism: 100,000 residents—one fifth of the pre-flood population—have returned to New Orleans . . . and find desolation and hope among the ruins. *Macleans*, pp. 26–30.

Brecht, R. D., & Rivers, W. P. (2002). Language, national security, and the nation's Schools. *Basic Education*, *46*(8), pp. 13–6.

Brown, C. L. (2002). Early language learning: A national necessity. *Basic Education*, *46*(8), 3–7.

Brooks, J. S., & Normore, A. H. (2005). An Aristotelian framework for the development of ethical leadership. *Journal of Values and Ethics in Educational Administration*, *3*(2), 1–8.

Burns, J. M. (1978). *Leadership*. New York, NY: Harper and Row.

Casey, L. (2003). Teaching the lessons of 9/11. *Dissent*, *50*(1), 50–7.

Cavanagh, S. (2004). Safe and secure. *Education Week*, *2*(25) 27–9.

Christians, C. (2003). The media and moral literacy. Ethical Space, The International Journal of Communications Ethics, 1(1). 1–17.

Christians, C. (1995). Communication ethics as the basis of genuine democracy. In P. Lee (Ed.), *The Democratization of Communication*, pp. 75–91. University of Wales Press, Cardiff.

Christians, C., Ferre, J., & Fackler, M. (1993). *Good News: Social Ethics and the Press*. New York, NY: Oxford University Press.

Dantley, M. E., & Tillman, L. C. (2006). Social justice and moral transformative Leadership. In C. Marshall, and M. Oliva (Eds.), *Leadership for Social Justice: Making Revolutions in Education*, pp. 16–30. Boston, MA: Pearson Education.

Diem, R. A. (2002). Some reflections on social studies and one high school: Post September 11. *Theory and Research in Social Education, 30*(1), 145–7.

Fairclough, N. (1995). *Media Discourse.* London, UK: Arnold.

Foster, L. A. (1989). Breaking down racial isolation. *Educational Leadership, 47*(2), 76–7.

Franklin, C. G. (2002). Coping in the face of terror. *Children and Schools, 24*(1), 3–5.

Gardner, J. W. (1990). *On Leadership.* New York, NY: Free Press.

Gibbs, N. (2006), The truth about stem-cells: The hope, the hype and what it means for you. *Time,* August 7, pp. 40–6.

Giroux, H. A. (2002). Democracy, freedom, and justice after September 11th: Rethinking the role of educators and the politics of schooling. *Teachers College Record, 104*(6), 1138–62.

Goodman, D. (2004). NCLB accesses high-schools for the military in war time. *The Education Digest, 69*(9), 4–6.

Harf, J. E. (1989). National security in the curriculum. Retrieved from, http://thememoryhole. org/edu/eric/ed307222.html

Hardy, L. (2006). Katrina exposes our schools' shameful inequality. *The Education Digest, 71*(7), 27–31.

Hines, M. E. (2003). Foreign language curriculum concerns in times of conflict. *The Delta Kappa Gamma Bulletin, 70*(1), 15–21.

Lantieri, L. (2002). After 9/11: Addressing children's fears. *Principal, 81*(5), 35–6.

Lee-Boggs, G. (2007). Inside and outside school walls. *Michigan Citizen,* January, Detroit, MI.

Levy, T. (2002). Should 9–11 change K-12? *Social Education, 66*(1), 2.

MacIntyre, A. (1966). *A Short History of Ethics.* New York, NY: Macmillan.

Marginson, S. (1987). Is there a human face behind that tough teacher mask? *The Australian Teacher, 19,* 14–16.

Marsch, C. (2006). Aristotelian ethos and the new orality: Implications for media literacy and media ethics. *Journal of Mass Media Ethics, 21*(4), 338–52.

Mindware Publishing (2006). Classroom game teaches students global awareness about life in emerging markets. Retrieved from, www.MindWarePublishing.com.

Nelson, M. (2002). Responding to the crisis: Reflections on educating the public. *Theory and Research in Social Education, 30*(1), 155–7.

Normore, A.H., Paul-Doscher, S., Riaz, O., Delval, R., & Martinez, J. (2006). In search of authentic educational leadership: Pursuing, cultivating, and supporting special moral agency. A symposium presented at the 11 Annual Values and Educational Leadership Conference, Victoria, British Columbia, October, 5–7.

Normore, A. H. (2004). Ethics and values in leadership preparation programs: Finding the North Star in the dust storm. *Journal of Values and Ethics in Educational Administration, 2*(2), 1–7.

Paul-Doscher, S., & Normore, A. H. (2006). The moral agency of the educational leader in times of national crisis and conflict. Paper presented at the 11 Annual Values and Educational Leadership Conference, Victoria, British Columbia, October, 5–7.

Petrou, M. (2006a). Tyrants of the Caribbean: A summit in Cuba. *Macleans,* September 25, pp. 34–7.

Petrou, M. (2006b). Russia goes to hell: Vladimir Putin is quashing freedoms, stifling opposition, bullying neighbors, encouraging Iran, promising an arms race and threatening a new Cold war. *Macleans,* May 22, pp. 26–33.

Petrou, M. (2006c). The scariest man on earth: The nuke-happy, Jew-hating lunatic president of Iran. *Macleans,* January 23, pp. 28–32.

Ravitch, D. (2001, October 17), Now is the time to teach democracy. *Education Week*, available at: http://edweek.org/ew/articles/2001/10/17/07ravitch.h21.html?querystring=ravitch

Rouse, K., Bentley, J., & Nicholson, K. (2006). Vocal teacher back in class: student critic mum. *The Denver Post*, March 14, pp. A01.

Sanders, T., & Stewart, V. (2004). International education: From community innovation to national policy. *Phi Delta Kappan*, 86(3), 200–5.

Sanoff, A. P. (2002). Change in course. *ASEE Prism*, 8, 30–2.

Savage, L. (2006). Israel's fight with Hezbollah: Another round of Middle east violence or a part of something far more ominous—World War III. *Macleans*, July 31, pp. 32–40.

Sergiovanni, T. J. (2006). *The Principalship: A Reflective Practice Perspective*, Boston, MA: Pearson Education, Inc.

Seyfer, J. (2003). San Jose, Calif., vocational school offers 'homeland security' training. *Knight Ridder Tribune Business News*, pp. 1.

Shapiro, S. H. (1989). New directions for sociology of education: Reconstructing the public discourse in education. *Education and Society*, 7(2), 21–38.

Shapiro, J. P., and Stefkovich, J. A. (2005). *Ethical Leadership and Decision Making in Education*. Mahweh, NJ: Lawrence Erlbaum, Associates.

Singer, A. (2002). A response to Diane Ravitch. *Educational Leadership*, 60(4), 92–3.

Smith, R. W. (2005). What is homeland security? Developing a definition grounded in the Curricula. *Journal of Public Affairs Education*, 11(3), 233–46.

Smith, P. (1999). Sex, lies and Hollywood's administrators: The (de)construction of school leadership in contemporary films. *Journal of Educational Administration*, 37(1), 50–65.

Starratt, R. J. (2005). Responsible leadership. *The Educational Forum*, 69(2), 124–33.

Stockman, F, (2006). Tomorrow's homework: Reading, writing, and Arabic; Bush announces language training against terrorism. *Boston Globe*, January 6, pp. A.6.

Suskind, R. (2006). Al-Qaeda's plot: To attack the NYC subway. *Time*, pp. 26–35.

Taylor, S. (1997). Critical policy analysis: exploring contexts, texts and consequences. *Discourse: Studies in the Cultural Politics of Education*, 18(1), 23–35.

Thomsen, S.R. (1993). A worm in the apple: Hollywood's influence on the public's perception of teachers. Paper presented at the Joint Meeting of the Southern States Communication Association and the Central States Communication Association, Lexington, KY, April, 2006.

Thornburgh, N. (2006). Inside America's secret workforce: A surprising look at the real people behind the debate over illegal immigration. *Time*, 34–45.

Tichy, N. M., & DeVanna, M. A. (1990). *The transformational leader*. 2nd ed. New York, NY: John Wiley.

Tompkins, R. B. (2005). Disaster equity: Keeping rural schools and communities in the picture as rebuilding begins. Retrieved from *Education Week*, http://edweek.org/ew/articles/2005/11/16/12tompkins.h25.html?querystring=katrin a&levelId=1000

Tuana, N. (2003). Moral literacy. Retrieved from, *Online Research/Penn State* http://rps.psu.edu/0305/literacy.html

Tumulty, K. (2006). Who gets to be an American? Inside the immigration debate that is dividing the nation. *Time*, April 10, 30–40.

U.S. Department of State. (2006). National security language initiative. Retrieved from, http://state.gov/r/pa/prs/ps/2006/58733.htm

Van Biema, D. (2006). The Opus Dei Code: The real story about the mysterious group that has a direct line to the Vatican. *Time*, April 24, 52–63.

Wallace, M. (1994). Discourse of derision: Role of the mass media within the education policy process. *Journal of Education Policy, 8*(4), 321–37.

Weber, M. (1947). *The theory of social and economic organizations* (T. Parsons, Trans.). New York, NY: Free Press.

Webster's Revised Unabridged Dictionary. (1913). Moral agency. Retrieved from, http://dictionary.reference.com/search?q=moral%20agent

Widdowson, H.G. (1995). Discourse analysis: A critical view. *Language and Literature, 4*(3), 157–72.

CHAPTER 6

Pedagogical Leadership

Pedagogical leadership can empower learners to "design their own representations of knowledge rather than absorbing representations preconceived by others; that it can be used to support the deep reflective thinking that is necessary for meaningful learning; and that it enables mindful and challenging learning" (Maclellan, 2008, p. 1986). With powerful connections to the other chapters in this volume and for our purposes, pedagogical leadership is deeply connected to content knowledge, teaching and learning, and assessment and evaluation (Ludwig & Herschell, 1998)—all which make up the multiple practices which account for the students' experience. It is within this context that teachers and education leaders need to ask the following two questions: How is effective instruction conducted to students with diverse backgrounds? How do students learn about and use multiple literacies in the complex, dynamic and interactive environments of the home, the classroom, and beyond (Smith, 1999, 2007, 2009, 2012a, 2012b)? Some key concepts discussed in this chapter include the following:

- Pedagogues
- Pedagogy
- Assessment literacy
- Theory of teaching
- Leadership pedagogy
- Leadership educator.

In this chapter, we focus on the teaching and *learning* aspect of pedagogy and leadership. An introduction to educational leadership concepts such as assessment, curriculum, pedagogy, evaluation, learning, and instruction is articulated. Next, we turn to *literacy* and introduce a series of activities designed to help readers identify and analyze the way that the above concepts are practiced in their schools, local communities and throughout the world. Then, we focus on educational *leaders'* ability to influence the pedagogical dynamics of a school through formal and informal means. It emphasizes skills that include observation and feedback, curriculum alignment and audits, assessing discrete, standardized, developing content knowledge, and norm-referenced assessments. Finally, we will articulate a series of *reflective* questions, prompts and activities to help the reader understand the personal, interpersonal and organizational consequences of their actions.

In recent years, interest has grown in "pedagogy" within English-language discussions of education. The impetus has come from different directions. There have been those like Paulo Freire seeking a "pedagogy of the oppressed" or "critical pedagogy"; practitioners wanting to rework the boundaries of care and education via the idea of social pedagogy; and, perhaps most significantly, governments wanting to constraint the activities of teachers by requiring adherence to preferred "pedagogies" (Smith, 2012a, 2012b). A common way of approaching pedagogy is as the art and science (and maybe even craft) of teaching. We suggest that a good way of exploring pedagogy is as the process of accompanying learners; caring for and about them; and bringing *learning* into life. The following section draws heavily from the work of Smith (2012a, 2012b), and his research on "What is pedagogy?," as published in the encyclopedia of informal education.

THE NATURE OF EDUCATION

The nature of education creates some confusion due to how easy it is to confuse education with schooling (Smith, 2012a). Education is a deliberate process of drawing out learning (*educere*), of encouraging and giving time to discovery. It is an intentional act. At the same time it is, as John Dewey (1963, cited in Smith, 2012a) put it, a social process—"a process of living and not a preparation for future living." For many concerned with education, it is also a matter of grace and wholeness, wherein we engage fully with the gifts we have been given. As Pestalozzi constantly affirmed, education is rooted in human nature; it is a matter of head, hand and heart (Brühlmeier 2010, as cited in Smith, 2012b). We find identity, meaning, and purpose in life "through connections to the community, to the natural world, and to spiritual values such as compassion and peace" (Miller, 2000, p. 3).

To educate is, in short, to set out to create and sustain informed, hopeful and respectful environments where learning can flourish. As such, education is a deeply practical activity, something that we can do for ourselves (what we could call self-education), and with others (see Smith, 2012a). This is a process carried out by parents and caregivers, friends and colleagues, and specialist educators. It is to the emergence of the last of these in ancient Greece that we will now turn as they have become so much a part of the way we think about, and get confused by, the nature of pedagogy.

Pedagogues and Teachers in Ancient Greek Society

According to Smith (2012b), within ancient Greek society there was a strong distinction between the activities of pedagogues (*paidagögus*) and subject teachers (*didáskalos*). The first pedagogues were slaves—often foreigners and the "spoils of war" (Young 1987). They were trusted and sometimes learned members of rich households who accompanied the sons of their "masters" in the street, oversaw their meals etc., and sat beside them when being schooled. These pedagogues were generally seen as representatives of their wards' fathers and literally "tenders" of children. Children were often put in their charge at around 7 years and remained with them until late adolescence (Smith, 2012b).

Plato talks about pedagogues as "men who by age and experience are qualified to serve as both leaders (hëgemonas) and custodians (paidagögous)" of children (Longenecker 1982, p. 53). Their role varied but two elements were common (Smith 2006). The first was to be an accompanist or companion—carrying books and bags, and ensuring their wards were safe. The second, and more fundamental task in relation to boys, was to help them learn what it was to be men. This they did by a combination of example, conversation and disciplining. Pedagogues were moral guides who were to be obeyed (Young, 1987, p. 156). The pedagogue was responsible for every aspect of the child's upbringing from correcting grammar and diction to controlling his or her sexual morals. Reciting a pedagogue's advice, Seneca said, "Walk thus and so; eat thus and so, this is the proper conduct for a man and that for a woman; this for a married man and that for a bachelor" (Smith, 2006, p. 201).

The relation of the pedagogue to the child is a fascinating one. It brings new meaning to Friere's (1972, cited in Smith, 2016) notion of the "pedagogy of the oppressed"—this was the education of the privileged by the oppressed. Apparently, it was a matter that, according to Plato, did not go unnoticed by Socrates. In a conversation between Socrates and a young boy Lysis, Socrates asked, "Someone controls you?" Lysis replied, "Yes, he is my tutor [or pedagogue] here." "Is he a slave?" Socrates queried. "Why, certainly; he belongs to us," responded Lysis, to which Socrates mused, "What a strange thing, I exclaimed; a free person controlled by a slave!" (Plato, 1925, cited in Smith, 2006).

Theories of Teaching

At the center of Herbart's theory of education and of schooling is the idea of "educational teaching" or "educating instruction" (*erzieinder Unterricht*). Hilgenheger (1993, p. 652) makes the following observations: like practical and theoretical educationalists before him, Herbart also makes a distinction between education (Latin: *educatio*) and teaching (Latin: *instructio*). "Education" means shaping the development of character with a view to the improvement of man. "Teaching" represents the world, conveys fresh knowledge, develops existing aptitudes and imparts useful skills.

Before Herbart, it was unusual to combine the concepts of "education" and "teaching." Consequently, questions pertaining to education and teaching were initially pursued independently ... Herbart ... took the bold step of "subordinating" the concept of "teaching" to that of "education" in his educational theory. As he saw it, external influences, such as the punishment or shaming of pupils, were not the most important instruments of education. On the contrary, appropriate teaching was the only sure means of promoting education that was bound to prove successful. In Herbart's own words, teaching is the "central activity of education." What Herbart and his followers achieved with this was to focus consideration of instruction and teaching (didactics) around schooling rather than other educational settings (Gundem 1998, pp. 239–40). Herbart also turned didactics "into a discipline of its own"—extracting it from general educational theory (*op. cit.*). Simplified and rather rigid versions of his approach grew in influence with the development of mass schooling and state-defined curricula.

This approach did not go unchallenged at the time. There were those who argued that teaching should become part of the human rather than "exact" sciences (Hamilton 1999, pp. 145–6). Rather than seeking to construct detailed systems of instruction, the need was to explore the human experience of teaching, learning and schooling. It was through educational practice and reflection upon it ("learning by doing") and exploring the settings in which it happens that greater understanding would develop. In Germany some of those arguing against an overfocus on method and state control of curricula looked to social pedagogy with its focus on community and democracy.

Initially, interest in pedagogy was reawakened by the decision of Paulo Freire to name his influential book *Pedagogy of the Oppressed* (first published in English in 1970). Based on Smith's work (2012b), the book became a key reference point on many education programs in higher education and central to the establishment of explorations around critical pedagogy. It was followed another pivotal text—Basil Bernstein's (1971) "On the classification and framing of educational knowledge." He drew upon developments in continental debates. He then placed them in relation to the different degrees of control people had over their lives and educational experience according to their class position and cultures. Later, he was to look at messages carried by different pedagogies (Bernstein 1990). Last, we should not forget the influence of Jerome Bruner's discussion of the culture of education (1996). He argued that teachers need to pay particular attention to the cultural contexts in which they are working and of the need to look to "folk theories" and "folk pedagogies" (Bruner 1996, 44–65). "Pedagogy is never innocent," he wrote, "It is a medium that carries its own message" (p. 44).

Pedagogy is about teaching. But we take a broad view of teaching as a complex activity, which encompasses more than just "delivering" education. Another way to explain it is by referring to:

- the art of teaching—the responsive, creative, intuitive part;
- the craft of teaching—skills and practice; and
- the science of teaching—research-informed decision making and the theoretical underpinning.

It is also important to remember that all these are grounded in ethical principles and moral commitment—teaching is never simply an instrumental activity, a question just of technique. While we can welcome the warnings against viewing teaching as an instrumental activity, whether it is satisfactory to describe it as pedagogy is a matter for some debate. Indeed, Hamilton (1999) has argued that much of what passes for pedagogy in UK education debates is better understood as didactics. We can see this quickly when looking at the following description of didactics from Künzli (1994, cited in Gundem 2000, 236). Simplified, we may say that the concerns of didactics are: what should be taught and learnt (the content aspect); how to teach and learn (the aspects of transmitting and learning): to what purpose or intention something should he taught and learned?

In looking to continental concerns and debates around pedagogy, a number of specialist pedagogues have turned to the work of Pestalozzi and to those concerned with more holistic forms of practice (see, for example, Cameron & Ross, 2011). As Brühlmeier (2010) has commented, "Pestalozzi has shown that there is more to [education] than attaining prescribed learning outcomes; it is concerned with the whole person, with their physical, mental and psychological development" (p. 5). Learning is a matter of head, hand and heart. Heart here is a matter of, *spirit*—the passions that animate or move us; *moral sense or conscience*—the values, ideals and attitudes that guide us; and *being*—the kind of person we are, or wish to be, in the world (Doyle & Smith 1999, 33–4). As Palmer (1998, p. 10) has argued, "*good teaching cannot be reduced to technique; good teaching comes from the identity and integrity of the teacher.*" However, the focus of pedagogues frequently takes them directly into questions around identity and integrity. This then means that their authenticity and the extent to which they are experienced as wise are vital considerations.

Accompanying

The greatest gift that we can give is to "be alongside" another person. Green and Christian (1998, p. 21) have described this as accompanying. It is in times of crisis or achievement or when we have to manage long-term difficulties that we appreciate the depth and quality of having another person to accompany us. In Western society at the end of the twentieth century, this gift has a fairly low profile. Although it is pivotal in establishing good communities, its development is often left to chance and given a minor status compared with such things as management structure and formal procedures. It is our opinion that the availability of this sort of quality companionship and support is vital for people to establish and maintain their physical, mental, and spiritual health and creativity. It is easy to overlook the sophistication of this relationship and the capacities needed to be "alongside another." It entails "being with", and this involves attending to the other.

It is our relationship with a young person upon which most of our work, as a practitioner, hinges. And this is a relationship that can "*develop only when the persons involved pay attention to one another*" (Barry & Connolly, 1986, p. 47). What effective workers with individual young people do is highly skilled work, drawing on, through different stages in the process, a range of diverse roles and capacities. Done well, the practitioner moves seamlessly through the stages, but the unifying core is the relationship between young person and the worker (Collander-Brown 2005, p. 33).

Caring for and Caring About

Pedagogues have to *be around* for people; in places where they are directly available to help, talk and listen. They also have to *be there* for people: ready to respond to the emergencies of life—little and large (Smith & Smith, 2008, p. 18). In recent years, our understanding of what is involved in "caring" has been greatly enhanced by the work of Nel Noddings. She distinguishes between caring for and caring about. Caring for involves face-to-face encounters in which one person attends directly to the needs of another. We learn first what it means to be cared for. "Then, gradually, we learn both to care for and, by extension, to care about others" (Noddings, 2002, p. 22). Such caring about, Noddings suggests, can be seen as providing the foundation for our sense of justice. Noddings then argues that caring relations are a foundation for pedagogical activity (by which she means teaching activity): first, as we listen to our students, we gain their trust and, in an ongoing relation of care and trust, it is more likely that students will accept what we try to teach. They will not see our efforts as "interference" but, rather, as cooperative work proceeding from the integrity of the relation. Second, as we engage our students in dialogue, we learn about their needs, working habits, interests, and talents. We gain important ideas from them about how to build our lessons and plan for their individual progress. Finally, as we acquire knowledge about our students' needs and realize how much more than the standard curriculum is needed, we are inspired to increase our own competence (Noddings, 2005).

For many of those concerned with social pedagogy (e.g., Smith, 2009) it is a place where care and education meet—one is not somehow less than the other (Cameron & Moss, 2011). For example, in Denmark "care" can be seen as one of the four central areas that describe the pedagogical tasks: care (take care of), socialization (to and in communities), formation (for citizenship and democracy) and learning (development of individual skills) . . . [T]he "pedagogical" task is not simply about development, but also about looking after . . . [P]edagogues not only put the individual child in the center, but also take care of the interests of the community. What we have here is a helping relationship. It "involves listening and exploring issues and problems with people; *and* teaching and giving advice; *and* providing direct assistance; *and* being seen as people of integrity" (Smith & Smith, 2008, 14).

While Paulo Freire (1972) and others talked about pedagogy in relation to working with adults, there are plenty who argue that it cannot escape the fact that its roots is bound up with practice with children. For example, Malcolm Knowles (1970) was convinced that adults learned differently to children—and that this provided the basis for a distinctive field of enquiry. He, thus, set andragogy—the art and science of helping adults learn—against pedagogy. While we might question whether children's processes of learning differ significantly from adults, it is the case that educators tend to approach them differently and employ contrasting strategies. There are also questions around the extent to which, in the English language at least, the notion of pedagogy has been tainted by its association with schooling. When we use the term, to what extent are we importing assumptions and practices that we may not intend? "At the heart of this language", wrote Street and Street (1991, cited in Smith & Smith, 2012b), "in contemporary society, there is a relentless commitment to instruction." While didactics may be the most appropriate or logical way of thinking about the processes, ideas and commitments involved in teaching, there is some doubt that the term "pedagogy" can take root in any sensible way in debates where English is the dominant language (p. 163).

In recent years, increasing numbers of professional development programs have dealt with assessment and evaluation literacy for teachers and/or administrators. After dividing educators' measurement-related concerns into either classroom assessments or accountability assessments, it is argued that educators' inadequate knowledge in either of these arenas can cripple the quality of education. Assessment literacy is seen, therefore, as a sine qua non for today's competent educator. As such, assessment literacy must be a pivotal content area for current and future staff development endeavors. Until preservice teacher education programs begin producing assessment-literate teachers, professional developers must continue to rectify this omission in educators' professional capabilities.

ASSESSMENT LITERACY

For the past few years, assessment literacy has been increasingly touted as a fitting focus for teachers' professional development programs. The sort of assessment literacy that is typically recommended refers to a teacher's familiarity with those measurement basics related directly to what goes on in classrooms. Given today's ubiquitous, externally imposed scrutiny of schools, we can readily understand why assessment literacy might be regarded as a likely target for teachers' professional development. Yet, is assessment literacy a legitimate focus for teachers' professional development programs or, instead, is it a fashionable, but soon forgettable, fad?

Assessment Literacy for Teachers

Many of today's teachers know little about educational assessment. For some teachers, test is a four-letter word, both literally and figuratively. The gaping gap in teachers' assessment-related knowledge is all too understandable. The most obvious explanation is, in this instance, the correct explanation. Regrettably, when most of today's teachers completed their teacher-education programs, there was no requirement that they learn anything about educational assessment. For these teachers, their only exposure to the concepts and practices of educational assessment might have been a few sessions in their educational psychology classes or, perhaps, a unit in a methods class (La Marca, 2006; Stiggins, 2006). Thus, many teachers in previous years usually arrived at their first teaching assignment quite bereft of any fundamental understanding of educational measurement. Happily, in recent years, we have seen the emergence of increased preservice requirements that offer teacher education candidates' greater insights regarding educational assessment. Accordingly, in a decade or two, the assessment literacy of the nation's teaching force is bound to be substantially stronger. But for now it must be professional development—completed subsequent to teacher education—that will supply the nation's teachers with the assessment-related skills and knowledge they need.

Two Types of Assessments

The term assessment in this instance should not be regarded as a traditional paper and pencil test or, for that matter, any kind of formal test. On the contrary, an assessment might consist of a wide variety of evidence-eliciting techniques such as asking students to respond to teacher-presented questions by using individual, erasable white boards during a class discussion, or conducting oral interviews with solo students or with groups of students. Similarly, an assessment of students' attitudes might feature the use of anonymous, self-report inventories. To assess students' cognitive skills, teachers might employ an elaborate performance test in which students must complete, then describe in writing, a series of independent, scientific experiments. Assessment, therefore, should most definitely not be regarded as synonymous with test. But, granted that the significance of teachers' assessment-related decisions can bounce all over the place, a key question remains: what kinds of assessments do teachers most need to understand? Several sensible ways to subdivide our current educational assessment cake are currently available. For instance, one increasingly popular distinction is to contrast summative assessment and formative assessment (McMillan, 2007).

Summative assessment refers to the use of assessment-based evidence when arriving at decisions about already-completed instructional events such as the quality of a year's worth of schooling or the effectiveness of a semester-long algebra course. Summative assessment is intended to help us arrive at go/no-go decisions based on the success of a final-version instructional program. In contrast, formative assessment is a process in which assessment-elicited evidence is used by teachers to adjust their ongoing instructional activities, or by students to adjust the ways they are trying to learn something. In contrast to its summative sibling, formative assessment has a powerful improvement orientation, because it is intended to stimulate ameliorative adjustments in teachers' still-malleable instructional programs or in students' current learning-tactics. For instance, formative assessment would be seen when a teacher frequently administers brief dip-stick quizzes, not for grading purposes but, instead, to let the teacher and the students see whether they need to make any changes in what they are doing in class. The function of the formative assessment process is to supply evidence that will enhance students' learning (Popham, 2008). Chiefly because of formative assessment's relatively recent arrival on the measurement scene, and because there are still some serious definitional disputes regarding what the precise nature of formative assessment is and is not (McMillan, 2007). Accountability assessments are those measurement devices, almost always standardized, used by governmental entities such as states, provinces or school districts to ascertain the effectiveness of educational endeavors.

Teachers who are genuinely assessment literate will not only know how to create more suitable assessments, but will also be conversant with a wide array of potential assessment options. All teachers assess their students, some more vigorously than others, and almost all of those assessments have an impact on instruction, some more substantial than others. Accordingly, all teachers need to possess sufficient assessment literacy so their classroom assessments are at least satisfactory or, preferably, substantially better. Thus, it seems that assessment literacy is a commodity needed by teachers for their own long-term wellbeing, and for the educational wellbeing of their students. For the foreseeable future, teachers are likely to exist in an environment where test-elicited evidence plays a prominent instructional and evaluative role. In such environments, those who control the tests tend to control the entire enterprise. Until preservice teacher educators routinely provide meaningful assessment literacy for prospective teachers, the architects of professional development programs will need to offer assessment-literacy programs. We can only hope they do it well.

LEADERSHIP PEDAGOGY

The word *pedagogy* has roots in the Greek *paidagōgeō*, which literally translates to "lead the child." The emphasis on leadership as the foundation of successful pedagogy, then, means educators should conceptualize pedagogy as larger than teaching strategies, where educators serve as leaders themselves in helping students learn and grow. Successful pedagogy encompasses three distinct areas: (i) the implementation of effective instructional strategies, (ii) environmental/classroom management techniques, and (iii) program design (Marzano, 2007). Therefore, educators who maximize their potential in building student leadership capacity must be intentional in matching their intended program or course outcomes with relevant student and leadership development theory, and then apply effective strategies for the delivery of material to a diverse student population. For example, supervisors of students should have an explicit set of outcomes in mind for the leadership development of these students; they should understand the incoming developmental level of typical students they supervise and construct an overall plan for building their leadership capacity; and lastly, they should utilize an effective set of educational techniques within their meetings, interactions, and overall supervision of students to achieve their goals. Clearly, intentionality is essential for success.

Despite the overwhelming number of popular definitions of leadership, there is a growing consensus around the general structure of effective leadership practice. Northouse (2009) summarizes this consensus by describing leadership as a combination of individual traits, abilities, skills, and behaviors practiced within one or more relationships with others to achieve common goals. Given this inclusive yet diffuse definition, an increasing number of leadership educators are beginning to adapt their programs and services around a three-tiered structure focused on student attitudes, knowledge, and behaviors. The importance of an emerging leader's "being," "knowing," and "doing" is seen in such diverse leadership development programs as the US Army Official Leadership Manual (Hesselbein & Shinseki, 2004) the Harvard Business School (Nohria & Khurana, 2010), and the popular student leadership textbook, *Exploring Leadership* (Komives, Lucas, & McMahon, 2007). Being (Attitudes). Kouzes and Posner (2010) state that, after decades of surveys in government, business, and education, inner qualities such as character, credibility, optimism, and integrity were first and foremost requisites for successful leaders across these disparate sectors. A popular quote often attributed to Ralph Waldo Emerson, "Your actions speak so loudly, I cannot hear what you say," is instructive in regard to the importance of credibility in engaging in effective leadership practices. Therefore, programs and interventions designed to build student leadership capacity should explicitly focus on nurturing and developing these inner qualities in students. Knowing (Knowledge). The practice of effective leadership looks much different today than it did in recent generations, owing to significant global demographic, economic, and technological shifts (Friedman, 2007; Kanter, Stein, & Jick, 2003).

Contemporary leaders must understand the complexities and inter-relatedness of systems and organizations (Allen & Cherry, 2000), know how to connect to and build relationships with diverse populations (Kezar & Moriarty, 2000), and recognize the difficulty of acting with integrity and a sense of ethics in ambiguous situations (Johnson, 2011). Success in these areas cannot simply be gained through practice or repetition, but must be learned through study. People will only willingly be led by those who know what they are doing.

Doing (Skills). One of the key reasons for leadership failure is that the leader in question, even when possessing adequate knowledge and a requisite attitude, is not sure what to do when under pressure to act in real time. Katz (1955) was the first to describe effective leadership as encompassing technical skill (e.g., hands-on ability at specialized tasks), interpersonal skill (e.g., perspective taking, making and building relationships), and conceptual skill (e.g., shaping policy, strategic planning). Capacity-building programs in higher education should therefore focus an aspect of their curriculum on helping students practice these three skills areas in different contexts, so they can learn how to apply them regardless of their particular environment.

Many leadership capacity-building programs do not explicitly distinguish the level of focus they apply to their curricula or outcomes. Day (2001) describes this as a failure to distinguish between leadership and leader development. Leadership development, he explains, is focused on building capacity within collectives for the practice of leadership within an organizational context—that is, where individuals within those organizations can more easily and successfully practice effective leadership. Leader development, by contrast, deals with the development of skill within individuals. More specifically, Yammarino, Dionne, Uk Chun, and Dansereau (2005) describe four inter-related "levels of analysis" relevant to leadership educators: (i) the Person level, where the focus of programs is on individuals and their traits, skills, abilities, and behaviors; (ii) the Dyad level, where the focus is on interpersonal relationships, often within a leader-group member context; (iii) the Group/Team level, which includes both hierarchical work teams with supervisors or non-hierarchical social or nonwork teams; and (iv) the Collective/System level, where programs are focused on leadership within systems, communities, and society as a whole. Competent leadership educators, therefore, should extend their own curricula to incorporate aspects of each of these four levels, attending to students' individual competencies, their ability to connect and collaborate with other students and organizations, and their desire and skill in creating positive large-scale impact.

The Role of the Leadership Educator

The true success of effective leadership programs is measured, not by the relationship students have with their instructor, but by students' ability to apply their learning to the challenges they will face after program completion (Magolda & King, 2004). Therefore, educators should attend to learning more than teaching. This student-centered approach places educators in the role of conduit rather than distributor, and requires attention to be given to collaborative learning practices, personal responsibility for growth and development, and the construction of an inclusive learning community. Leadership educators should, therefore, practice transparent teaching practices and embrace their own learning within the process. It is important for practitioners to model the type of leadership that is being taught. If, for example, the Relational Leadership

Model (Komives et al., 2007) is chosen as the theoretical frame for the educational experience, does the leadership educator practice the values and behaviors described within the model? If the programs and training that students receive are not integrated into the personal practice of the educator, then students will see that as inconsistent with what is being taught, and are therefore likely to disengage from the experience.

A value that educators and students tend to overlook or discount within leadership education is spirituality. Spirituality, broadly defined as "the deepest values and meanings by which people live" (Sheldrake, 2007), is often integral to the value-orientation of leaders, and therefore affects how leaders interact with others. Spirituality may also determine how, why, and to what extent leaders will impact the world around them. Utilizing the being, knowing, doing framework referenced earlier in this chapter, leadership educators must model how to effectively and transparently incorporate one's personal values and spirituality into the practice of leading. Doing so allows students and educators to be authentic in how they discuss being, knowing, and doing in practice, and an attention to spirituality creates an inclusive space where students can bring all parts of themselves into their experience as a leader, learner, and pedagogue.

Discussion

1. We need to move discussions of pedagogy beyond seeing it as primarily being about teaching. We must look at those traditions of practice that flow from the original pedagogues in ancient Greece. We have much to learn through exploring through the thinking and practice of specialist pedagogues who look to accompany learners; care for and about them; and bring learning into life. Teaching is just one aspect of their practice.

2. Reliability of educational assessments, especially the three forms in which consistency evidence is reported for groups of test-takers (stability, alternate-form, and internal consistency) and how to gauge consistency of assessment for individual test-takers. Many educators place absolutely unwarranted confidence in the accuracy of educational tests, especially those high-stakes tests created by well-established testing companies. When educators grasp the nature of measurement error, and realize the myriad factors that can trigger inconsistency in a student's test performances, those educators will regard with proper caution the imprecision of the results obtained on even some of our most time-honored assessment instruments.

3. How to identify and eliminate assessment bias that offends or unfairly penalizes test takers because of personal characteristics such as race, gender, or socioeconomic status. During the past two decades, the measurement community has devised both judgmental and empirical ways of dramatically reducing the amount of assessment bias in our large-scale educational tests. Classroom teachers need to know how to identify and eliminate bias in their own teacher-made tests.

4. Designing and implementing formative assessment procedures consonant with both research evidence and experience-based insights regarding such procedures' likely success. Formative assessment is a process, not a particular type of test. Because there is now substantial evidence at hand that properly employed formative

assessment can meaningfully boost students' achievement, today's educators need to understand the innards of this potent classroom process.

5. How to collect and interpret evidence of students' attitudes, interests, and values. When considering the importance of students' acquisition of cognitive versus affective outcomes, it could be argued that inattention to students' attitudes, interests, and values can have a lasting, negative impact on those students. Teachers, therefore, should at least learn how to assess their students' affect so that, if those teachers choose to do so, they can get an accurate fix on their students' affective dispositions.

6. Assessing English Language Learners and students with disabilities. Although most of the measurement concepts that educators need to understand will apply across the board to all types of students, there are special assessment issues associated with students whose first language is not English and for students with disabilities. Because today's educators have been adjured to attend to such students with more care than was seen in the past, it is important for all teachers to become conversant with the assessment procedures most suitable for these subgroups of students.

REFERENCES

Alexander, R. (2000). *Culture and Pedagogy. International comparisons in primary education.* Oxford, UK: Blackwell.

Alexander, R. (2008). *Essays on Pedagogy.* London: Routledge.

Allen, K. E., & Cherry, C. (2000). *Systemic leadership: Enriching the meaning of our work.* Lanham, Md: American College Personnel Association and National Association for Campus Activities; University Press of America.

Atherton, C. (1998). "Children, animals, slaves and grammar," In Y. L. Too & N. Livingstone (eds.), *Pedagogy and Power: Rhetorics of classical learning.* Cambridge: Cambridge University Press.

Barry, W. A., and Connolly, W.J. (1986). *The Practice of Spiritual Direction.* New York, NY: Harper and Collins.

Beere, J. (2010). *The perfect Ofsted lesson.* Bancyfelin: Crown House Publishing.

Bernstein, B. (1971). "On the classification and framing of educational knowledge." In M. F. D. Young (ed.), *Knowledge and Control: New directions for the sociology of knowledge.* London: Collier-Macmillan.

Bernstein, B. (1990). *The structuring of pedagogical discourse. Class, codes and control,* Vol. 4. London: Routledge.

Black, P., & Wiliam, D. (1998a). Assessment and classroom learning. *Assessment in Education: Principles, Policy, and Practice,* 5(1), 7–73.

Board of Education (1944). Teachers and Youth Leaders. *Report of the Committee appointed by the President of the Board of Education to consider the supply, recruitment and training of teachers and youth leaders.* London: HMSO. [Part 2 is reproduced in the informal education archives, www.infed.org/archives/e-texts/mcnair_part_two.htm. Retrieved October 23, 2012].

Brühlmeier, A. (2010). *Head, heart and hand. Education in the spirit of Pestalozzi.* Cambridge, UK: Sophia Books.

Bruner, J. (1996). *The Culture of Education*. Cambridge, Mass: Harvard University Press.

Cameron, C. (2004). "Social Pedagogy and Care: Danish and German practice in young people's residential care." *Journal of Social Work*, 4(2), 133–51.

Cameron, C., & Moss, P. (eds.). (2011). *Social Pedagogy and Working with Children and Young People: Where Care and Education Meet*. London: Jessica Kingsley.

Castle, E. B. (1961). *Ancient Education and Today*. Harmondsworth: Pelican.

Cohen, B. (2008). "Introducing 'The Scottish Pedagogue'" in Children in Scotland. *Working it out: Developing the children's sector workforce*. Edinburgh: Children in Scotland.

Collander-Brown, D. (2005). "Being with another as a professional practitioner: uncovering the nature of working with individuals." *Youth and Policy*, (86), 33–48.

Comenius, J. A. (1907). *The Great Didactic*, translated by M. W. Keatinge. London: Adam & Charles Black. [http://archive.org/details/cu31924031053709. Accessed October 4, 2012].

Day, D. V. (2001). Leadership development: A review in context. *Leadership Quarterly, 11*(4), 581–613.

Dewey, J. (1963). *Experience and Education*. New York: Collier Books. [First published in 1938].

Dewey, J. (1966). *Democracy and Education, An introduction to the philosophy of education*. New York: Macmillan. First published 1916.

Doyle, M. E., and Smith, M. K. (1999). *Born and Bred? Leadership, heart of informal education*. London: The Rank Foundation. [http://rankyouthwork.org/bornandbred/index.htm Retrieved October 16, 2012].

Freire, P. (1972). *Pedagogy of the Oppressed*. Harmondsworth: Penguin.

Friedman, T. L. (2007). *The world is flat 3.0: A brief history of the twenty-first century*. New York, NY: Picador,

Green, M., & Christian, C. (1998). *Accompanying young people on their spiritual quest*. London: National Society/Church House Publishing.

Gundem, B. B. (1998). *Understanding European didactics—an overview: Didactics* (Didaktik, Didaktik(k), Didactique). Oslo: University of Oslo. Institute for Educational Research.

Gundem, B. B. (December 07, 1992). Vivat Comenius: A Commemorative Essay on Johann Amos Comenius, 1592–1670. *Journal of Curriculum and Supervision*, 8(1), 43–55.

Hamilton, D., & Gudmundsdottir, S. (1994). Didaktik and/or curriculum. *Curriculum Studies*, 2, 345–50.

Hamilton, D. (1999). The pedagogic paradox (or why no didactics in England?). *Pedagogy, Culture & Society*, 7(1), 135–52.

Hamilton, M. (2006). Just do it: Literacies, everyday learning and the irrelevance of pedagogy. In *Studies in the Education of Adults*, 38(2), Autumn 125–40.

Herbart, J. F (1892). *The Science of Education: its general principles deduced from its aim and the aesthetic revelation of the world*, translated by H. M. & E. Felkin. London: Sonnenschein.

Herbart, J. F., Felkin, H. M., & Felkin, E. (1908). *Letter and lectures on education: By Johann Friedrich Herbart; Translated from the German, and edited with an introduction by Henry M. and Emmie Felkin and a preface by Oscar Browning*. London: Sonnenschein.

Hesselbein, F., & Shinseki, E. K. (2004). *Be, know, do: Leadership the army way: Adapted from the official army leadership manual*. San Francisco: Jossey-Bass.

Higher Education Research Institute (1996). *A social change model of leadership development*. Los Angeles, CA: University of California Higher Education Research Institute.

Hilgenheger, N. (1993). Johann Friedrich Herbart. *Prospects: the quarterly review of comparative education* vol. XXIII, no. 3/4, 649–64. Paris, UNESCO: International Bureau of Education. http://ibe.unesco.org/fileadmin/user_upload/archive/publications/ThinkersPdf/herbarte.pdf (accessed October 11, 2012).

Jeffs, T., & Smith, M. K. (2005). *Informal Education. Conversation, democracy and learning.* Ticknall: Education Now.

Johnson, C. E. (2011). *Meeting the ethical challenges of leadership: Casting light or shadow.* Thousand Oaks, CA.: Sage.

Kansanen, P., & Meri, M. (1999). The didactic relation in the teaching-studying-learning process. In B. Hudson et al. (eds.), *Didaktik/Fachdidaktik as Science(s) of the Teaching Professions.* Umeå: Thematic Network on Teacher Education in Europe.

Kant, I. (1900). *Kant on education (Ueber pa?dagogik).* Translated by A. Churton. Boston: D.C. Heath. [http://files.libertyfund.org/files/356/0235_Bk.pdf (accessed October 10, 2012)].

Kanter, R. M., Stein, B. A., & Jick, T. D. (2003). *The challenge of organizational change: How companies experience it and leaders guide It.* New York: Free Press.

Katz, R. L. (1955). Skills of an Effective Administrator. *Harvard Business Review, 33*(1), 33–42.

Kelly, A. V. (2009). *The Curriculum: Theory and Practice.* 6th ed. London: Sage.

Kezar, A. J., & Moriarty, D. (2000). Expanding our understanding of student leadership development: A study exploring gender and ethnic identity. *Journal of College Student Development, 41*(1), 55–69.

Kyriacou, C. (2009). The five dimensions of social pedagogy within schools. *Pastoral Care in Education: An International Journal of Personal, Social and Emotional Development,* 27(2), [http://tandfonline.com/doi/abs/10.1080/02643940902897681?journalCode=rped20 Retrieved June 23, 2011].

Kouzes, J. M., & Posner, B. Z. (2007). *The leadership practices inventory.* San Diego: Pfeiffer and Company/University Associates.

Kouzes, J. M., & Posner, B. Z. (2008). *The leadership challenge.* 4th ed. San Francisco: Jossey-Bass.

Kouzes, J. M., & Posner, B. Z. (2010). *The truth about leadership: The no-fads, heart-of-the-matter facts you need to know.* San Francisco: Jossey-Bass.

Kahneman, D. (2011). *Thinking Fast and Slow.* London: Allen Lane.

Kennell, N. M. (1995). *The gymnasium of virtue: Education & culture in ancient Sparta.* Chapel Hill: University of North Carolina Press.

Künzli, R. (1994). *Didaktik: Modelle der Darstellung. des Umgangs und der Erfahrung.* Zurich: Zurich University, Didaktikum Aarau.

La Marca, P. (2006, June). Assessment literacy: Building capacity for improving student learning. Paper presented at the National Conference on Large- Scale Assessment, Council of Chief State School Officers, San Francisco, CA.

Lindeman, E. C. (1926). *The Meaning of Adult Education.* New York: New Republic, republished in 1989 by Oklahoma Research Center for Continuing Professional and Higher Education. [Online version from http://archive.org/details/meaningofadulted00lind. Retrieved October 23, 2012].

Lindeman, E. C. (1951). Building a social philosophy of adult education In S. Brookfield (ed.) (1987), *Learning Democracy: Eduard Lindeman on adult education and social change.* Beckenham: Croom Helm.

Longenecker, R. N. (1982). The Pedagogical Nature of the Law in Galatians 3:19–4:7. *Journal of the Evangelical Theological Society 25.*

Lorenz, W. (1994). *Social Work in a Changing Europe.* London: Routledge.

Magolda, M. B. B., & King, P. M. (2004), *Learning partnerships: Theory and models of practice to educate for self-authorship*. Sterling, Va.: Stylus.

Marzano, R. J. (2007). *The art and science of teaching: A comprehensive framework for effective instruction*. Alexandria, Va.: Association for Supervision and Curriculum Development.

McMillan, J. H. (Ed.). (2007). *Formative classroom assessment: Theory into practice*. New York, NY: Teachers College Press.

Miller, R. (2005). *Holistic Education: A Response to the Crisis of Our Time*. Paper was presented at the Institute for Values Education in Istanbul, Turkey in November. [http://pathsoflearning. net/articles_Holistic_Ed_Response.php Retrieved: March 7, 2012].

Mills, C. W. (1959) *The Sociological Imagination*. New York: Oxford University Press. The appendix 'On intellectual craftsmanship' can be read here.

Murphy, P. (1996). Defining pedagogy. In P. Murphy & C. Gipps (eds.), *Equity in the Classroom: towards effective pedagogy for boys and girls*. London: Falmer Press. [Also reprinted in Hall, K., Murphy, P., & Soler, J. (2008). *Pedagogy and practice: Culture and identities*. London: Sage. It can be downloaded from: http://corwin.com/upm-data/32079_Murphy%28OU_Reader_2%29_Rev_Final_Proof.pdf Retrieved February 12, 2012].

Noddings, N. (2002). *Starting at Home. Caring and social policy*. Berkeley: University of California Press.

Noddings, N. (2005). Caring in education. *the encyclopaedia of informal education*, [www.infed. org/biblio/noddings_caring_in_education.htm Retrieved October 16, 2012].

Nohria, N., & Khurana, R. (2010), *Handbook of leadership theory and practice*. Boston, Mass: Harvard Business School Press.

Northouse, P. G. (2009). *Introduction to leadership concepts and practice*. Thousand Oaks, CA: Sage.

Northouse, P. G. (2010). *Leadership: Theory and practice*. 5th ed. Thousand Oaks, CA: Sage.

Ofsted (2011). *Lesson observation—key indicators*. London: Ofsted. [https://ncetm.org.uk/public/files/725865/Ofsted+key+indicators.pdf Retrieved October 10, 2012].

Ofsted (2012). *The framework for school inspection from September 2012*. London: Ofsted. [http://ofsted.gov.uk/resources/framework-for-school-inspection-september-2012–0 Retrieved October 10,2012].

Pestalozzi, J. H. (2010). *Leonard and Gertrude* (from the 1885 edition published by D. C. Heath). Memphis: General Books.

Plato (1925). *Lysis* 208 C, trans. W. R. M. Lamb, Loeb Classical Library. Cambridge: Harvard University Press.

Popham, W. J. (2006). *Mastering assessment: A self-service system for educators*. New York, NY: Routledge.

Popham, W. J. (2007). Instructional sensitivity: Educational accountability's dire deficit. *Phi Delta Kappan*, 89(2), 149–55.

Popham, W. J. (2008). *Transformative assessment*. Alexandria, VA: Association for Supervision and Curriculum Development.

Popham, W. J. (2009). Assessment Literacy for Teachers: Faddish or Fundamental? *Theory into Practice*, 48, 4–11.

Rogers, C. (1967). The interpersonal relationship in the facilitation of learning. reprinted in H. Kirschenbaum & V. L. Henderson (eds.) (1990), *The Carl Rogers Reade*, 304–11. London: Constable.

Simon, B. (1981). Why no pedagogy in England? In B. Simon & W. Taylor (eds.), *Issues for the 80's*. London: Batsford. Also reprinted in J. Leach & B. Cole (eds.) (1999), *Learners and Pedagogy*. London: Paul Chapman Publishing.

Sheldrake, P. (2007). *A brief history of spirituality*. Malden, Mass.: Blackwell.

Smith, M. J. (2006). The role of the pedagogue in Galatians. *Faculty Publications and Presentations*. Paper 115. Lynchburg, VA: Liberty University.

Smith, M. K. (2012a). "What is education?" In *the encyclopaedia of informal education*. Retrieved from, www.infed.org/mobi/what-is-education/

Smith, M. K. (2012b). "What is pedagogy?," *the encyclopaedia of informal education*. Retrieved from, http://infed.org/mobi/what-is-pedagogy/

Smith, H., & Smith, M. (2008). *The art of helping others: Being around, being there, being wise*. London: Jessica Kingsley Publishers.

Smith, M. E., & Smith, M. K. (2002). "Friendship and informal education." *the encyclopaedia of informal education*. [http://infed.org/biblio/friendship_and_education.htm Retrieved October 23, 2012].

Smith, M. K. (1994). *Local Education. Community, conversation, action*. Buckingham: Open University Press.

Smith, M. K. (1999, 2007, 2009). "Social pedagogy" In *the encyclopaedia of informal education*. [http://infed.org/biblio/b-socped.htm Retrieved October 16, 2012].

Washington, B. T. (1963). *Up from slavery: An autobiography*. Garden City, NY: Doubleday.

Yammarino, F. J., Dionne, S. D., Uk Chun, J., & Dansereau, F. (2005). Leadership and levels of analysis: A state-of-the-science review. *Leadership Quarterly*, 16(6), 879–919.

Young, N. H. (1987). Paidagogos: The Social Setting of a Pauline Metaphor. *Novum Testamentum*, 29, 150.

Young, K. (1999). *The Art of Youth Work*. Lyme Regis: Russell House.

CHAPTER 7

Information Leadership

The combined effect of the rapid growth of information is an increasingly fragmented information base, a large component of which is available only to people with money and/or acceptable institutional affiliations. In the recent past, the outcome of these challenges has been characterized as the "digital divide" between the information "haves" and "have nots" along racial and socio-economic lines that seem to widen as time passes (del Val & Normore, 2008). The digital divide addresses issues concerning equal opportunity, equity and access that have an effect on the development of marginalized and otherwise disadvantaged students in education systems (del Val & Normore, 2008; Selwyn, Gorard, & Williams, 2001). As a result, those with limited access become less prepared for the increasingly global market that is emerging in the twenty-first century. Research (e.g., Carvin, 2006; Hage, 2005; Picciano, 2006; Tansley, 2006; Welner & Weitzman, 2005) clearly indicates that this is a global phenomenon that has caused a widening equity gap in primary, secondary and higher education across all continents. Consequently, information leadership has become more critical than ever as discourses about the knowledge economy focus on the necessity of educating ALL students with skills for the global workplace.

School leaders and those who prepare them will need to know why, when, and how to use all of these tools and think critically about the information they provide. To do so will enable educators to interpret and make informed judgments as users of information sources. It will also enable them to become producers of information in their own right, and thereby become more powerful participants in society. This is part of the basic entitlement of every citizen, in every democracy in the world, to freedom of expression and the right to information (Abdelaziz, 2004). It is instrumental in building and sustaining democracy. These skills are viewed by many policy makers and educators as critical to the creation of an equitable global "Information Society" in which both developed and developing nations can share in social and economic development. Information leadership aims to develop *both* critical understanding *and* active participation. Some key concepts discussed in this chapter include the following:

- Digital divide
- Social justice leadership
- Integrated learning systems
- Access and equity

- Information literacy
- Ethical paradigms.

Consistent with previous chapters, we begin with an introduction to the *learning* about the digital divide, Integrated Learning systems (ILSs), the gap in the digital divide, social justice, and concepts such as technology, Internet, effective technology professional development, and technology access and equity. These are explained through the text, which also include a brief supplemental case study. Next, we present the concept of information *literacy*, and what that looks like. This is further enhanced by a focus on the role of *leadership* in which we focus on an educational leaders' ability to influence the information dynamics of the education process through formal and informal means. It emphasizes skills that include technology integration, technology support, online instruction/learning and generational technology differences in learning. Finally, we offer a series of *reflective* questions, prompts and activities focused on information leadership to help the reader understand the personal, interpersonal and organizational consequences of their actions. Additionally, we embed a series of discussion activities designed to help readers identify and analyze the way that the above concepts are practiced in their schools, local communities and throughout the world.

LEARNING ABOUT THE "DIGITAL DIVIDE"

Recent years have demonstrated a surge of computers and access to the Internet in public schools as an integrated effort to infuse information technology (IT) into the curriculum. It is estimated that 98 percent of public schools in the United States have computers and Internet access (Bull & Bull, 2003; Cattagni & Farris, 2001; Parsad, Jones, & Greene, 2005; Rathbun, West, & Hausken, 2003; U.S. Department of Education, 2000). Yet many researchers have asserted that education continues to reflect a "digital divide" between the information "haves" and "have nots" in society along racial and socio-economic factors that seems to widen as time passes (e.g., Hage 2005; Harrington-Lueker, 2001; Hoffman & Novak, 2000; Judge, Puckett, & Cabuk, 2004; Kaiser Family Foundation, 2004; Tansley, 2006). This digital divide addresses issues concerning equal educational opportunity and equity that have an effect on the development of disadvantaged students in public schools.

Disadvantaged students are usually the ones who do not have access to computer technology outside of their schools, thereby creating a digital divide. As a result of this digital divide, minority students and the poor living in urban and rural areas become less prepared for the increasingly competitive global market that is emerging in the twenty-first century. Meanwhile, it has been reported that 8 out of the 10 fastest growing occupations are computer-related (Education Reform Network, 2003; U.S. Department of Labor, 2000; Wilhelm, Carmen, & Reynolds, 2002). With these statistics at the nexus of public school, one pervasive issue that needs to be addressed is whether public schools can serve to bridge the widening gap of the digital divide. According to the Education Reform Network (2003), state governments, nonprofit agencies, and private enterprises all continue to make significant contributions to meet the changing needs of students and invest considerable time and money to make sure schools have computers for students. Yet public schools in the United States during the last 20 years continue to be faced with the challenge of a widening digital divide. The digital divide is not limited to the United States: it is a global phenomenon that encompasses a widening equity gap in primary, secondary, and higher education (Carvin, 2006; Hage, 2005; Layer, 2005; Levy & Murname, 2004; McGrath, 2004; Picciano, 2006; Tansley, 2006).

Over the past two decades, educational leadership scholars have made significant contributions to our understanding of social justice (Adams, Bell, & Griffin, 1997; Applebaum, 2004; Bigelow, Christensen, Karp, Miner, & Peterson, 2002; Delpit, 1988; Giroux, 1994; Marshall & Oliva, 2006; Marshall & Ward, 2004). Important conceptual research suggests that a social justice orientation to educational leadership practice and research can address "how institutionalized theories, norms, and practices in schools and society lead to social, economic, and educational inequities" (Dantley & Tillman, 2006, p. 17). In response to a more equitable practice in urban schools, this research explored social justice leadership and the digital divide, which have both garnered increased attention (Education Reform Network, 2003; Marshall & Oliva, 2006).

According to Marshall and Oliva, (2006), finding conceptual inspiration and guidance in notions of equity and equality, researchers and practitioners have begun to develop a pedagogy of leadership based on an ethic of care. Furthermore, they have embraced the moral imperative of improving "practice and student outcomes for minority, economically disadvantaged, female, gay/lesbian, and other students who have not traditionally served well in schools" (Marshall & Oliva, 2006, p. 6). As a result, the influence of leadership activity on institutional racism, gender discrimination, inequality of opportunity, inequity of educational processes, and justice have gained currency and attention. According to Rawls (2001), each individual has the same indefeasible claim to a fully adequate scheme of equal basic liberties, which scheme is compatible with the same scheme of liberties for all; and social and economic inequalities are to be attached to offices and positions open to all under conditions of fair equality of opportunity. He further asserts that these inequalities are to be the greatest benefit of the least-advantaged members of society (p. 291).

The unjust reality of the world has been explained with concepts such as hegemony (Gramsci, 1975), a culture of power (Delpit, 1988), and an inter-relationship of cultural inequalities in cultural politics (Giroux, 1994). In order to understand, promote, and enact social justice, school leaders must first develop a heightened and critical awareness of oppression, exclusion, marginalization, and justice. Awareness of social injustices, however, is not sufficient; school leaders must act when they identify inequity. School leaders are not only uniquely positioned to influence equitable educational practices, their proactive involvement is imperative. As Larson and Murtadha (2002) note, "throughout history, creating greater social justice in society and in its institutions has required the commitment of dedicated leaders" (p. 135).

Defining Social Justice Leadership

The discourse of social justice and leadership appears to be inextricably linked. According to Marshall and Oliva (2006, p. 5) social justice "has generated a great deal of scholarship over the last decade" which, in essence, capitalizes on the relevance of such a discourse. Recent commemorations of the 50th anniversary of the *Brown v. Board of Education* and the 40th anniversary of the *Civil Rights Act* have emphasized how movements for social justice have helped to define American history. These commemorations continue to serve as catalysts to refocus thinking on how school leaders have become social justice advocates and activists. Furthermore, discussions about social justice in the field of education have typically framed the concept of social justice around several issues including race, diversity, marginalization, morality, heterosexism, anti-Semitism, ableism, classism, spirituality, and gender (Adams et al., 1997; Normore & Brooks, 2014). Dantley and Tillman (2006, p. 17) add age, ability, and sexual orientation to the discourse. Some research (e.g., Bogotch, 2005, p. 7) asserts that social justice has no one specific meaning. Rather, "its multiple *a posterori* meanings emerge[d] differently from experiences and contexts." Bogotch (2005, p. 8) zeroes in on a key component of social justice by stating that "social justice, like education, is a deliberate intervention that requires the moral use of power" and concludes that it is "both much more than what we currently call democratic schooling and community education, and much less than what we hold out as the ideals of progressing toward a just and democratic society and a new humanity worldwide." Furman and Shields (2005, p. 123) argue the "need for social justice to encompass education that is not only just, democratic, emphatic, and optimistic, but also academically excellent" (as cited in Firestone & Riehl, 2005). The notion of social justice is hard to capture. Tillman (2005, p. 261) asserts that "it is demanding, fraught with controversy, and highly contextualized. Most people believe it is important but far fewer take the time or energy to actively pursue it. Thinking about social justice from a theoretical or historical perspective is a necessary but insufficient condition for actually achieving social justice."

While a review of the literature on social justice leadership does not present a clear definition of social justice, there is a general framework for delineating it. Lee and McKerrow (2005, p. 1) suggest that social justice is defined "not only by what it is but also by what it is not, namely injustice. By seeking justice, we anticipate the ideal. By questioning injustice, we approach it. Integrating both, we achieve it." These authors further assert that individuals for social justice seek to challenge political, economic and social structures that privilege some and disadvantage others. They challenge unequal power relationships based on gender, social class, race, ethnicity, religion, disability, sexual orientation, language, and other systems of oppression.

Technology "Haves" and "Have Nots"

Current literature indicates that poor disenfranchised minority students have limited opportunities to prepare for the economic demands of the twenty-first century (e.g., Freeman, 2005; Welner & Weitzman, 2005). Over 20 years ago, researchers at Johns Hopkins University reported that public schools located in the poorer districts were least likely to own microcomputers (Ascher, 1984). The issue 20 years ago was access to IT. Access meant actually having the physical components of computers (hardware and software) in the classrooms or somewhere in the schools (e.g., media center). Inequalities in gender, social class, and race in relation to equal access to computer technology were predominant in the 1980s. It may seem that 20 years later there are more students than ever before with access to computers in schools; however, this does not mean that the digital divide may be closing as schools have more computers. Equal access to IT continues to be a struggle for poor and other minority students in the United States.

There are differences in the ratio of computers to individuals that cut across socio-economic lines. For example, the ratio of computers to students in schools with a higher percentage of poor students is 1:16. Contrastingly, the ratio in schools with lower percentage of poor students is 1:7 (Cattagni & Farris, 2001; Picciano, 2006). Interestingly, the gender gap in computer access has been closing faster than the gap measured in terms of race and social class (Hoffman & Novak, 1999). The last 10 years have indicated that the digital divide between the technology "haves" and "have nots" may actually be increasing (Hoffman & Novak, 1994; Kaiser Family Foundation, 2004). The digital divide is conceptualized in a way that addresses the issue of equity in students' access and successful utilization of computer technology in schools. An assumption is made that education, and specifically public schooling, can assist in "bridging" the digital divide by incorporating high quality ILSs into the curricula.

Integrated Learning Systems. ILSs are advanced computer-based instructional systems consisting of a set of computerized courseware covering several grade levels, content areas, and complex classroom management and reporting features (Lawson-Martin & Normore, 2005). According to Picciano (2006), ILS is defined as "systems of hardware, software, curriculum, and management components" (p. 102) that become the technology infrastructure of the school. An ILS built on computer technology is a costly endeavor that requires considerable time and money to develop and sustain in schools. Public schools equipped with the appropriate IT components of an ILS would then serve all students, particularly the disadvantaged students, by teaching the necessary specialized skills (i.e., use of computers) to compete in a global economy that increasingly relies on IT (Levy & Murname, 2004).

ILS is part of a new breed of instructional computer programs that utilize recent developments in computer memory, computational speed capabilities, new computer programming languages, and research in human cognition and learning. An ILS is a computer-based learning system designed to help users develop specific skills, such as literacy and mathematical competency (Becker, 1994; Martin & Normore, 2006). Through expert system technology and artificial intelligence, ILS is able to carry on intelligent "dialogues" with students and flexibly adjust to the knowledge and skill level of individuals. It can also provide a variety of methods of representing and accessing information (Mandle & Lesgold, 1988). Some systems are oriented to discovery-learning, while others are more didactic, or "teaching" oriented. For instance, ILS in mathematics education is currently more adaptive to individual students, and better matched with current goals in mathematics, than earlier computer-assisted instructional tools (Mandle & Lesgold, 1988, p. 26). Key decision makers in schools responsible for introducing ILS into school programs believe that ILS are effective in raising standardized test scores for high and low achievers, older students, and students who have difficulty in learning from traditional classroom-based methods (Brush, 1997). In recent years, many schools have turned to ILS to facilitate instruction and assist with raising state standardized test scores (Becker, 1994; Picciano, 2006: Rathbun, West & Hausken, 2003; U.S. Dept. of Education, 2000; Wilhelm, Carmen, & Reynolds, 2002).

Digital Access and Equity

Current literature examines equity in terms of curriculum content and how students are taught in schools (Gerstl-Pepin & Woodside-Jiron, 2005; McGrath, 2004; Wilhelm, Carmen, & Reynolds, 2002). Research suggests that public schools with higher percentages of poorer students engaged them in "drill and practice" and "tutorial" exercises (repetition and lower level thinking) instead of other applications involving higher order (critical) thinking (Judge, Puckett, & Cabuk, 2004; McGrath, 2004; Picciano, 2006). Digital equity is defined contextually to address fair access to IT for children. Moreover, the content and use of the hardware and software are crucial to the optimal use of computer technology in teaching and learning. In its IT Blueprint, Miami-Dade County Public Schools, the 4th largest district in the United States, addresses equity as the "fair and equitable distribution of those resources" in technology (M-DCPS, *IT Blueprint*, 2006, p. 46). In this sense what is equitable is also just (Beckner, 2004).

Technology in the home is another factor that affects the education of students in school (Fairlie & McNulty, 2005; Kaiser Family Foundation, 2004; Wilhelm, Carmen, & Reynolds, 2002). Poorer students are less prepared as they enter schooling and lag behind other students from higher SES groups. The literature suggests that having a home computer may increase the probability that students will graduate high school (Fairlie & McNulty, 2005). It is estimated that 84 percent of low-income households in inner-city neighborhoods do not have computers (Wilhelm, Carmen, & Reynolds, 2002). About half of Black and Latino children have access to a home computer, compared to 85.5 percent of White children (Fairlie & McNulty, 2005).

Public schools can serve as the bridge to close the digital divide for students who do not have access to IT in their homes. The advent of the Internet in the mid 1990s increased the capacity of microcomputers to be used as effective tools to help students learn the necessary skills required in a changing job market. At least 98 percent of public schools are now connected to the Internet compared to 35 percent of public schools in 1994 (Cattagni & Farris, 2001; Lonergan, 2000). This does not mean that students have direct access to computers or the Internet in their classrooms. Other studies have suggested that only 15 percent of classrooms have Internet access (Hoffman & Novak, 1999). On the other hand, the ratio of computers to students in the United States public schools is averaged at 1:4 (Picciano, 2006). This ratio is considered "reasonable for effective learning" (Cattagni & Farris, 2001; Lonergan, 2000); however, this figure can be misleading as it misrepresents the access to technology experienced by poorer and disadvantaged students. Those who have more access include teachers, administrators, and office personnel in lieu of students.

The Gap in the Digital Divide

Internet access between Whites and minorities (Hispanics, Blacks) differ considerably in homes as well as in schools (Cattagni & Farris, 2001; del Val, 2006; Lonergan, 2000;

Parsad, Jones, & Greene, 2005). For example, 83 percent of non-Hispanic Whites had home computers with 50 percent connected to the Internet, compared to 46 percent of Black with 25 percent Internet access, and 47 percent Hispanic with 20 percent Internet access; and Asians surpass Whites in having home computers by 2 percent (Wilhelm, Carmen, & Reynolds, 2002). Other studies cite that 50.6 percent of Blacks and 48.7 percent of Latinos, compared to 74.6 percent of Whites, have access to computers at home (Fairlie, 2002; Heim, 2006). The ratio of computers with Internet access to students remained greater in schools with poorer students than in schools with the lowest concentration of poverty (1:9 compared to 1:6) (Cattagni & Farris, 2001). Other studies show that there was a disparity between children in highest SES groups having more access to computers and the Internet than children in lowest SES groups (Lonergan, 2000; Rathbun, West, & Hausken, 2003). At the same time, 90.2 percent of private college freshman reported using the Internet for research, compared to 77.6 percent of freshman entering Black public colleges (Hoffman & Novak, 1999). Subsequently, 80.1 percent of private college freshman used e-mail, compared to 41.4 percent of students in Black public colleges (Hoffman & Novak, 1999). Although schools can serve as vehicles of digital equity, the gap in the digital divide may begin to widen as early as first grade (Judge, Puckett, & Cabuk, 2004). The literature indicates that the digital divide appears at all levels of schooling.

The digital divide is a term that entered the collective psyche in the 1990s, with national and global implications. It describes the inability to access computer technology and the use of the Internet by certain segments of society (i.e., the poorest) from participation "in the global information society" (Hage, 2005). The digital divide affects one-sixth of the world's population—approximately 1 billion people. Low income families face added disadvantages because of lack of access to computers in the home (inability to pay for equipment and services). Moreover, public schools in poorer neighborhoods may not adequately provide an effective infrastructure with the tools that students need to learn computer technology outside of their homes. In 2003, the National Center for Education Statistics of the US Department of Education published a report that indicated 93 percent of instructional rooms in US public schools had Internet access (Parsad, Jones, & Greene, 2005). This may have meant that at least teachers may have had at least a personal computer installed in their classrooms. Notwithstanding, the digital divide seems to have increased over time in the United States and all around the world along lines demarcated by race and social class (Carvin, 2006; Harrington-Lueker, 2001; Hoffman & Novak, 1999; Judge, Puckett, & Cabuk, 2004; Kaiser Family Foundation, 2004).

Students have a necessity, and some would say a right, to learn the computer skills demanded by the current job market (Levy & Murname, 2004). At a time when more computers are made available in schools than ever before, the digital divide continues to widen and fewer people in the lowest SES groups are given the opportunity to join the world of computer technology and the Internet. This socio-economic digital divide is a global phenomenon (Bull & Bull, 2003; Carvin, 2006; Fairlie, 2002; Hage, 2005; Heim, 2006). Digital equity is about the "social justice goal" of "equitable access" and "effective use of technology for teaching and learning, access to content that is of high quality and culturally relevant" (Judge, Puckett, & Cabuk, 2004, p. 383).

Increases in government funding at federal and state levels, investments made by the private sector to provide technology resources to public schools, and advances in computer technology have yet to close the digital divide in education (Bull & Bull, 2003; Cattagni & Farris, 2001; Parsad, Jones, & Greene, 2005; Picciano, 2006). For example, ambitious goals were set by the Clinton administration during the 1990s to guarantee "universal access" to computers and the Internet at home and in schools. The 1994 Elementary and Secondary Education Act led to the creation of the E-Rate program in 1996. E-Rate provides discounts to public schools in purchasing the equipment and services needed to develop an appropriate technology infrastructure in schools. In 2001, $5.8 billion was earmarked to E-rate applicants in the United States (Cattagni & Farris, 2001). Interestingly, the No Child Left Behind Act (NCLB) of the Bush Administration addresses the achievement gap in general without increasing overall federal funding for education. However, NCLB contains a section called Enhancing Education through Technology (ED-Tech) program. ED-Tech is geared to improve the use of technology by students in schools (NCLB, 2001). ED-Tech also focuses on teacher training in the use of computer technology in the classroom.

Using Ethical Paradigms to Address the Digital Divide

A theoretical framework for applying ethics using multiple paradigms is suggested here for the purpose of addressing the issue of equity and social justice in the information age of computers. These paradigms consist of the ethics of justice, critique, care, profession (Shapiro & Stefkovich, 2005), and community (Furman, 2004). The ethic of justice highlights the right of equal educational opportunity that is of high quality available to all students (fairness, equity, equality) whereas the ethic of critique examines the current policies and practices that may perpetuate inequalities inherent in public schools (bureaucracy). As changes in policy and practice lead to digital equity in providing equal access to computer technology and its effective use, then disadvantaged students would not be affected by race/ethnicity or SES in learning computer skills in order to succeed in school and (later on) in the work force. The ethic of care ensures that children are put first and education serves the best interest of students. As these paradigms merge, the ethic of the profession acts as a call to action for educational leaders to plan, implement, and sustain efficient and effective ILS in their schools. The ethic of community addresses the greater good for the greatest number in supporting excellence in education and digital equity for all students in public schools.

These paradigms support social justice education—in particular the work of Freire (1970/2003) and Smith-Maddock and Solozano (2002) who assert that we must engage in problem-posing methodology in order to identify and name inequities, analyze the cause of the inequities, and find solutions. Gillian and Ward (2004) claim that social justice education is a "belief in our own humanity and the power to assert our moral authority in the face of continuing injustice and intolerance" (p. 69). Moreover, IT integration in public schools must be relevant and meaningful to students (Hung & Seng Koh, 2004; Eberwein, 2005), contain culturally responsive content (Furman & Sheilds, 2005) and confront digital inequity (Carvin, 2006; Fairlie, 2002).

According to the Education Reform Network (2003) there are several dimensions of digital equity that must be taken into consideration in order to help bridge the divide: content creation (i.e., opportunities for learners and educators to create their own content), effective use (i.e., educators must be skilled in using these resources effectively for teaching and learning), quality content (i.e., access to high quality digital content), cultural relevance (access to high quality, culturally relevant content), and technology resources. The literature pinpoints the importance of curriculum content in the integration of computer technology in schools (ILS—hardware, software, management, wiring, connectivity, etc.). Moreover professional development of teachers to utilize the latest technology in the classroom is crucial to the success of increased student access to computers in schools. Equity incorporates efficient and effective ILS utilization by teachers and students in schools. High quality, culturally relevant ILS in schools can help ensure that students have access to successful experiences as long as teachers keep pace with the acquisition of new knowledge and skills. Pedagogical content knowledge is essential with respect to integrating technology in the classroom effectively.

To address the issues of digital equity, school leaders are in a position to ensure opportunities are made available for all students in schools. Social justice is constructed in relation to experiential knowledge of social injustice. At a time when criticisms are being voiced about the eroding ethics of society, it becomes vital that decisions and actions for twenty-first century educational leaders be based on ethical and moral foundations. Successful social justice leadership will involve moral choices with an emphasis on sense and meaning, morality, self-sacrifice, duty, and obligation. Recent research reflects a distinct trend emphasizing that effective school leaders advocate for social justice and maintain an ethical orientation (Bogotch, 2005; Furman & Sheilds, 2005; Lee & McKerrow, 2005; Normore & Blanco, 2006). According to Jazzar and Algozzine (2007), in order for school and district leaders to be successful in the new millennium, "the pendulum must swing back to values and moral dimension" (p. 155). When moral authority overcomes bureaucratic leadership in a school, the outcomes can be extraordinary for all students. The multiple paradigm approach as outlined by Shapiro and Stefkovich (2005) may help to revolutionize the field of educational leadership to successfully bridge the achievement gap and meet the challenges of the twenty-first century.

CASE OF A MIDDLE SCHOOL IN FLORIDA

Florida has the 10th highest poverty rate in the nation and ranks 16th in home Internet access (Wilhelm, Carmen, & Reynolds, 2002). Indeed, educational leaders in Florida face significant challenges in changing the way teaching and learning take place in the classrooms. All educational leaders (federal and state government officials, superintendents, principals, assistant principals, and teachers) are given the charge to advocate for and support the integration of technology (computers and multimedia) in public schools. According to Levy and Murname (2004), these leaders are given the charge to address the need for the most vulnerable students (poor, disadvantaged minority groups) to have a "more equal" educational opportunity to learn the skills necessary to be successful in the job market. For purposes of our argument, and as an example, we now introduce one of the top six largest urban school districts in the United States. The district faces the challenge of developing an appropriate ILS and the supporting technology infrastructure to meet the educational needs of its students. The district has a student population of more than 300,000 students. It has a comprehensive IT strategic plan conducted by CELT Corporation (Massachusetts). The strategic plan provides a blueprint for the years 2005–2008 (Miami-Dade County Public Schools, 2006). The plan is to help "all students to be fully prepared to succeed as workers, citizens, and leaders" (p. 1). This blueprint is meant to ensure that "all students have access to current, appropriate, and sufficient information resources" (p. 46) among other goals that address the issue of equity in IT to bridge the digital divide. Best-practices research cited in the blueprint emphasizes project-based learning (McGrath, 2004) in helping students gain information literacy skills in its more than 300 schools. The district is moving toward critical mass in infusing IT to continue to increase access and raise the standards of curriculum content in the use of computers in schools. The district defines critical mass as computer to student ratios of 1:2 in grades K-5, and 1:1 in grades 6–12 (p. 48). E-Rate, ED-Tech, Title I, and other funding sources are utilized to cover the increasing costs in closing the digital divide in the schools. As stated in the district IT Blueprint, "it is important to recognize that in highly effective learning environments, one-to-one student-to-computer access is often a requirement" (p. 49). The expansion of Internet access in schools is a component of its IT plan and implementation district-wide.

One of its average size middle schools (1,500 students) is located in a rural/suburban area of the county. The school has expanded its IT infrastructure significantly in the last decade. It is a Title I school, with more than 70 percent of the student population eligible for free or reduced lunch. The majority of students are Hispanic-American (57 percent), with a smaller percentage of African-American (27 percent), a diminishing number of White-American (14 percent), and a small percentage of Asian-American (2 percent) (Miami-Dade County Public Schools, 2005). In 1997, IT in the school consisted of 11 computers in a small classroom with drill and practice and tutorial software that was then obsolete and hardly used by the students. Today, the school is constructing an ILS that currently has more than 500 computers for administrators, staff, faculty, and students. Technically, the ratio of computers to students is 1:3, although this does not reflect actual student access to computers (personal communication, December, 2006). Most classrooms have at least two computers (one for the teacher's use), and some have up to 4 computers (classroom size average at 30). A couple of classrooms have multiple computers for student use. Furthermore, all counselors, office staff, and administrators have a PC and are on-line. The school has a full-time IT administrator on staff, working under the principal, who has been developing, implementing, and managing the growing ILS in the school for the past several years. Presently, there are three computer labs (40 computers per lab) that are regularly used by students for classroom assignments in math, science, language arts, and social studies. Two labs are actual classrooms wired with multiple PCs, and one lab is in the Media Center. Teachers have been offered training courses in computer technology and curriculum content to infuse IT in their lesson plans. Students use the computers in these labs during classroom time on a rotating basis.

Over the years, the school has oscillated between a C and a D grade from the state A+ plan (Florida Comprehensive Assessment Test scores—FCAT). The school recently received a B grade. ILS infusion in this school may have been a significant contributing factor in its acquisition of a higher letter grade as a result of improved FCAT scores. It may be true that FCAT scores may not measure all the gains in student learning that has occurred at this school as a result of increasing student access to computer technology. Nevertheless, many students are poor and do not have computers, let alone Internet access, at home. These students are having the opportunity to experience working with computers in school that they would otherwise not have at home. The expanding ILS infrastructure in the school is bridging the digital divide in providing students with the acquisition of computer skills that improves their competitive advantage in school and in the future job market.

An adequate infusion of ILS in the school curricula can facilitate the development of skills in students necessary to succeed in the emerging job market of the twenty-first century. School leaders now have a moral imperative to not only acquire basic IT competency in order to help develop and implement effective ILS in schools, but also to promote the use of new technology to enhance teaching and learning. Schools and school leaders then can become the equalizing agents in providing educational opportunities to their communities and nation that help bridge the digital divide for equal access and equitable opportunity.

INFORMATION LITERACY

We contend that information literacy forms the basis for lifelong learning and should be introduced wherever possible within national curricula as well as in tertiary, nonformal and lifelong education. Drawing on the work of Reich (1990), Mitchell and Boyd (2001) suggest that "under the influence of the new information technologies (IT), machines can easily outthink and outperform anyone whose academic skills do not include understanding as well as efficiency" and that "Managing the productivity of information-age machinery will require workers who have a more comprehensive and a subtler grasp of both reading and mathematics than has heretofore been expected of public school students" (p. 73). Information literacy is concerned with teaching and learning about the whole range of information sources and formats. Thus, the various technologies of public communication (i.e., print, Internet, television, radio, etc.,) ought to engender information literacy. As a result, information literacy is a social process for understanding, finding, evaluating, communicating, and using information— activities that may be accomplished in part by fluency with IT, in part by sound investigative methods, but most important, through critical discernment and reasoning. Using print media as an integral part of the educational leadership experience, for example, can stimulate the moral imagination and help produce information literate citizens. Research on media representations provides comment on the media coverage directed at various social, cultural, and political issues. Texts, film, television, and books have focused on analyses of public debates during political campaigns, assessment processes of schools and education policies, and social and cultural issues (Shapiro, 1989; Smith, 1999; Taylor, 1997). Studies have reported that media such as film, newspapers, and magazines, for example, influences popular beliefs about current affairs (Giroux, 2002). For example, Thomas (2006) cited a study that investigated the content, effect, and intent, or influence, of Brisbane newspaper reports on the issues of entrance to tertiary education.

A strong correlation between content of press items and public opinion was found, together with evidence of agenda setting involving the selection and omission of items and preferential media access to public elites. As such, it reflects the emphasis on news found in much of the work on media discourse and questions the ability of journalists and news reporters to adequately inform the public and policymakers on national and global issues (Afflerbach & Moni, 1994). Tuana (2003) argued, for example, that "the news media . . . in striving to provide interesting sound bites about human cloning has often been ethically irresponsible in failing to adequately explain the science of cloning" and "politicians debating cloning legislation often do not acknowledge the full range of scientific options that are available" (p. 3). Media knowledge—as an integral form of information literacy and communication is always a form of social practice (Giroux, 2002). Researchers (e.g., Thomas, 2006) have argued that the press constructs a hegemonic consensus within a framework given by "the powerful and the privileged of society who are seen by the press to be legitimate spokespersons for society . . . depicting reported crises as a symbol of moral decay . . . the work ethic and moral order" (p. 34). Thomas emphasized the ideological dominance to the process of hegemonic struggle—a struggle in which the news media can work to give hegemonic consent to the maintenance of existing political, social, and economic arrangements. According to Fairclough (1995),

> Theorization of news as discourse highlights the discursive nature of media power and its influence on knowledge, beliefs, values, social relations and social identities through its particular ways of representing the world, its particular constructions of social identities and its particular constructions of social relations (p. 49).

As suggested in the research (e.g., Abdelaziz, 2004; Burkhardt, MacDonald, & Rathemacher, 2005; Correia, 2002), information literacy initiates, sustains, and extends lifelong learning through abilities that may use technologies but are ultimately independent of them. As information is increasingly codified in digital forms (Correia, 2002), new skills are needed to operate the technology to search for, organize, manage information, and use it to solve problems and create new knowledge and cultural products. Because the Internet is a common information and communication tool globally, IL is often understood as digital literacy in which computer literacy, media literacy, and media education are integral components. As Abdelaziz (2004) claims,

> Introducing new media technology—let alone the kinds of "critical thinking" and the new pedagogies associated with IL–is almost bound to meet with considerable inertia, if not overt resistance . . . Still, a vigorous IL campaign could result in the long run in the emergence of an "information culture." (p. 3).

DISCUSSION

1. At first glance it appears that the inundation of computers in public schools, showing an average of five students to every computer counted, has provided the sufficient digital equity to close the digital divide. Upon closer observation, recent literature indicates that the digital divide between extreme SES groups, and the divide between Whites and Blacks, may be widening and not closing in the first two decades of the twenty-first century. The problem is home access to computers and the Internet by the poorest students outside of public schools. Of course, there are public libraries that can be utilized to use computers and access the Internet across America, yet this is not utilized optimally, or may be inadequate for use for a large number of people. A preliminary literature review of this subject indicates that the overall digital divide is widening in some sectors of society and closing in others in spite of the efforts of public schools to close the digital divide in education. Yet time may be the critical factor to reveal the effect of the trend of implementing and sustaining ILS in schools to improve student learning. The lack of ILS in public schools seems to perpetuate social injustice for disadvantaged students. Therefore, how can educational leaders alleviate the challenges to act in ways that help bridge the digital divide for students and help them gain the necessary computer skills to be successful and productive members of society? How do we ensure that school leaders have basic knowledge of ILS and state-of-the-art technology infrastructure to develop a vision of what students need to learn?

2. Developing a strategic plan is essential in addressing issues of information literacy and digital equity for efficient and effective utilization of IT in schools (Picciano, 2006). Implementation of a plan requires constant monitoring and feedback. Sustainability of an efficient and effective ILS in schools requires long-term planning including added costs for maintenance, service, and upgrade of equipment to keep the infrastructure running smoothly. Toward this end, how can educational leaders collaborate in an integrated effort involving all stakeholders in developing a viable system that works? Could a balance of professional development (teacher training) and state-of-the-art computer technology for student learning provide stability in the implementation of the curriculum? Should educational leaders stop investing in IT—computers and multimedia equipment installed and utilized in teaching and learning—but to invest more money and time in the strategic planning, implementation, and sustainability of IT in the curricula of public schools?

3. IT may be the essential tools that need to be made accessible to students in public schools to meet the demands of the twenty-first century. How can leadership in nonprofit and for-profit private enterprises benefit from investing in the technology infrastructure in public schools to supplement what government is providing? Moreover, closing the digital divide may require additional financial support. For example, Computers for Youth (CFY) has provided 6,000 computers to low-income families in middle schools throughout New York City (Carvin, 2006). Various organizations, such as Hewlett-Packard and Microsoft, are also investing in the development and support of IT in public schools. These types of collaborative ventures are required to meet the challenges of the twenty-first century for students

in public schools. It requires a collective effort—the "village" concept—of all sectors of society to effectively address the challenge posed by the digital divide. With this, how does the ethic of community culminate in its effort to bring about a more caring and just society in the education of its children?

4. Providing digital equity in public schools can play a vital role in closing the digital divide in the new millennium if ILS and state-of-the-art technology infrastructure infused in schools continues to be a priority for districts across the country. Should special attention be given to the disadvantaged students in schools to ensure their success in school and a job market that demands a skilled labor force in the twenty-first century? If so, how do educational leaders engage in this special attention?

5. Given the demographic shift of the US population which is becoming increasingly more diverse, there is a need to look at practices (i.e., the types of discourse, preparation, training, experiences, processes, and structures) that promote the development and support of educational leaders committed to social justice and principles of access and equity. School leaders have a moral obligation to respond to the changing political, moral, and social landscapes in which they live and work. What would such a response look like for educational leaders? Could the response involve a curricular focus in their leadership training and preparation on inter-relating social justice, democracy, and equity and values so that school leaders can identify practices that explicitly and implicitly deter social progress? How do they develop the knowledge base on how to respond to these injustices in school practices? How must leaders' critical engagement in dialogue and reflective practice about social justice, access and equity be well-informed about a greater, more robust and inclusive form of democratic schooling, and a substantively egalitarian education system?

6. Educators and policy makers need to focus on the critical need for students to acquire crucial skills and empower them to obtain their basic educational require-ments. How could leaders create ways of developing balanced programs while still meeting the requirements of legislation? Further, in our "new millennium" genera-tion, this amounts to a high school diploma plus some post-secondary educational experience. The desire to achieve the "American Dream" that includes at least a high school diploma is one that often goes unrealized for many marginalized students. How then must public schools serve to prepare students to live better lives in the future, or will they serve to hinder their growth and ultimately that of society? By definition, educational leadership also means addressing the issue of the digital divide that can perpetuate social injustice in education.

7. District leaders and school-site administrators are in a unique position to make a difference in urban and rural public schools. The crisis of the apparent widening of the digital divide can become the opportunity for public schools throughout the nation to answer the call to prepare students to meet the challenges of the new information age, and help make all students information literate. When developing programs for under-represented students, how can educators at all levels create ways of developing balanced programs while still meeting the requirements of legislation and simultaneously serving the needs of all students—as in any teaching and leadership intervention?

REFERENCES

Abdelaziz, A. (2004). Information competency for lifelong learning. Paper presented at the World Library and Information Congress: 70th IFLA General Conference and Council, p. 4. Available [online]: http://ifla.org/IV/ifla70/papers/116e-Abid.pdf

Adams, M., Bell, L. A., & Griffin, P. (1997). *Teaching for diversity and social justice*. New York: Routledge.

Afflerbach, P., & Moni, K. (1994). Legislators, reporters, and reading assessment. *Reading Research Report, 31*. National Research Center, College Park, MD.

Anderson, G. L. 1991. Cognitive politics of principals and teachers: Ideological control in an elementary school. In J. Blase (Ed.), *The Politics of life in schools: Power, conflict, and cooperation*, 120–30. Newbury Park: Sage.

Anderson, G., and Herr, K. (1993). The micropolitics of student voices: Moving from diversity of bodies to diversity of voices in schools. In C. Marshall (Ed.), *The New Politics of Race and Gender*, 58–68. New York: Falmer.

Anderson-Levitt, K. (2003). A world culture of schooling? In K. Anderson-Levitt (Ed.), *Local meanings, global schooling: Anthropology and world culture theory*, 1–26. New York: Palgrave Macmillan.

Apple, M., Kenway, J., & Singh, M. (Eds.). (2005). *Globalizing education: Policies, pedagogies, & politics*. New York: Peter Lang.

Applebaum, B. (2004). Social justice education, moral agency, and the subject of resistance. *Educational Theory, 54*(1), 59–72.

Archer, J. (September, 2004). Leading for learning. Education. *Week on the Web*. http://edweek. org/sreports/special_reports_article.cfm?slug=leadpack_2004.htm

Ascher, C. (1984). *Microcomputers: Equity and quality in education for urban disadvantaged students*. ED242801. New York, NY: Eric Clearinghouse on Urban Education.

Association for Supervision and Curriculum Development (2000). The contemporary principal: New skills for a new age. *Education Update, 42*(3), 1–8.

Barnett, B. (April, 2003). *Catching the tiger by the tail: The illusive nature of principal preparation*. Paper presented at the Annual Meeting of the American Educational Research Association, Chicago, IL.

Barro, R. (2000). *Education and economic growth*. Paris: OECD.

Barth, R. S. (2003) *Lessons learned: Shaping relationships and the culture of the workplace*. Thousand Oaks, CA.: Corwin Press, 2003.

Bauman, Z. (1998) *Globalization: The human consequences*. New York: Columbia UP.

Becker, H. J. (1994). Mindless or mindful use of integrated learning systems. *International Journal of Educational Research, 21*(1), 65–79.

Beckner, W. (2004). *Ethics for educational leaders*. Boston, MA: Pearson Education, Inc.

Begley, P. T. (2000). *School leadership in Canada*. 2nd ed. Hillsdale, ON, Canada: Paul Begley & Associates.

Begley, P. T., & Cambell-Evan, G. (1992). Socializing experiences of aspiring principals. *The Alberta Journal of Educational Research, 38*(4), 285–99.

Bennis, W. (1985). *Leaders: The strategies for taking charge*. New York: Harper & Row.

Benson, M. (2001). The professional principals series. *OPC Register: The Magazine for Ontario's Principals and Vice-principals, 3*(1), 6.

Bigelow, W., Christensen, L., Karp, S., Miner, B., & Peterson, B. (2000). *Rethinking our classroom: Teaching for equity and justice*. Milwaukee, WI: A Rethinking Schools Publication.

Blood, R. (1966). The function of experience in professional preparation: *Teaching and the principalship*. Unpublished doctoral dissertation. Claremont, CA: Claremont Graduate School.

Bogotch, I. E. (2005). Social justice as an educational construct: Problems and possibilities. Paper presented at the annual meeting of the University Council of Educational Administration, Nashville, TN, November.

Bolman, L. G., & Terrance E. D. (2003). *Reframing organizations*. 3rd ed. San Francisco: Jossey-Bass.

Bracher, P., Panoch, J. V., Piediscalzi, N., & Uphoff, J. K. (1974). *Public education religion studies: Questions and answers*. Dayton, OH: Public Education Religion Studies Center, Wright State University.

Bransford, J., Brown, A., & Cocking, R. (Eds.). (1999). *How people learn: Brain, mind, experience, and school*. Washington, DC: National Academy Press.

Bredeson, P.V. (1996). New directions in the preparation of educational leaders. In *International handbook of educational leadership and administration*, 251–77. Springer Netherlands.

Briskin, L., & Priegert-Coulter, R. (1992). Introduction: Feminist pedagogy: Challenging the normative. *Canadian Journal of Education*, *17*(3), 247–63.

Brooks, J. S. (2006). Tinkering toward utopia or stuck in a rut? School reform implementation at Wintervalley High. *Journal of School Leadership*, *16*(3), 240–65.

Brooks, J. S., & Jean-Marie, G. (2007). Black leadership, white leadership: Race and race relations in an urban high school. *Journal of Educational Administration*, *45*(6), 756–68.

Brooks, J. S., & Miles, M. T. (2008). From scientific management to social justice . . . and back again? Pedagogical shifts in educational leadership. In A. H. Normore (Ed.), *Leadership for social justice: Promoting equity and excellence through inquiry and reflective practice*, 99–114. Charlotte, NC: Information Age Publishing.

Browne-Ferrigno, T. (2003). Becoming a principal: Role conception, initial socialization, role identity transformation, purposeful engagement. *Educational Administration Quarterly*, *39*(4), 468–503.

Brush, T. A. (1997). The effects on student achievement and attitudes when using integrated learning systems with cooperative pairs. *Educational Technology Research and Development*, *45*(2), 51–64.

Brydon, D. (2004, fall). Cross-talk, postcolonial pedagogy, and transnational competency. *Situation Analysis*, *4*, 70–87.

Bull, G., & Bull, G. (2003). The digital disconnect: A recent Pew study. *Learning and Leading with Technology*, *31*(4), 28–31.

Burbules, N., & Torres, C. (2000). *Globalization and education: Critical perspectives*. New York, NY: Routledge.

Burkhardt, J. M., MacDonald, M. C., & Rathemacher, A. J. (2005). *Creating a comprehensive information competency plan: a how-to-do-it manual and CD-ROM for librarians*. New York, NY: Neal-Schuman Publishers.

Campbell, R. F., Fleming, T., Newell, L. J., & Bennion, J. W. (1987). *A history of thought and practice in educational administration*. New York: Teachers College Press.

Capra, F. (1996). *The web of life: A new scientific understanding of living systems*. New York: Anchor Books.

Carlson, R. O. (1961). Succession and performance among school superintendents. *Administrative Science Quarterly*, *6*, 210–27.

Carnoy, M., & Rhoten, D. (2002). What does globalization mean for education change? A comparative approach. *Comparative Education*, *46*(1), 1–9.

Carvin, A. (2006, March). *The gap: The digital divide network*. Reed Business Information, p. 70.

Carvin, A. (2006, March). The gap: The digital divide network. *Reed Business Information*.

Cascadden, D. (1998). Principals as managerial leaders: A qualitative study of the perspective of selected elementary school principals. *Journal of School Leadership*, 8(2), 137-70.

Castetter, W. B., & Young, I. P. (2000). *The human resource function in educational administration*. 7th ed. Upper Saddle River, NJ: Merrill/Prentice Hall.

Cattagni, A., & Farris, E. (2001). *Internet access in U.S. public schools and classrooms: 1994-2000* (NCES 2001-071). U.S. Department of Education. Washington, DC: National Center for Education Statistics.

Chirichello, M. (2001, January). *Preparing principals to lead in the new millennium: A response to the leadership crisis in American schools*. Paper presented at the 14th International Congress for School Effectiveness and Improvement, Toronto, ON, Canada.

Christians, C. (2003). The media and moral competency. *Ethical Space, The International Journal of Communications Ethics*, 1(1), 1-17.

Christians, C., Ferre, J., & Fackler, M. (1993). *Good News: Social Ethics and the Press*. New York, NY: Oxford University Press.

Clark, T. (2007). *EPIC change: How to lead change in the global age*. San Francisco, CA: Jossey-Bass.

Collins, J. C. (2001). *Good to great: Why some companies make the leap . . . and others don't*. New York, NY: Harper Business.

Correia, A. (2002). Information Competency for an active and effective citizenship. White paper prepared for UNESCO, the U.S. National Commission on Libraries and Information Science, and the National Forum on Information Competency, for use at the Information Competency Meeting of Experts, Prague, The Czech Republic.

Courchene, T. J. (1995). Glocalization: The regional/international interface. *Canadian Journal of Regional Science*, 18(1), 1-20.

Crawford, J., Carlton, P., & Stengel, L. (November, 2003). *The effects of principal succession on school climate in Urban settings*. Paper presented at the Annual Meeting of the University Council for Educational Administration, Portland, OR.

Cunningham, W. G., & Gresso, D. W. (1993). *Cultural leadership: The culture of excellence in education*. Needham Heights, MA: Allyn & Bacon.

Dantley, M. E. (2005). African American spirituality and Cornel West's notions of prophetic pragmatism: Restructuring educational leadership in American urban schools. *Educational Administration Quarterly*, 41(4), 651-74.

Dantley, M. E., & Tillman, L. C. (2006).Social justice and moral transformative leadership. In C. Marshall & M. Oliva (Eds.), *Leadership for social justice: Making revolutions in education*, 16-30. Boston, MA: Pearson Education.

Daresh, J. C. (1997). Improving principal preparation: A review of common strategies. *NASSP Bulletin*, 81(585), 3-8.

Daresh, J. C. (2000). *New principals: new induction programs*. Paper presented at the Annual Meeting of the American Educational Research Association, New Orleans, LA.

Deal, T. E., & Peterson, K. D. (1991). *The principal's role in shaping school culture*. Washington, DC: United States Department of Education.

Deal, T. E., & Peterson, K. D. (1999). *Shaping school culture: The heart of leadership*. San Francisco, CA: Jossey-Bass.

del Val, R. E. (2006). Book review: Closing the equity gap, edited by Geoff Layer, 2005. *Adult Education Quarterly*, 57(1), 90-1.

del Val, R. E., & Normore, A.H. (2008). Leadership for social justice: Bridging the digital divide. *University Council for Educational Administration (UCEA, International Journal of Urban Educational Leadership*, 2, 1–15. Available [On-line]: http://uc.edu/urbanleadership/current_issues.htm

Delpit, L. (1988). The silenced dialogue: Power and pedagogy in educating other people's children. *Harvard Education Review, 58*(3), 280–98.

Dill, W. R. (1960). How aspiring managers promote their own careers. *California Management Review*, 2, 9–15.

Earle, J., & Kruse, S. (1999). *Organizational competency for education: Topic in educational leadership.* Mahwah, NJ: Lawrence Erlbaum Associates, Inc.

Eberwein, J. (2005, fall). 10 ways to integrate technology in a meaningful way. *FETC Connections.* Florida Educational Technology Corporation, Inc., 2–3.

Education Reform Network (2003). The five dimensions of digital equity. http://digitalequity.edreform.net/

Educational Research Service (1999). Is there a shortage of qualified candidates for openings in the principalship? An exploratory study. For the National Association of Elementary School Principals (NAESP) and National Association of Secondary School Principals (NASSP), Washington, DC.

Educational Research Service, National Association of Elementary School Principals and National Association of Secondary School Principals (2000). The principal, keystone of a *high achieving school: Attracting and keeping the leaders we need.* For the National Association of Elementary School Principals (NAESP) and National Association of Secondary School Principals (NASSP), Washington, DC.

English, F. W. (2002). The point of scientificity, the fall of the epistemological dominos, and the end of the field of educational administration. *Studies in Philosophy and Education, 21*(2), 109–36.

English, F. W. (2003a). Cookie-cutter leaders for cookie-cutter schools: The teleology of standardization and the de-legitimization of the university in educational leadership preparation. *Leadership and Policy in Schools, 2*(1), 27–46.

English, F. W. (2003b). *The postmodern challenge to the theory and practice of educational administration.* Springfield, IL: Charles C. Thomas Publishers.

English, F. W. (2006). The unintended consequences of a standardized knowledge base in advancing educational leadership programs. *Educational Administration Quarterly, 42*(3), 461–72.

Fairclough, N. (1995). *Media discourse.* London, UK: Arnold.

Fairholm, G. (1997). *Capturing the heart of leadership: Spirituality and community in the new American workplace.* Westport: Praeger.

Fairlie, R. (2002). *Race and the digital divide.* Chicago, IL: Joint Center for Poverty Research.

Fairlie, R., & McNulty, J. (2005, October). Kids with access to home computer more likely to graduate. *AScribe Newswire.* Santa Cruz, CA: University of California.

Freebody, P., & Luke, A. (2003). Competency as engaging with new forms of life: The 'four roles' model. In: G. Bull & M. Anstey (eds.), *The competency lexicon.* 2nd ed, 52–7. Sydney, AUS: Prentice Hall.

Freeman, E. (2005). No child left behind and the denigration of race. *Equity and Excellence in Education, 38*(3), 190–9.

Freire, P. (1970/2003). *Pedagogy of the oppressed.* New York: Continuum.

Friedman, T. L. (1999). *The Lexus and the olive tree: Understanding globalization.* New York, NY: Anchor.

Friedman, T. L. (2005). *The world is flat: A brief history of the twenty-first century*. New York, NY: Farrar, Straus and Giroux.

Fullan, M. (1993). Coordinating school and district development in restructuring. In J. Murphy & P. Hallinger (Eds.), *Restructuring schooling: Learning from ongoing efforts.* (pp. 224–36). Newbury Park, CA: Corwin Press.

Fullan, M. (1997). *What's worth fighting for in the principalship?* 2nd ed. New York: Teachers College Press.Fullan, M. (2001). *Leading in a culture of change*. San Francisco, CA: Jossey-Bass.

Furman, G. C. (2004). The ethic of community. *Journal of Educational Administration, 42*(2), 215–35.

Furman, G. C., & Sheilds, C. M. (2005). How can educational leaders promote and support social justice and democratic community in schools? In W. A. Firestone & C. Riehl (Eds.), *A new agenda for educational leadership*, 119–37. New York, NY: Teachers College Press.

Fyfe, I. (2007). Hidden in the curriculum: political competency and education for citizenship in Australia. *Melbourne Journal of Politics*. Retrieved on January 23, 2016 from, http://find books.com/p/books/

Gaudelli, W. (2003). *World class: Teaching and learning in global times*. Mahwah, NJ: Lawrence Erlbaum.

Gee, J. P. (1991). The legacies of competency: From Plato to Freire through Harvey Graff: Competency, discourse, and linguistics. *Harvard Educational Review, 58*(2), 195–212.

Gerstl-Pepin, C. I., & Woodside-Jiron, H. (2005). Tensions between the "science" of reading and a "love of learning": One high-poverty school's struggle with NCLB. *Equity and Excellence in Education, 38*(3), 232–41.

Gillian, C., & Ward, J. (2004). *Racing moral formation: African American perspectives on care and justice*. Forward. In V. Siddle Walker & J.R. Snarey (Eds.), ix-xii. New York: Teachers College Press.

Giroux, H. A. (1994). Teachers, public life and curriculum reform. *Peabody Journal of Education, 69*(3), 35–47.

Giroux, H. A. (2002). Democracy, freedom, and justice after September 11th: Rethinking the role of educators and the politics of schooling. *Teachers College Record, 104*(6) 1138–62.

Gramsci, A. (1975). *Selections from the prison notebook*. (Q. Hoare & G. N. Smith, Trans. and Edit.). New York: International Publishers.

Green, A. (1997). *Education, globalization and the nation state*. New York, NY: Macmillan.

Greenfield, W. (1985). *Being and becoming a principal: Responses to work contexts and socialization processes*. Paper presented at the annual meeting of the American Educational Research Association, Chicago.

Gutherie, J. W., & Saunders, T. (2001, January). *Who will lead the public schools?* Education Supplement. The New York Times.

Hage, M. (2005, November). *The digital divide continues to hinder development in rural areas*. Food and agriculture organization of the United Nations: Second world summit on the information society, Available: [on-line]: www.fao.org

Hage, M. (2005, November). *The digital divide continues to hinder development in rural areas*. Food and Agriculture Organization in the United Nations: Second World Summit on the Information Society. Available [online]: www.fao.org.

Hall, E. T. (1959). *The silent language*. New York, NY: Doubleday Publishing Group, Inc.

Hall, G. E., & Mani, M. N. G. (1992). Entry strategies: Where do I begin? In F. W. Parkay & G. E. Hall (Eds.), *Becoming a principal: The challenges of beginning leadership*, 48–69. Needham Heights, MA: Simon & Shuster.

Hargreaves, A., & Fullan, M. (1999). *What's worth fighting for out there?* Toronto, ON, Canada: Ontario Public School Teachers' Federation.

Harrington-Lueker, D. (2001, June). New networks, old problems: Technology in urban schools. *Technology in Urban Schools: EWA Special Report*, 2–7. Washington, DC: Education Writers Association.

Hargreaves, A., & Fink, D. (2004). The seven principles of sustainable leadership. *Educational Leadership*, 61(7), 8–13.

Hart, A. W. (1993). *Principal succession: Establishing leadership in schools.* Albany, NY: SUNY Press.

Harvey, T. R., & Drolet, B. (2004). *Building teams-building people: Expanding the fifth resource.* 2nd ed. New York, NY: ScarecrowEducation.

Heim, K. (2006, March). Global digital divide grows. *The Seattle Times*, March 21, 3–5, Seattle, WA.

Hess, F. M. (1999). *Spinning wheels: The politics of urban school reform.* Washington, DC: Brookings Institute.

Hoban, G. (2002). *Teacher learning for educational change: A systems thinking approach.* Buckingham, UK: Open University Press.

Hoffman, D. L., & Novak, T. P. (2000). The growing digital divide: Implications for an open research agenda. In B. Kahin & E. Brynjolffson (Eds.),*Understanding the digital economy: Data, tools and research.* Cambridge, MA: MIT Press. Available [on-line]: http://ecommerce. vanderbilt.edu/

Hung, D., & Seng Koh, T. (2004, March-April). A social-cultural view of information technology integration in school contexts. *Educational Technology*, 48–54.

Institute of Educational Leadership (2000, October). *Leadership for student learning: Reinventing the principalship. School leadership for the 21st Century.* Initiative, A Report of the task Force on the Principalship. Washington, DC: Institute for Educational Leadership.

Jackson, B. L., & Kelley, C. (2002). Exceptional and innovative programs in educational leadership. *Educational Administration Quarterly*, 38(2), 192–212.

Jazzar, M., & Algozzine, R. (2007). *Keys to 21st century educational leadership.* Boston, MA: Pearson Education/Allyn & Bacon.

Johnson, B. (2001, January). *The dynamics of succession: A qualitative study of principal succession in four elementary schools of the Toronto Catholic District School Board.* Paper presented at the 14th Annual International Congress for School Effectiveness and Improvement, Toronto, ON, Canada.

Judge, S., Puckett, K., & Cabuk, B. (2004). Digital equity: New findings from the early childhood longitudinal study. *Journal of Research on Technology in Education*, 36(4), 383–96.

Jungck, S., & Kajornsin, B. (2003). "Thai wisdom" and globalization: Negotiating the global and local in Thailand's national education reform. In K. Anderson-Levitt (Ed.), *Local meanings, global schooling: Anthropology and world culture theory*, 27–49. New York: Palgrave Macmillan.

Kaiser Family Foundation (2004). The digital divide. *Survey Snapshot*, August. Washington, DC: Kaiser Family Foundation. Available:[on-line]: www.kff.org

Kaiser Family Foundation (2004, September). Children, the digital divide, and federal policy. *Issue Brief.* 2–4, Washington, DC: Kaiser Family Foundation.

Kapur, D., & McHale, J. (2005). *Give us your best and brightest: The global hunt for talent and its impact on the developing world.* Washington, DC: Center for Global Development.

Kaufman, R., & Herman, J. (1991). *Strategic planning in education: Rethinking, restructuring, revitalizing.* Lancaster, PA: Technomic Publishing.

Kaye, M. J. (1995). *Measuring professional socialization in a distant program.* Available [Online]: http://nu.edu/nuri/llconf/confll995/kaye.html

Kelley, C., & Peterson, K. (2000, November). *The work of principals and their preparation: Addressing critical needs for the 21st century.* Paper presented at the annual meeting of the University Council for Educational Administration, Albuquerque, NM.

Klenke, K. (2006). The "S" factor in leadership: education, practice and research. *Journal of Education for Business, 79*(1), 56–60.

Kohn, A. (1997, February). How not to teach values: A critical look at character education. *Phi Delta Kappan,* 429–39.

Ladson-Billings, G. J. (1995a). Toward a theory of culturally relevant pedagogy. *American Education Research Journal, 35,* 465–91.

Ladson-Billings, G. (1995b). But that's just good teaching! The case for culturally relevant pedagogy. *Theory into Practice, 34*(3), 159–65.

Layer, G. (2005). *Closing the equity gap: The impact of widening participation strategies in the UK and the USA.* Leicester, England: National Institute of Adult Continuing Education.

Lechner, F., & Boli, J. (2005). *World culture: Origins and consequences.* Malden, MA: Blackwell.

Lee, S. S., & McKerrow, K. (2005).Advancing social justice: Women's work. *Advancing Women in Leadership, 19,* 1–2.

Leithwood, B. E., Marginson, S., Preston, R., McClellan, B. E., & Arnove, R. F. (2003). The political economy of education reform in Australia, England, and Wales, and the United States.

Leithwood, K., Riedlinger, B., Bauer, S., & Jantzi, D. (2003). Leadership program effects on student learning: The case of the greater New Orleans school leadership center. *Journal of School Leadership, 13*(6), 707–29.

Leithwood, K., Steinbach, R., & Begley, P. (1992). Socialization experiences: Becoming a principal in Canada. In F. Parkay & G. Hall (Eds.), *Becoming a principal: Challenges of leadership,* 284–307. Needham Heights, MA: Allyn & Bacon.

Levy, F., & Murname, R. J. (2004). Education and the changing job market. *Educational Leadership, 62*(2), 80–3.

Lonergan, J. M. (2000). *Internet access and content for urban schools and communities.* New York, NY: Eric Clearinghouse on Urban Education.

Ludwig, C., & Herschell, P. (1998). The power of pedagogy: Routines, school competency practices and outcomes. *Australian Journal of Language and Competency, 21.*

Maclellan, E. (2008). Pedagogical competent: What it means and what it allows. *Teaching and Teacher Education, 24* (8), 1986–92.

MacMillan, R. (1996). *The relationship between school culture and principal's practices at the time of succession.* Unpublished doctoral dissertation, OISE/University of Toronto, Toronto, Ontario, Canada.

Malley, J. (2005). *Ethics corner: Should we teach ethics in K-12?* Available at: http://ccamain.com/pdf/k-12.pdf

Mandle, H., & Lesgold, A. (1988). *Learning issues for intelligent tutoring systems.* New York, NY: Springer-Verlag.

Marshall, C., & Gerstl-Pepin, C. (2005), *Reframing educational politics for social justice.* Boston, MA: Allyn & Bacon.

Marshall, C., & Ward, M. (2004), "Yes, but. . .": Educational leaders discuss social Justice. *Journal of School Leadership, 14*(5), 530–63.

Marshall, C., & Oliva, O. (2006), *Leadership for social justice: Making revolutions in education.* Pearson Education: Boston, MA.

Martin, R., & Normore, A. H. (2005, April). Effects of cooperative and individual integrated learning system on attitudes and achievement in mathematics. Paper presented at the fifth annual College of Education Research Conference, Miami, Florida, April 26.

Martin, R. L., & Normore, A. H. (2006, April). Effects of cooperative and individual instructional learning system on attitudes and achievement in mathematics. In M. Cleary, S. Nielson, & M. Plakhotnik (Eds.),*Supporting Interdisciplinary Inquiry: Proceedings of the Fifth Annual College of Education Conference*, 64–9. Miami, FL: Florida International University.

Marx, G. T. (2006a). *Sixteen trends: Their profound impact on our future.* Alexandria, VA: Educational Research Service.

Marx, G. T. (2006b). Using trend data to create a successful future for our students, our schools, and our communities. *ERS Spectrum.* Alexandria, VA: Educational Research Service.

McCarthy, M. M. (1999). The evolution of educational leadership preparation programs. In J. Murphy & K. S. Louis (Eds.), *Handbook of research on educational administration*, 135–47. San Francisco, CA: Jossey-Bass.

McCleary, M. (2006, February). Bridging the digital divide. *The Washington Times*, February 2, A18.

McGrath, D. (2004). Equity revisited: PBL and the digital divide. *Learning and Leading with Technology, 32*(9), 36–9.

Merriam, S. B. (1998). *Qualitative research and case study applications in education.* San Francisco, CA: Jossey-Bass.

Merrill, J. C. (1990). *The imperative of freedom: A philosophy of journalistic autonomy.* Latham, MD: Freedom House.

Merton, R. K. (1963). *Social theory and social structure.* New York, NY: Free Press.

Miami-Dade County Public Schools (2005). *District and school profiles 2004–2005.* M-DCPS assessment and data analysis, Miami, FL.

Miami-Dade County Public Schools (2006). *Information technology blueprint.* http://itblueprint.dadeschools.net/

Mintzberg, H. (1994). *The rise and fall of strategic planning.* London, UK: Prentice Hall International.

Molinaro, V., & Drake, S. (1998). Successful educational reform: Lessons for leaders. *International Electronic Journal for Leadership in Learning, 2*(9). Retrieved June 22, 2016 from, http://ucalgary.ca/~iejll/

Murphy & P. Hallinger (Eds.). (1993). *Restructuring schooling: Learning from ongoing efforts*, 224–36. Newbury Park, CA: Corwin Press.

Murphy, J., & Forsyth, P. B. (Eds.). (1999). *Educational administration: A decade of reform.* Thousand Oaks, CA: Corwin Press.

Muth, R., & Barnett, B. (2001). Making the case for professional preparation: Using research for program improvement and political support. *Educational Leadership and Administration: Teaching and Program Development, 13*, 109–20.

National Association of Secondary School Principals (1992). *Salaries paid principals and assistant principals.* Arlington, VA: Educational Research Service.

Newton, R. M. (2001). A recruitment strategy: Retooling the principal's role. *AASA Professor, 24*(4), 6–10.

No Child Left Behind Act of 2001, P.L. No. 107–10, 115 Stat. 1425 (2002).

Normore, A. H. (2001). Leadership succession planning. In P.T. Begley & C. Slater (Eds.), *School leadership in Canada series*, 23–8. Hillsdale, ON, Canada: Begley & Associates.

Normore, A. H. (2002). Recruitment, socialization and accountability of school administrators in two Ontario school districts: A research report Ontario Principals Council Register. *Professional Journal for Ontario's Vice-Principals and Principals*, 4(3), 22–40.

Normore, A. H. (2004a). Leadership success in schools: Planning, recruitment and socialization. *International Electronic Journal for Leadership in Learning*, 8(10), Available [On-line]: http://ucalgary.ca/~iejll

Normore, A. H. (2004b). Recruitment and selection: Addressing the leadership shortage in one large Canadian school district. *Canadian Journal of Educational Administration and Policy*, 30, May 12, 2004. Available [On-line]: http://umanitoba.ca/publications/cjeap

Normore, A. H. (2004c). Socializing school administrators to meet leadership challenges that doom all but the most heroic and talented leaders to failure. *International Journal of Leadership in Education, Theory and Practice*, 7(2), 107–25.

Normore, A. H. (2004d). The edge of chaos: School administrators and accountability. *Journal of Educational Administration*, 42(1), 55–77.

Normore, A. H. (2006). Leadership recruitment and selection in school districts: Trends and issues. *Journal of Educational Thought*, 40(1), 41–73.

Normore, A. H., & Blanco, R. (2006, Dec. 20). Leadership for social justice and morality: Collaborative partnerships, school-linked services and the plight of the poor. *International Electronic Journal for Leadership in Learning*, (10), Special issue. Available [On-line]: http://ucalgary.ca/~iejll/

Normore, A. H., & Paul Doscher, S. (2007). Using media as the basis for a social issues approach to promoting moral competency in university teaching. *Journal of Educational Administration*, 45(4), 427–50.

Ogawa, R. T. (1994) Leadership succession. In S.B. Bacharach & B. Mundell (Eds.), *Organizational behavior in schools*, 359–89. Thousand Oaks, CA: Corwin Press.

Olson, D. (1994). *The world on paper*. Cambridge, UK: Cambridge University Press.

Olson, D. (2001). Competent minds; competent societies. In: P. Tynjälä, K. Mason & K. Lonka (Eds.), *Writing as a learning tool: Integrating theory and practice*, 1–5. Academic Publishers, London: Kluwer.

Olson, D. (2003). *Psychological theory and educational reform*. Cambridge: Cambridge University Press.

Organization for Economic Cooperation and Development (2003). *Source of economic growth in OECD countries*. Paris: OECD.

Ortiz, F. I. (1982). *Career patterns in education: Women, men and minorities in public school administration*. New York, NY: Praeger.

Parsad, B., Jones, J., & Greene, B. (2005). *Internet Access in U.S. Public Schools and Classrooms: 1994–2003* (NCES 2005–015). U.S. Department of Education. Washington, DC: National Center for Education Statistics.

Patton, M. (1998). Discovering process use. *Evaluation Journal*, 4(2), 225–33.

Paul-Doscher, S., & Normore, A. H. (2009, in press). The moral agency of the educational leader in times of national crisis and conflict. *Journal of School Leadership*, 18(1).

Piacciano, A. (2007). *Educational leadership and planning for technology*. 4th ed. Upper saddle river, NJ: Pearson Education.

Picciano, A.G. (2006). *Educational leadership and planning for technology*. 4th ed. Upper Saddle River, NJ: Pearson Education, Inc.

Pieter, J. (1994). Succession and the elementary school principal: An exploratory study. (Doctoral dissertation, University of California, 1990). Dissertation Abstracts International, UMI No. 9517779.

Pounder, D. G., & Young, P. (1996). Recruitment and selection of educational administrators: priorities for today's schools. In K. Leithwood, J. Chapman, D. Corson, P. Hallinger, & A. Hart (Eds.), *International handbook of educational leadership and administration*, 279–308. Netherlands: Kluwer Academic Publishers.

Pounder, D. G., & Merrill, R. J. (2001). Job desirability of high school principalship: Job choice theory perspective. *Educational Administration Quarterly*, 37(1), 27–57.

Ranly, D. (1992). *The lessons of general semantics*. In D. Brentari, G. N., Larson, L. A. & K. MacLeod (Eds.), *The Joy of Grammar*, 251–67. Amsterdam, The Netherlands: John Benjamins Publishing Company.

Rathbun, A., West, J., & Hausken, E. G. (2003). *Young children's access to computers in the home and at school in 1999 and 2000* (NCES 2003–03–00). Washington, DC: National Center for Education Statistics.

Rawls, J. (2001). *Justice as fairness: A restatement*. Cambridge, Mass: The Belnap Press of Harvard University Press.

Rebore, R. W. (2001). *Human resources administration in education*. 6th ed. Boston, MA: Allyn & Bacon.

Renihan, P. (1999). *In-school leadership for Saskatchewan schools: Issues and strategies*. Saskatchewan Educational Leadership Unit, University of Saskatchewan (S.S.T.A. Research Centre Report. No. 99–02). Regina, SK, Canada: S.S.T.A.

Riaz, O., & Normore, A. H. (2008). Examining the spiritual dimension of educational leadership. *University Council for Educational Administration (UCEA), Journal of Values and Ethics in Educational Administration*, 6(4), 1–8.

Robertson, R. (1995). Glocalization: Time-space and homogeneity. In M. Featherstone, S. Lash, & R. Robertson (Eds.), *Global modernity*, 25–44. London, UK: Sage.

Robinson, J. (2000). Training teachers to be principals. *The Ontario Principal's Council Register: The Magazine for Ontario's principals and vice-principals*, 2(4), 23–6.

Rosenau, J. N. (1994). New dimensions of security: The interaction of globalizing and localizing dynamics. *Security Dialogues*, 25(3), 255–81.

Ross, P. N. (1989). *Socialization in the preparation of principals*. Unpublished manuscript, York Region Board of Education, Toronto, ON, Canada.

Rothwell, W. J. (2001). *Effective succession planning: ensuring leadership continuity and building talent from within*. New York: American Management Association.

Sachs, J. (2005). *The end of poverty: Economic possibilities for our time*. New York, UK: Penguin Press.

Saphier, J., & King, M. (1985). Good seeds grow in strong cultures, *Educational Leadership*, 42(6), 67–74.

Sassen, S. (2006). *Territory, authority, rights: From medieval to global assemblages*. Princeton, NJ: Princeton University Press.

Schein, E. H. (1992). *Organizational culture and leadership*. San Francisco, CA: Jossey-Bass.

Scholte, J. A. (2000). *Globalization: a critical introduction*. New York: St. Martin's Press Inc.

Selwyn, N., Gorard, S., & Williams, S. (2001). Digital divide or digital opportunity? The role of technology in overcoming social exclusion in U.S. education. *Educational Policy*, 15, 258–77.

Senge, P., Smith, P., Kruschwitz, N., Laur, J., & Schley, S. (2008). *The necessary revolution: How individuals and organizations are working together to create a sustainable world*. Cambridge, MA: Doubleday Currency.

Sergiovanni, T. J. (2001). *The principalship: A reflective practice perspective*. Needham Heights, MA: Allyn & Bacon.

Seyfarth, J. T. (1999). *The principal: new leadership for new challenges.* Upper Saddle River, NJ: Prentice Hall.

Shafritz, J. M., & J. S. Ott, eds. (2005). *Classics of Organization Theory.* 5 th ed. New York, UK: Harcourt Brace.

Shapiro, J. P., & Stefkovich, J. A. (2005). *Ethical leadership and decision making in education: Applying theoretical perspectives to complex dilemmas.* 2nd ed. Mahwah, NJ: Lawrence Erlbaum Associates, Inc.

Shapiro, S. H. (1989). New directions for sociology of education: Reconstructing the public discourse in education. *Education and Society,* 7(2), 21–38.

Slaughter, A. M. (2006). *A new world order.* Princeton, NJ: Princeton University Press.

Smith, P. (1999). Sex, lies and Hollywood's administrators: The (de)construction of school leadership in contemporary films. *Journal of Educational Administration,* 37(1), 50–65.

Smith-Maddock, R., & Solorzano, D. G. (2002). Using critical race theory, Paulo-Freire's problem-posing method, and case study research to confront race and racism in education. *Qualitative Inquiry,* 8(1), 66–84.

Spillane, J. P., Diamond, J. B., Burch, P., Hallett, T., Jita, L., & Zoltners, J. (2002). Managing in the middle: School leaders and the enactment of accountability policy. *Educational Policy,* 16(5), 731–62.

Spring, J. (1998). *Education and the rise of the global economy.* Mahwah, NJ: Lawrence Erlbaum.

Spring, J. (2008). Research on globalization and education. *Review of Educational Research,* 78(2), 330–63.

Stevens, P., & Weale, M. (2003). *Education and economic growth.* London: National Institute of Economic and Social Research.

Stout, R. I. (1973). *New approaches to recruitment and selection of educational administration.* Danville, IL: University Council for Ed. Administration. (ERIC/Clearinghouse on Educational Management, No. 61832 72–86751).

Stromquist, N. (2002). *Education in a globalized world: The connectivity of economic power, technology, and knowledge.* Lanham, MD: Rowman & Littlefield.

Sutton, R. E. (1991). Equity and computers in the schools: A decade of research. *Review of Educational Research,* 61(4), 475–503.

Tansley, D. (2006, February). *Mind the gap: 2006 will witness the deepening of the digital divide. London.* England: *The Financial Times,* February 13, 21

Tansley, D. (2006, February). Mind the gap: 2006 will witness the deepening of the digital divide. London, UK: *The Financial Times,* 13, p. 21.

Taylor, S. (1997). Critical policy analysis: exploring contexts, texts and consequences. *Discourse: Studies in the Cultural Politics of Education,* 18(1), 23–35.

Tekeste, M. (1996). *The recruitment and selection of in-school administrators in Saskatchewan* (S.S.T.A. Research Center Report. No. 96–05). Regina, SK, Canada: S.S.T.A. Townsend, T. (April, 2003). A partnership approach to the training of school leaders: Issues of capability and succession planning. Paper presented at the Annual Meeting of the American Educational research Association, Chicago, IL.

Thomas, S. (2006). *Education policy in the media: Public discourse on education.* Teneriffe, Queensland: Post Pressed.

Thompson, S. (2004). Leading from the eye of the storm. *Educational Leadership,* 61(7), 60–3.

Tuana, N. (2003) Moral competency. *Online Research/Penn State,* 24(2). Available at: http://rps.psu.edu/0305/competency.html

Turner, B. S. (2002). Cosmopolitan virtue, globalization and patriotism. *Theory, Culture & Society, 19*(1–2), 45–63.

U.S. Department of Education (2000). *Teacher use of computers and the internet in public schools* (NCES 2000–090).Washington, DC: National Center for Education Statistics.

U.S. Department of Labor (2000). *2000–2010 employment projections*. Washington, DC: U.S. Bureau of Labor Statistics. Available [on-line]: www.bls.gov/emp

Uphoff, J. K. (2001). Religious diversity and education. In J. Banks & C. A. M. Banks (Eds.), *Multicultural education: Issues & perspectives*. 4th ed, 103–21. New York: Wiley.

Van Berkum, D. W., Richardson, M. D., & Lane, K. E. (1994). *Professional development in educational administration programs: Where does it exist?* Educational Resources Information Center (ERIC No. 026 260)

Wallace Foundation (2003). *Beyond the pipeline: Getting the principals we need, where they are needed most*. A policy brief by the Wallace Foundation. New York: Wallace Foundation.

Wanous, J. P. (1980). *Organizational entry: Recruitment, selection and socialization of school administration*. Reading, MA: Addison-Wesley Publishing Company.

Weber, E. (2007). Globalization, "glocal" development, and teachers' work: A research agenda. *Review of Educational Research, 77*(3), 279–309.

Welner, K. G., & Weitzman, D. Q. (2005). The soft bigotry of low expenditures. *Equity and Excellence in Education, 38*(3), 242–8.

Wenzel, J. (2000). Grim Fairy Tales: Taking a risk. In A. Amireh & L. Suhair Maja, (eds.), *Imaginary maps. Going global: The transnational reception of Third World women writers*, 229–51. New York: Garland.

Wilhelm, T., Carmen, D., & Reynolds, M. (2002, June). Connecting kids to technology: Challenges and opportunities. *Kids Count Snapshot*. Available[online]: http://kidscount.org

Willinsky, J. (1998). *Learning to divide the world: Education at empire's end*. Minneapolis: University of Minnesota Press.

Winter, P. A., & Dunaway, D. M. (1997). Reactions of teachers, as applicants, to the principal recruitment practices in a reform environment: The effects of job attributes, job information sources, and school level. *Journal of Research and Development in Education, 30*(3), 144–53.

Wolcott, H. F. (1991). Propriospect and the acquisition of culture. *Anthropology and Education Quarterly, 22*(3), 251–73.

Wolcott, H. F. (2003). *Teachers versus technocrats*. Walnut Creek, CA: AltaMira Press.

Yin, R. K. (1994). *Case study research*. 2nd ed. Thousand Oaks, CA: Sage.

CHAPTER 8

Organizational Leadership

More than ever, leaders are expected to be change agents in their respective organizations. Yet, leadership turnover continues to rise and organizations continue to struggle in their efforts to confront the fearsome adaptive challenges of the global age (Clark, 2007). We contend that educational leaders need to understand theories of organizations, socialization patterns and how their leadership practices influence organizational dynamics. Teachers and administrators who understand the politics in schools can operate more successfully to facilitate change. However, possessing the skill set necessary to identify and influence common social patterns that affect their work in school organizations.

Research on organizational dynamics, socialization, recruitment, succession planning, behavior and learning (e.g., Barth, 2003; Bolman & Deal, 2007; Clark, 2007; Collins, 2001; Harvey & Drolet, 2004; Hoban, 2002; Normore, 2006; Senge, Smith, Kruschwitz, Laur, & Schley, 2008; Shafritz & Ott, 2005) identified several social patterns common to organizations. Among these patterns are organizational culture, diversity, values and goals. Goals, derived from the organization's mission and strategic planning process, provide purpose and direction for organizational members and work groups. Goals have the most impact on people's behavior if they are clear and owned by individual members and/or by the collective (Fullan, 2001; Senge et al, 2008). Of course, people differ with respect to the way they respond to and internalize organizational goals. Some of these differences have little influence on organizational life, while others have a substantial affect. Diversity may be in terms of personality, motivation, cognitive style, leadership/followership style, gender, ethnicity, class, age, competency, seniority, organizational function and so on. Understanding and appreciating these differences is necessary for successful collaboration. Some key concepts in this chapter include the following:

- Socialization
- Professional socialization
- Organizational socialization
- Recruitment
- Selection
- Induction.

Consistent with previous chapters, we begin with an introduction to the *learning* about organizational leadership. Focus is on school leadership and administration. The concepts explored include organization, hierarchy, succession planning, communication, bureaucracy, recruitment, structure, committees, task forces and professional learning communities. Next, we will discuss the importance of *literacy* and how these elements of organization are analyzed and practiced in schools, local communities and throughout the world. Then, we focus on an educational *leaders'* ability to influence the organizational dynamics of a school through formal and informal means. It emphasizes skills that include restructuring, organizational analysis, forming and dissolving structures, aligning organizational structures to learning processes and outcomes. Finally, we offer a series of *reflective* questions, prompts and activities to help the reader understand the personal, interpersonal and organizational consequences of their actions.

ORGANIZATIONAL LEADERSHIP

More than ever, leaders are expected to be change agents in their respective organizations. Yet, leadership turnover continues to rise and organizations continue to struggle in their efforts to confront the fearsome adaptive challenges of the global age (Clark, 2007). Universities in particularly experience vast president, provost, and dean leadership turnover for various reasons. Sometimes, it's due to using one position as a stepping stone to another position while other times they seek a more amenable and friendly oriented campus (Clark, 2007). We contend that these leaders need to understand theories and politics of organizations, organizational norms, and unexamined professional and organizational socialization processes, issues of social patterns that impact student experiences at universities and how their leadership and instructional practices can influence how the organizations can operate more successfully to facilitate change as a primary goal. When goals are clear and collectively owned they have the most impact on people's behavior while simultaneously addressing other important organizational processes (Earl & Kruse, 1999). Research on organizational dynamics, socialization, behavior and learning (e.g., Bolman & Deal, 2007; Clark, 2007; Fullan, 2001; Normore, 2006; Senge, Smith, Kruschwitz, Laur, & Schley, 2008) identified several social patterns common to organizations. Among these patterns are organizational and institutional culture, diversity, values and goals. Despite the increase rate of leadership turnover and the challenges to confront struggles of the global age leaders are expected to be change agents in their respective organizations. Leaders who understand the politics in higher education can operate more successfully as change facilitators when they have the skill set necessary to identify and influence common social patterns that affect their work in the organizations (Normore, 2006).

Senge and colleagues (2008) maintain that a revolution is underway in today's organizations. According to these authors, organizations around the world are boldly leading the change from dead-end, business-as-usual tactics to transformative strategies that are essential for creating a flourishing, sustainable world. Today's most innovative leaders, educational and otherwise, are recognizing that, for the sake of organizations and our world, we must implement revolutionary—not just incremental—changes in the way we live and work. Other important organizational processes requiring attention include communication, decision making, conflict management, and bureaucratic social patterns. Earle and Kruse (1999) discuss the importance of bureaucratic social patterns, which are characterized by a fixed division of labor, hierarchy of offices, explicit rules, and specialized job training. When translated to school systems, these authors contend that certain political, social communal patterns, and patterns of inequality based on social class, race, and gender unfortunately, yet predictably, influence organizational norms. Each of these patterns describes a variety of often unexamined social patterns that affect how students experience the practices of schooling. The complexity of school change and how understanding these patterns can help create collaborative school organizations of promise and optimism. By working collaboratively across boundaries, organizations are already exploring and putting into place unprecedented solutions that move beyond just being "less bad" to creating pathways that will enable us to flourish in an increasingly interdependent world (Senge et al., 2008).

In his ground-breaking contribution to the study of leadership and organizational change, Clark (2007) argues that, in order for leaders—and those who prepare and train them—to improve on organizational competence, they will need to develop the essential habits of facilitating change in a critically different era and change how they determine what's relevant. Only the discretionary efforts of people can make change happen and this requires leadership and energy management (Normore & Brooks, 2015; Clark, 2007). Obtaining organizational competence through collaboration with others is crucial for education leaders if they hope to make significant contributions and obtain satisfaction on tasks that enhance the development of an increasingly interconnected system. The big picture created by this "systems perspective" (see Senge et al., 2008) is the foundation for developing and maintaining a collaboratively interdependent organization. The systems perspective should guide organizational design, work design, strategic planning, communication, compensation plans, decision-making procedures, problem solving, and so on.

All education leaders need a conceptual road map for successfully navigating the roles they play in the various school organizations of which they are a part. If educators have little understanding of organizational processes, they may fail to influence effectively and may even inadvertently inhibit organizational effectiveness as we now see more than ever in university after university. Organizational competency is necessary for education leaders to make a contribution and obtain satisfaction in joining with others in tasks that clearly see the interconnectedness of the organization to the larger world.

Socialization

Socialization involves the processes by which members of an organization learn the skills, knowledge, and dispositions required to perform their role in an effective manner (Bennis, 1985; Merton, 1963). Bennis asserts that socialization involves a complex set of human relationships within an organization that includes all the people in it and their relationships to each other and to the outside world. The preparation of these members involves both professional and organizational socialization (Hart, 1993). *Professional socialization* involves acquiring knowledge, skills, and behaviors through which values and norms of the profession are internalized and a professional identity is established (Daresh, 2000; Pounder & Young, 1996). Begley and Cambell-Evan, (1992) assert that professional socialization generally begins in the pre-appointment phase of a leader's education career and continues into early post-appointment growth and ongoing development. It requires dialogue, collaboration, and mentoring by an experienced professional to serve as a guide (Daresh, 1997; Greenfield, 1985). Pre-appointment professional socialization includes mandatory and voluntary courses for certification; first-hand experience of leadership and management tasks; modeling and social learning by observing both good and bad leadership; and deliberate mentoring by some existing leaders who see importance in their role in preparing future leaders (Barnett, 2003; Muth & Barnett, 2001).

Formal preparation is important for developing the technical knowledge and skills that administrators require to be successful (Greenfield, 1985; Normore, 2002, 2004a). Devoting more time, energy and resources to programs that focus on meaningful content in a form consistent with good principles of adult education is one promising suggestion for improving socialization experiences (Jackson & Kelley, 2002). On-the-job leadership activities are viewed as the most helpful of all socialization activities (Greenfield, 1985; Normore, 2002).

Organizational socialization is specific to the educational context. Each organization is comprised of a complex array of people, policies, processes, and priorities to which leaders must adjust (Greenfield, 1985a; Hart, 1993; Leithwood et al., 1992). As members make the transition to organizational ranks so does the emergence of new socialization experiences (Browne-Ferrigno, 2003; Ortiz, 1982). When preparing for their new leadership roles, aspiring leaders begin to take on a different role as an educator. Consequently, the need to be resocialized becomes crucial and a new professional identity unfolds. The need to fit into the immediate work environment and organizational norms tend to replace those learned during professional socialization.

There are mediating influences on leader's socialization such as work setting, culture and relationships with peers, superiors, district policies and procedures, formal training, and outcomes. Experiences can range from carefully planned training and induction programs to unplanned, on the job experiences (Daresh, 1997) and include workshops, formal courses, job shadowing, leaders' meetings, peer coaching, and mentoring (Hart, 1993; Sergiovanni, 2001). Induction experiences and ongoing professional development opportunities are key to organizational socialization (Barnett, 2003; Hall & Mani, 1992; Leithwood et al., 1992; McCarthy, 1999). This suggests that the profession adopt a longer-term view of the preparation and development of organizational leaders that extends not only into the induction period but provides planned socialization experiences each time a new leadership assignment is made (Daresh, 2000; Pounder & Young, 1996).

Many formal university courses are considered of little value to the administrator role (Normore, 2004b) and has little or no impact on how well they perform their tasks as school administrators (Begley, 2000; Bredeson, 1996). The lack of leadership practicality in university courses and certification programs are often admonished and criticized (Begley, 2000; Bredeson, 1996; Leithwood et al., 1992). For example, universities and school districts can use a variety of bridging strategies to provide aspiring administrators with practical leadership experience including internships (Muth & Barnett, 2001), and knowledge to help them succeed in the principalship prior to their first position. It is naive to believe that pre-service training or even out-of-district in-service programs will provide aspiring leaders with all they need to know about how to be an effective leader in a particular school district (Begley, 2000; Bredeson, 1996; Daresh, 2000). School districts, therefore, must continue training new and veteran administrators with a variety of supportive induction activities to help them continue their professional growth as school leaders for the new millennium.

A wide body of literature suggests that socialization experiences and structured opportunities for interaction with colleagues promote growth of aspiring and practicing school leaders (Begley & Cambell-Evan, 1992; Bennis, 1985; Hall & Mani, 1992; Kaye, 1995; Leithwood et al., 1992; Seyfarth, 1999). As supported by previous research (e.g., Daresh, 1997; Greenfield, 1985; Hart, 1993; Leithwood et al., 1992; Normore, 2004a), both of these districts provided a range of formal activities such as training programs, mentoring, and job shadowing. They also provided a range of informal activities such as in-services, opportunities for relationship building with subordinates and super-ordinates, as well as on the job experiences and discussions about policies, procedures and priorities. As documented in research, mentoring, on-the-job leadership experiences and the administration preparation program are considered to be most valuable in preparing school administrators for their role (Leithwood et al., 1992; Daresh, 2000; Normore, 2002).

Leadership Succession

A crucial element in preparing school leaders for success is individual school districts. Research indicates that when school districts are willing to invest funds in succession planning and development it will likely lead to a qualified pool of candidates for leadership positions (Bennis, 1985; Leithwood et al., 1992; Pieter, 1994). Leadership/ executive succession is of tremendous importance to those who work in organizations. Some of the seminal research conducted in this area (e.g., Blood, 1966; Carlson, 1961; Dill, 1960; Stout, 1973) and other inquiry (e.g., Crawford, Carlton, & Stengel, 2003; Hargreaves, Moore, Fink, Brayman, & White, 2003; Hargreaves & Fink, 2004; Hart, 1993; Muth & Barnett, 2001; Normore, 2001, 2002; Rothwell, 2001; Townsend, 2003) conclude that leadership succession is an interactive process that can be very disruptive, and its results can be ineffective and dysfunctional if the new leader does not become an integrated and respected member of the social system whose leadership has received popular affirmation. Carlson (1961) asserted that succession often disrupts lines of authority and communication, disturbs power and decision-making systems, and generally upsets the organization's normal activities. In contrast, disruption can have a positive impact on a school such that performance is substantially enhanced (Hart, 1993). As this process develops and unfolds in organizational settings, a leader under-goes a group membership boundary passage resulting in varying degrees of acceptance and legitimacy by the membership (Hargreaves et al., 2003; Johnson, 2001; Normore, 2004a; Pounder & Merrill, 2001).

In the past, organizations focused succession planning efforts on the preparation of high leadership potential individuals (Blood, 1966). For example, some School

Boards engaged in succession planning via career-bound successors (those who are active in preparation for the administrative position), while others focused on place-bound successors (those who take more time to prepare for leadership positions and are considerably less progressive in views about schooling) to lead their institutions (Carlson, 1961). Carlson asserted if school districts choose leaders from within the organization, the central tendency of his/her performance would be to stabilize what exists, whereas for leaders who are chosen outside the containing school system, the central tendency of his or her performance would be to alter what already exists.

Today, school organizations are learning that the focus must be not only on high potential individuals, but also on the context of these individuals and the value they can add to the school and district leadership team (Leithwood, Riedlinger, Bauer, & Jantzi, 2003; Normore, 2001). Succession planning can help school districts in several ways: (a) by engaging senior management in a disciplined review of leadership talent, (b) guiding development activities of administrative teams, (c) bringing selection systems, rewards systems and leadership development into alignment with the process of leadership renewal, (d) assuring continuity of leadership, (e) avoiding transition problems, and (f) preventing premature promotion of principals through professional development (Johnson, 2001; MacMillan, 1996). During succession, a successor who possesses knowledge about social influencing processes and skill in applying that knowledge can have a substantial impact on the outcomes of his or her own succession practices and experiences (Barnett, 2003; Hart, 1993; Johnson, 2001).

Various researchers (e.g., Begley, 2000; Ogawa, 1994; Pieter, 1994) maintain that district leaders can assess their current practices by allocating funds to design flexible preparation processes that support leaders undergoing succession and lead to outcomes that advance district policies and goals including: (a) training and support specifically designed to assist leaders in a new assignment, (b) recognizing that they face challenges common to major transitions, (c) acknowledging that a unique mix between the leader and the school will give rise to the outcomes of the succession, and (d) preparing the leaders for the impact the school will have on them as well as the sustainable impact they hope to have on the school (Hargreaves & Fink, 2004). According to Fullan (1997), districts can capitalize on the expectations for change and sustainability that succession brings to implement new programs and work toward the improvement of schools by shaping and expanding the professional orientation, knowledge, and skills of those in leadership roles (Archer, 2004; Fullan, 1993, 1997; Hargreaves et al., 2003; Hargreaves & Fink, 2004; Hart, 1993; MacMillan, 1996). To avoid potential succession problems school districts can implement well-planned strategies during the stages of recruitment and selection, and provide effective socialization experiences for enhanced development.

Recruitment and Selection

Effective recruitment and selection of school administrators continue to be one of the more challenging human resource tasks in educational organizations. This challenge is due, in part, to the inexact science of attracting, screening, and identifying candidates to fit the complex leadership needs of schools today (McCarthy, 1999; Pounder &

Merrill 2001; Pounder & Young, 1996; Young & Castetter, 2003). In 1992, a special report from the National Association of Secondary School Principals (NASSP) called for "all stakeholders to unite in a rational attack on the common problems associated with the recruitment, identification, selection, preparation, and development of school administrators" (p. 34). Since that call, major efforts have resulted in the development of a knowledge and skill base for the preparation of potential school administrators for the role (Castetter & Young, 2000; Johnson, 2001; Muth & Barnett, 2001; Rebore, 2001; Robinson, 2000; Seyfarth, 1999; Young & Castetter, 2003). In the past, attracting teachers into the ranks of school administrators was relatively easy because educators saw administration as a normal part of career advancement that usually occurred in mid-career (Fullan, 1997; Hargreaves & Fullan, 1999; Winter & Dunaway, 1997). Teachers no longer see administration as a way to improve their salaries, prestige or respect among other colleagues (ERS, NAESP & NASSP, 2000; Pounder & Merrill, 2001; Seyfarth, 1999). Many highly qualified, competent, and talented teachers dismiss careers in administration because they do not want to sit in an office all day, hassle teachers, discipline students, work with unhappy parents, or push paper—all activities frequently associated with the stereotypical role of the school administrator (Rebore, 2001; Renihan, 1999). Many individuals do not consider the fact that alternative images of school leadership are possible. Until some of those alternatives become better accepted and understood, there may always be a problem of individuals pre-screening and self-selecting (ASCD, 2000; Cascadden, 1998; Chirichello, 2001; Rebore, 2001; Wallace Foundation, 2003).

Recruitment practices must be extensive and aggressive and focus on placing and keeping an effective and satisfied administrator (Castetter & Young, 2000). Common methods of recruiting administrators range from internal searches, referrals, and contacting employment agencies, to advertising vacancies with college and university placement services (Young & Castetter, 2003). Factors that affect recruitment and selection practices range from job complexity and size of school district, to fringe benefits, increase or decrease in student population, and poor remuneration, as it relates to responsibilities and the expectations of the job (Castetter & Young, 2000; Renihan, 1999; Robinson, 2000; Tekeste, 1996). The selection process requires a choice of best candidates to fill the administrative positions (Benson, 2001; Pounder & Merrill, 2001; Renihan, 1999; Tekeste, 1996). Selection procedures and interviews are usually structured around information relating to the work history of the candidates, their education and training, motivation, and maturity (Rebore, 2001; Seyfarth, 1999; Tekeste, 1996). Some of the selection procedures include resumes, pre-screening interviews often done by telephone, employee testing, reference checks, and consulting services (Rebore, 2001).

Research indicates that most school districts have two pools of candidates from which they recruit: internal and external (Castetter & Young, 2000; Pounder & Merrill, 2001; Rebore, 2001). According to the literature, recruitment and selection activities begin shortly after staffing needs are determined (Castetter & Young, 2000; McCarthy, 1999; Seyfarth, 1999; Van Berkum, Richardson, & Lane, 1994). In a study conducted by Normore (2004a, 2004b, 2004c) on two urban school districts in Canada, findings revealed that, although self-selection was practiced, it was common practice in both districts for experienced administrators and area superintendents to identify and encourage potential candidates (Cascadden, 1998; Chirichello, 2001) to apply for administrative pools at an early career stage rather than in mid-career (Ortiz, 1982). Normore further emphasized that both districts engaged in a provocative practice of deliberately rotating school administrators every 3 to 5 years, based on the philosophy that regular rotation kept administrators alert and helped in the transplantation of change initiatives from one school to another. As supported by Johnson (2001), this trickle-down hypothesis may hold ground but it lacks any comprehensive dialogue or even planned inquiry related to the purpose or potential outcomes of regular rotation. The literature reiterates that selection is generally structured around the work history and leadership experiences of the candidates, portfolio, formal education and administrative training (Normore, 2004a; Rebore, 2001; Tekeste, 1996).

Expectations, guiding principles, structure and responsibility are aspects that guide and influence decision making through all stages of the leadership succession planning process. Clear expectations for leadership are central and must be understood consistently among all school leaders and aligned with future strategic direction. Aspiring and practicing administrators systemically need to know what leadership knowledge, skills, attitudes, behavior and roles are expected and supported in the district. This is especially important as the role of the school administrator continues to change and expand. The mission of succession planning also needs to be articulated. Some districts adopt the philosophy of internal promotion, some support external promotion, while others endorse a combination of both. The overall organization of the succession planning process should be clear outlining the organizational and support structures, timelines, events and assignments. Some districts appoint the responsibility to a superintendent and organize centrally, while other districts employ a shared leadership approach.

In order to attract and recruit potential leaders, principals and superintendents need to recognize leadership qualities among teachers and to encourage them to pursue and apply for administrative roles. The application process must be aligned with the selection process and include any contractual considerations that may hinder and/or support appointments. Emotional and financial support for a structured leadership preparation program is a key part of leadership succession planning. Leaders participate in both professional and organizational socialization experiences in order to learn about leading. These processes involve understanding culture, norms and values of the new schools, and district and consist of a range of formal and informal leadership for learning activities. Well-structured formal induction programs are important to support new administrators in the transition from a teaching role to an administrative role and should be considered an integral part of ongoing professional development.

Discussion

1. *Need for collaboration and support*
   There is a need to shift focus from the leadership of the principal alone to a more inclusive form of leadership, to the collaborative empowerment of all school

systems administrators. While it may seem to run contrary to the districts' mode of operation (i.e., how they move people without input), it seems appropriate for district offices to foster school and district cultures that are collaborative and support an atmosphere of inquiry. Even though some of the training structures have been used in the past (i.e., mentoring, job-shadowing) and have frequently been unsuccessful, how do we address and eliminate the barriers that prohibit these processes from occurring?

2. *Relevance of academic training programs and certification courses*
   Training programs need to be reconfigured around the redefined role of the school administrator. Higher standards and greater rigor should also be required for the accreditation of administrator training programs which will be responsible for delivering the upgraded and reconfigured training for the administrator role. How do school districts help transform the mindset of potential leadership candidates in an effort to balance perspectives? Considering the practice of internal hiring only, the same practice might be opposed to a program that produces students that question the present status quo. How can universities and districts form symbiotic relationships when designing and implementing leadership preparation and certification programs so common realities are addressed effectively?

3. *Leadership development*
   Districts engaged in leadership succession planning might consider an issue series as part of induction tailored to the needs of newly appointed school leaders. Given the findings from previous and current research, what should this leadership series include for first year principals? How do leadership development explore succession? How does leadership development include educational policy and management practices?

4. *Leadership succession success*
   Research indicates that specific steps are regularly taken by school districts and perceptions of participants are reported. Still, much in the individual plans is yet to unfold before long-term effects can be ascertained. Finding relevant information requires searching under other labels and categories of literature such as effective school districts, educational governance, transformational leadership, and organizational learning. How do we convey the links between leadership succession and more generalized school district leadership practices? Are there specific ways to address how it fits in the organizational governance and procedural structures within a school district?

5. *Rotating administrators*
   Further investigation on the policy of systematically rotating leaders is needed. An approach would be to use these qualitative data findings to develop a survey that could be administered to a broader range of districts and compare the findings to more generalizable data. Is this a desirable component of a leadership succession process? Is rotation a strategy related to succession of district administrators that impedes succession processes at the school level or does the process create opportunities for emerging assistants to be promoted? Can administrative rotation be shown to have positive effects on student learning outcomes?

REFERENCES

Abdelaziz, A. (2004). Information competency for lifelong learning. Paper presented at the World Library and Information Congress: 70th IFLA General Conference and Council, p. 4. Available [online]: http://ifla.org/IV/ifla70/papers/116e-Abid.pdf

Afflerbach, P.,& Moni, K. (1994). Legislators, reporters, and reading assessment. *Reading Research Report, 31*. National Research Center, College Park, MD.

Anderson, G. L. (1991). Cognitive politics of principals and teachers: Ideological control in an elementary school. In J. Blase (ed.), *The Politics of life in schools: Power, conflict, and cooperation*, 120–30. Newbury Park: Sage.

Anderson, G., & Herr, K. (1993). The micropolitics of student voices: Moving from diversity of bodies to diversity of voices in schools. In C. Marshall (ed.), *The New Politics of Race and Gender*, 58–68. New York: Falmer.

Anderson-Levitt, K. (2003). A world culture of schooling? In K. Anderson-Levitt (Ed.), *Local meanings, global schooling: Anthropology and world culture theory*, 1–26. New York: Palgrave Macmillan.

Apple, M., Kenway, J., & Singh, M. (Eds.). (2005). *Globalizing education: Policies, pedagogies, & politics*. New York: Peter Lang.

Archer, J. (September, 2004). Leading for learning Education. *Week on the Web*. http://edweek.org/sreports/special_reports_article.cfm?slug=leadpack_2004.htm

Association for Supervision and Curriculum Development (2000). The contemporary principal: New skills for a new age. *Education Update, 42*(3), 1–8.

Barnett, B. (April, 2003). *Catching the tiger by the tail: The illusive nature of principal preparation*. Paper presented at the Annual Meeting of the American Educational Research Association, Chicago, IL.

Barro, R. (2000). *Education and economic growth*. Paris: OECD.

Barth, R. S. (2003). *Lessons learned: Shaping relationships and the culture of the workplace*. Thousand Oaks, CA: Corwin Press.

Bauman, Z. (1998) *Globalization: The human consequences*. New York: Columbia UP.

Begley, P. T. (2000). *School leadership in Canada*. 2nd ed. Hillsdale, ON, Canada: Paul Begley & Associates.

Begley, P. T., & Cambell-Evan, G. (1992). Socializing experiences of aspiring principals. *The Alberta Journal of Educational Research, 38*(4), 285–99.

Bennis, W. (1985). *Leaders: The strategies for taking charge*. New York: Harper & Row.

Benson, M. (2001). The professional principals series. OPC Register: The Magazine for Ontario's Principals and Vice-principals, 3(1), 6.

Blood, R. (1966). *The function of experience in professional preparation: Teaching and the principalship*. Unpublished doctoral dissertation, Claremont Graduate School, Claremont, CA.

Bolman, L. G., & Terrance E. D. (2003). *Reframing organizations*. 3rd ed. San Francisco: Jossey-Bass.

Bracher, P., Panoch, J. V., Piediscalzi, N., & Uphoff, J. K. (1974). *Public education religion studies: Questions and answers*. Dayton, OH: Public Education Religion Studies Center, Wright State University.

Bransford, J., Brown, A., & Cocking, R. (Eds.). (1999). *How people learn: Brain, mind, experience, and school*. Washington, DC: National Academy Press.

Bredeson, P. V. (1996). New directions in the preparation of educational leaders. In Leithwood, B. E, Marginson,S, Preston, R, McClellan, B. E, & Arnove, R. F. (2003). The political economy of education reform in Australia, England, and Wales, and the United States.

Briskin, L., & Priegert-Coulter, R. (1992). Introduction: Feminist pedagogy: Challenging the normative. *Canadian Journal of Education, 17*(3), 247–63.

Brooks, J. S. (2006). Tinkering toward utopia or stuck in a rut? School reform implementation at Wintervalley High. *Journal of School Leadership, 16*(3), 240–65.

Brooks, J. S., & Jean-Marie, G. (2007). Black leadership, white leadership: Race and race Relations in an urban high school. *Journal of Educational Administration, 45*(6), 756–68.

Brooks, J. S., & Miles, M. T. (2008). From scientific management to social justice . . . and back again? Pedagogical shifts in educational leadership. In A. H. Normore (Ed.), *Leadership for social justice: Promoting equity and excellence through inquiry and reflective practice,* 99–114. Charlotte, NC: Information Age Publishing.

Browne-Ferrigno, T. (2003). Becoming a principal: Role conception, initial socialization, role identity transformation, purposeful engagement. *Educational Administration Quarterly, 39*(4), 468–503.

Brydon, D. (2004, fall). Cross-talk, postcolonial pedagogy, and transnational competency. *Situation Analysis, 4,* 70–87.

Burbules, N., & Torres, C. (2000). *Globalization and education: Critical perspectives.* New York, NY: Routledge.

Burkhardt, J. M., MacDonald, M. C., & Rathemacher, A. J. (2005) *Creating a comprehensive information competency plan: A how-to-do-it manual and CD-ROM for librarians.* New York, NY: Neal-Schuman Publishers.

Campbell, R. F., Fleming, T., Newell, L. J., & Bennion, J. W. (1987). *A history of thought and practice in educational administration.* New York: Teachers College Press.

Capra, F. (1996). *The web of life: A new scientific understanding of living systems.* New York: Anchor Books.

Carlson, R. O. (1961). Succession and performance among school superintendents. *Administrative Science Quarterly, 6,* 210–27.

Carnoy, M., & Rhoten, D. (2002). What does globalization mean for education change? A comparative approach. *Comparative Education, 46*(1), 1–9.

Carvin, A. (2006, March). The gap: The digital divide network. *Reed Business Information.*

Cascadden, D. (1998). Principals as managerial leaders: A qualitative study of the perspective of selected elementary school principals. *Journal of School Leadership, 8*(2), 137–70.

Castetter, W. B., & Young, I. P. (2000). *The human resource function in educational administration.* 7th ed. Upper Saddle River, NJ: Merrill/Prentice Hall.

Chirichello, M. (2001, January). *Preparing principals to lead in the new millennium: A response to the leadership crisis in American schools.* Paper presented at the 14th International Congress for School Effectiveness and Improvement, Toronto, ON, Canada.

Christians, C. (2003). The media and moral competency. *Ethical Space, The International Journal of Communications Ethics,*1(1), 1–17.

Christians, C., Ferre, J., & Fackler, M. (1993). *Good News: Social Ethics and the Press.* New York, NY: Oxford University Press.

Clark, T. (2007). *EPIC change: How to lead change in the global age.* San Francisco, CA: Jossey-Bass.

Collins, J. C. (2001). Good to great: Why some companies make the leap . . . and others don't. New York, NY: Harper Business.

Correia, A. (2002). Information Competency for an active and effective citizenship. White paper prepared for UNESCO, the U.S. National Commission on Libraries and Information Science, and the National Forum on Information Competency, for use at the Information Competency Meeting of Experts, Prague, The Czech Republic.

Courchene, T. J. (1995). Glocalization: The regional/international interface. *Canadian Journal of Regional Science*, 18(1), 1–20.

Crawford, J., Carlton, P., & Stengel, L. (November, 2003). T*he effects of principal succession on school climate in Urban settings*. Paper presented at the Annual Meeting of the University Council for Educational Administration, Portland, OR.

Cunningham, W. G., & Gresso, D. W. (1993). *Cultural leadership: The culture of excellence in education*. Needham Heights, MA: Allyn & Bacon.

Dantley, M. E. (2005). African American spirituality and Cornel West's notions of prophetic pragmatism: Restructuring educational leadership in American urban schools. *Educational Administration Quarterly*, 41(4), 651–74.

Daresh, J. C. (1997). Improving principal preparation: A review of common strategies. *NASSP Bulletin*, 81(585), 3–8.

Daresh, J. C. (2000). *New principals: New induction programs*. Paper presented at the Annual Meeting of the American Educational Research Association, New Orleans, LA.

Deal, T. E., & Peterson, K. D. (1991). *The principal's role in shaping school culture*. Washington, DC: United States Department of Education.

Deal, T. E., & Peterson, K. D. (1999). *Shaping school culture: The heart of leadership*. San Francisco, CA: Jossey-Bass.

del Val, R. E., & Normore, A. H. (2008). Leadership for social justice: Bridging the digital divide. *University Council for Educational Administration (UCEA, International Journal of Urban Educational Leadership*, 2, 1–15. Available [On-line]: http://uc.edu/urbanleadership/current_issues.htm

Dill, W. R. (1960). How aspiring managers promote their own careers. *California Management Review*, 2, 9–15.

Earle, J., Kruse, S. (1999). *Organizational competency for education: Topic in educational leadership*. Mahwah, NJ: Lawrence Erlbaum Associates, Inc.

Educational Research Service, National Association of Elementary School Principals and National Association of Secondary School Principals (2000). The principal, keystone of a *high achieving school: Attracting and keeping the leaders we need*. For the National Association of Elementary School Principals (NAESP) and National Association of Secondary School Principals (NASSP), Washington, DC.

Educational Research Service (1999). Is there a shortage of qualified candidates for openings in the principalship? An exploratory study. For the National Association of Elementary School Principals (NAESP) and National Association of Secondary School Principals (NASSP), Washington, DC.

English, F. W. (2002). The point of scientificity, the fall of the epistemological dominos, and the end of the field of educational administration. *Studies in Philosophy and Education*, 21(2), 109–36.

English, F. W. (2003a). Cookie-cutter leaders for cookie-cutter schools: The teleology of standardization and the de-legitimization of the university in educational leadership preparation. *Leadership and Policy in Schools*, 2(1), 27–46.

English, F. W. (2003b). *The postmodern challenge to the theory and practice of educational administration*. Springfield, IL: Charles C. Thomas Publishers.

English, F. W. (2006). The unintended consequences of a standardized knowledge base in advancing educational leadership programs. *Educational Administration Quarterly*, 42(3), 461–72.

Fairclough, N. (1995). *Media discourse*. London, UK: Arnold.

Fairholm, G. (1997). *Capturing the heart of leadership: Spirituality and community in the new American workplace*. Westport: Praeger.

Freebody, P., & Luke, A. (2003). Competency as engaging with new forms of life: The 'four roles' model. In G. Bull & M. Anstey (eds.), *The competency lexicon*. 2nd ed, 52–57. Sydney, AUS: Prentice Hall.

Friedman, T. L. (1999). *The Lexus and the olive tree: Understanding globalization*. New York, NY: Anchor.

Friedman, T. L. (2005). *The world is flat: A brief history of the twenty-first century*. New York, NY: Farrar, Sraus and Giroux.

Fullan, M. (1993). Coordinating school and district development in restructuring. In J. Murphy & P. Hallinger (Eds.), *Restructuring schooling: Learning from ongoing efforts*, 224–36. Newbury Park, CA: Corwin Press.

Fullan, M. (1997). *What's worth fighting for in the principalship?*. 2nd ed. New York: Teachers College Press.

Fullan, M. (2001). *Leading in a culture of change*. San Francisco, CA: Jossey-Bass.

Fyfe, I. (2007). Hidden in the curriculum: political competency and education for citizenship in Australia. *Melbourne Journal of Politics*. Retrieved on January 23, 2016 from, http://find books.com/p/books/

Gaudelli, W. (2003). *World class: Teaching and learning in global times*. Mahwah, NJ: Lawrence Erlbaum.

Gee, J. P. (1991). The legacies of competency: From Plato to Freire through Harvey Graff: Competency, discourse, and linguistics. *Harvard Educational Review, 58*(2), 195–212.

Giroux, H. A. (2002). Democracy, freedom, and justice after September 11th: Rethinking the role of educators and the politics of schooling. *Teachers College Record, 104*(6) 1138–62.

Green, A. (1997). Education, globalization and the nation state. New York, NY: Macmillan.

Greenfield, W. (1985). *Being and becoming a principal: Responses to work contexts and socialization processes*. Paper presented at the annual meeting of the American Educational Research Association, Chicago.

Gutherie, J. W., & Saunders, T. (2001, January). *Who will lead the public schools?* Education Supplement, The New York Times.

Hage, M. (2005, November). *The digital divide continues to hinder development in rural areas*. Food and Agriculture Organization in the United Nations: Second World Summit on the Information Society. Available [online]: http://fao.org

Hall, E. T. (1959). *The silent language*. New York, NY: Doubleday Publishing Group, Inc.

Hall, G. E., & Mani, M. N. G. (1992) Entry strategies: Where do I begin? In F.W. Parkay & G. E. Hall (Eds.), *Becoming a principal: The challenges of beginning leadership*, 48–69. Needham Heights, MA: Simon & Shuster.

Hargreaves, A., & Fink, D. (2004). The seven principles of sustainable leadership. *Educational Leadership, 61*(7), 8–13.

Hargreaves, A., & Fullan, M. (1999). *What's worth fighting for out there?* Toronto, ON, Canada: Ontario Public School Teachers' Federation.

Hargreaves, A., Moore, S., Fink, D., Brayman, C., & White, R. (2003). *Succeeding leaders? A study of principal succession and sustainability*. Toronto, ON, Canada: Ontario Principals Council.

Hart, A.W. (1993). *Principal succession: Establishing leadership in schools*. Albany, NY: SUNY Press.

Harvey, T. R., & Drolet, B. (2004). *Building teams-building people: Expanding the fifth resource*. 2nd ed. New York, NY: ScarecrowEducation.

Hess, F. M. (1999). *Spinning wheels: The politics of urban school reform*. Washington, DC: Brookings Institute.

Hoban, G. (2002). *Teacher learning for educational change: A systems thinking approach.* Buckingham, UK: Open University Press.

Institute of Educational Leadership (2000, October). *Leadership for student learning: Reinventing the principalship. School leadership for the 21st Century.* Initiative, A Report of the task Force on the Principalship. Washington, DC: Institute for Educational Leadership.

Jackson, B. L., & Kelley, C. (2002). Exceptional and innovative programs in educational leadership. *Educational Administration Quarterly, 38*(2), 192–212.

Johnson, B. (2001, January). *The dynamics of succession: A qualitative study of principal succession in four elementary schools of the Toronto Catholic District School Board.* Paper presented at the 14th Annual International Congress for School Effectiveness and Improvement, Toronto, ON, Canada.

Jungck, S., & Kajornsin, B. (2003). "Thai wisdom" and globalization: Negotiating the global and local in Thailand's national education reform. In K. Anderson-Levitt (Ed.), *Local meanings, global schooling: Anthropology and world culture theory* 27–49. New York: Palgrave Macmillan.

Kaye, M. J. (1995). *Measuring professional socialization in a distant program.* Available [On-line]: http://nu.edu/nuri/llconf/confll995/kaye.html

Kapur, D., & McHale, J. (2005). *Give us your best and brightest: The global hunt for talent and its impact on the developing world.* Washington, DC: Center for Global Development.

Kaufman, R., & Herman, J. (1991). *Strategic planning in education: Rethinking, restructuring, revitalizing.* Lancaster, PA: Technomic Publishing.

Kelley, C., & Peterson, K. (2000, November). *The work of principals and their preparation: Addressing critical needs for the 21st century.* Paper presented at the annual meeting of the University Council for Educational Administration, Albuquerque, NM.

Klenke, K. (2006). The "S" factor in leadership: education, practice and research. *Journal of Education for Business, 79*(1), 56–60.

Kohn, A. (1997, February). How not to teach values: A critical look at character education. *Phi Delta Kappan,* 429–39.

Ladson-Billings, G. J. (1995a). Toward a theory of culturally relevant pedagogy. *American Education Research Journal, 35,* 465–91.

Ladson-Billings, G. (1995b). But that's just good teaching! The case for culturally relevant pedagogy. *Theory into Practice, 34* (3), 159–65.

Lechner, F., & Boli, J. (2005). *World culture: Origins and consequences.* Malden, MA: Blackwell.

Leithwood, K., Riedlinger, B., Bauer, S., & Jantzi, D. (2003). Leadership program effects on student learning: The case of the greater New Orleans school leadership center. *Journal of School Leadership, 13*(6), 707–29.

Leithwood, K., Steinbach, R., & Begley, P. (1992). Socialization experiences: Becoming a principal in Canada. In F. Parkay & G. Hall (Eds.), *Becoming a principal: Challenges of leadership,* 284–307. Needham Heights, MA: Allyn & Bacon.

Ludwig, C., & Herschell, P. (1998). The power of pedagogy: Routines, school competency practices and outcomes. *Australian Journal of Language and Competency, 21.*

Maclellan, E. (2008). Pedagogical competent: What it means and what it allows. *Teaching and Teacher Education, 24*(8), 1986–92.

MacMillan, R. (1996). *The relationship between school culture and principal's practices at the time of succession.* Unpublished doctoral dissertation, OISE/University of Toronto, Toronto, Ontario, Canada.

Malley, J. (2005). *Ethics corner: Should we teach ethics in K-12?* Available at: http://ccamain.com/pdf/k-12.pdf

Marx, G. T. (2006a). *Sixteen trends: Their profound impact on our future.* Alexandria, VA: Educational Research Service.

Marx, G. T. (2006b). Using trend data to create a successful future for our students, our schools, and our communities. *ERS Spectrum.* Alexandria, VA: Educational Research Service.

McCarthy, M. M. (1999). The evolution of educational leadership preparation programs. In J. Murphy & K. S. Louis (Eds.), *Handbook of research on educational administration* 135–47. San Francisco, CA: Jossey-Bass.

Merriam, S. B. (1998). *Qualitative research and case study applications in education.* San Francisco, CA: Jossey-Bass.

Merton, R. K. (1963). *Social theory and social structure.* New York, NY: Free Press.

Merrill, J. C. (1990). *The imperative of freedom: A philosophy of journalistic autonomy.* Latham, MD: Freedom House.

Mintzberg, H. (1994). *The rise and fall of strategic planning.* London, UK: Prentice Hall International.

Molinaro, V., & Drake, S. (1998). Successful educational reform: Lessons for leaders. *International Electronic Journal for Leadership in Learning,* 2(9). Retrieved June 22, 2016 from, http://ucalgary.ca/~iejll/

Murphy, J., & Forsyth, P. B. (Eds.). (1999). *Educational administration: A decade of reform.* Thousand Oaks, CA: Corwin Press.

Muth, R., & Barnett, B. (2001). Making the case for professional preparation: Using research for program improvement and political support. *Educational Leadership and Administration: Teaching and Program Development,* 13, 109–20.

National Association of Secondary School Principals (1992). *Salaries paid principals and assistant principals.* Arlington, VA: Educational Research Service.

Newton, R. M. (2001). A recruitment strategy: Retooling the principal's role. *AASA Professor,* 24(4), 6–10.

Normore, A. H. (2001). Leadership succession planning. In P.T. Begley & C. Slater (Eds.), *School leadership in Canada series,* 23–8. Hillsdale, ON, Canada: Begley & Associates.

Normore, A. H. (2002). Recruitment, socialization and accountability of school administrators in two Ontario school districts: A research report Ontario Principals Council Register. *Professional Journal for Ontario's Vice-Principals and Principals,* 4(3), 22–40.

Normore, A. H. (2004a). Leadership success in schools: Planning, recruitment and socialization. *International Electronic Journal for Leadership in Learning,* 8(10), Available [On-line]: http://ucalgary.ca/~iejll

Normore, A. H. (2004b). Recruitment and selection: Addressing the leadership shortage in one large Canadian school district. *Canadian Journal of Educational Administration and Policy,* 30, May 12, 2004. Available [On-line]: http://umanitoba.ca/publications/cjeap

Normore, A. H. (2004c). Socializing school administrators to meet leadership challenges that doom all but the most heroic and talented leaders to failure. *International Journal of Leadership in Education, Theory and Practice,* 7(2), 107–25.

Normore, A. H. (2004d). The edge of chaos: School administrators and accountability. *Journal of Educational Administration,* 42(1), 55–77.

Normore, A. H. (2006). Leadership recruitment and selection in school districts: Trends and issues. *Journal of Educational Thought,* 40(1), 41–73.

Normore, A. H., & Brooks, J.S (2014). The department chair: The conundrum of leadership versus management. In Issa Lahera, A., Hamdan, K., & Normore, A. H. (Eds.), *Pathways to excellence: Developing and cultivating leaders for the classroom and beyond* (pp. 3–19). Bingley, UK: Emerald Group Publishing Limited.

Normore, A. H., & Paul Doscher, S. (2007). Using media as the basis for a social issues approach to promoting moral competency in university teaching. *Journal of Educational Administration, 45*(4), 427–50.

Ogawa, R. T. (1994). Leadership succession. In S. B. Bacharach & B. Mundell (Eds.), *Organizational behavior in schools,* 359–89. Thousand Oaks, CA: Corwin Press.

Olson, D. (2003). *Psychological theory and educational reform.* Cambridge: Cambridge University Press.

Olson, D. (2001). Competent minds; competent societies. In P. Tynjälä, K. Mason & K. Lonka (Eds.), *Writing as a learning tool: Integrating theory and practice,* 1–5. Academic Publishers, London: Kluwer.

Olson, D. (1994). *The world on paper.* Cambridge, UK: Cambridge University Press.

Organization for Economic Cooperation and Development (2003). *Source of economic growth in OECD countries.* Paris: OECD.

Ortiz, F. I. (1982). *Career patterns in education: Women, men and minorities in public school administration.* New York, NY: Praeger.

Patton, M. (1998). Discovering process use. *Evaluation Journal, 4*(2), 225–33.

Paul-Doscher, S., & Normore, A. H. (2009, in press). The moral agency of the educational leader in times of national crisis and conflict. *Journal of School Leadership, 18*(1).

Piacciano, A. (2007). *Educational leadership and planning for technology.* 4th ed. Upper Saddle River, NJ: Pearson Education.

Pieter, J. (1994). Succession and the elementary school principal: An exploratory study. (Doctoral dissertation, University of California, 1990). *Dissertation Abstracts International,* UMI No. 9517779.

Pounder, D. G., & Young, P. (1996). Recruitment and selection of educational administrators: Priorities for today's schools. In K. Leithwood, J. Chapman, D. Corson, P. Hallinger, & A. Hart (Eds.), *International handbook of educational leadership and administration,* 279–308. Netherlands: Kluwer Academic Publishers.

Pounder, D. G., & Merrill, R. J. (2001). Job desirability of high school principalship: Job choice theory perspective. *Educational Administration Quarterly, 37*(1), 27–57.

Ranly, D. (1992). *The lessons of general semantics.* In D. Brentari, G. N., Larson, L.A. and MacLeod. K. (Eds.), *The Joy of Grammar,* 251–67. Amsterdam, The Netherlands: John Benjamins Publishing Company.

Rebore, R. W. (2001). *Human resources administration in education.* 6th ed. Boston, MA: Allyn & Bacon.

Renihan, P. (1999). *In-school leadership for Saskatchewan schools: Issues and strategies.* Saskatchewan Educational Leadership Unit, University of Saskatchewan (S.S.T.A. Research Centre Report. No. 99–02). Regina, SK, Canada: S.S.T.A.

Riaz, O., & Normore, A. H. (2008). Examining the spiritual dimension of educational leadership. *University Council for Educational Administration (UCEA), Journal of Values and Ethics in Educational Administration, 6*(4), 1–8.

Robertson, R. (1995). Glocalization: Time-space and homogeneity. In M. Featherstone, S. Lash, & R. Robertson (Eds.), *Global modernity,* 25–44. London, UK: Sage.

Robinson, J. (2000). Training teachers to be principals. *The Ontario Principal's Council Register: The Magazine for Ontario's principals and vice-principals, 2*(4), 23–6.

Rosenau, J. N. (1994). New dimensions of security: The interaction of globalizing and localizing dynamics. *Security Dialogues, 25*(3), 255–81.

Ross, P. N. (1989). *Socialization in the preparation of principals.* Unpublished manuscript, York Region Board of Education, Toronto, ON, Canada.

Rothwell, W. J. (2001). *Effective succession planning: ensuring leadership continuity and building talent from within.* New York: American Management Association.

Saphier, J., & King, M. (1985). Good seeds grow in strong cultures. *Educational Leadership, 42*(6), 67–74.

Sassen, S. (2006).*Territory, authority, rights: From medieval to global assemblages.* Princeton, NJ: Princeton University Press.

Schein, E. H. (1992). *Organizational culture and leadership.* San Francisco, CA: Jossey-Bass.

Sachs, J. (2005). *The end of poverty: Economic possibilities for our time.* New York, UK: Penguin Press.

Scholte, J. A. (2000). *Globalization: a critical introduction.* New York: St. Martin's Press Inc.

Selwyn, N., Gorard, S., & Williams, S. (2001). Digital divide or digital opportunity? The role of technology in overcoming social exclusion in U.S. education. *Educational Policy, 15,* 258–77.

Senge, P., Smith, P., Kruschwitz, N., Laur, J., & Schley, S. (2008). *The necessary revolution: How individuals and organizations are working together to create a sustainable world.* Cambridge, MA: Doubleday Currency.

Sergiovanni, T. J. (2001). *The principalship: A reflective practice perspective.* Needham Heights, MA: Allyn & Bacon.

Seyfarth, J. T. (1999). *The principal: new leadership for new challenges.* Upper Saddle River, NJ: Prentice Hall.

Shafritz, J. M., & J. S. Ott, eds. (2005). *Classics of Organization Theory.* 5th ed. New York, UK: Harcourt Brace.

Shapiro, S. H. (1989). New directions for sociology of education: Reconstructing the public discourse in education. *Education and Society, 7*(2), 21–38.

Slaughter, A. M. (2006). *A new world order.* Princeton, NJ: Princeton University Press.

Smith, P. (1999). Sex, lies and Hollywood's administrators: The (de)construction of school leadership in contemporary films. *Journal of Educational Administration, 37*(1), 50–65.

Spillane, J. P., Diamond, J. B., Burch, P., Hallett, T., Jita, L., & Zoltners, J. (2002). Managing in the middle: School leaders and the enactment of accountability policy. *Educational Policy, 16*(5), 731–62.

Spring, J. (1998). *Education and the rise of the global economy.* Mahwah, NJ: Lawrence Erlbaum.

Spring, J. (2008). Research on globalization and education. *Review of Educational Research, 78*(2), 330–63.

Stevens, P., & Weale, M. (2003). *Education and economic growth.* London: National Institute of Economic and Social Research.

Stout, R. I. (1973). *New approaches to recruitment and selection of educational administration.* Danville, IL: University Council for Ed. Administration. (ERIC/Clearinghouse on Educational Management, No. 61832 72–86751).

Stromquist, N. (2002). *Education in a globalized world: The connectivity of economic power, technology, and knowledge.* Lanham, MD: Rowman & Littlefield.

Tansley, D. (2006, February). Mind the gap: 2006 will witness the deepening of the digital divide. London, UK: *The Financial Times, 13,* p. 21.

Taylor, S. (1997). Critical policy analysis: exploring contexts, texts and consequences. *Discourse: Studies in the Cultural Politics of Education, 18*(1), 23–35.

Tekeste, M. (1996). *The recruitment and selection of in-school administrators in Saskatchewan* (S.S.T.A. Research Center Report. No. 96–05). Regina, SK, Canada: S.S.T.A. Townsend, T. (April, 2003). *A partnership approach to the training of school leaders: Issues of capability and succession planning. Paper presented at the Annual Meeting of the American Educational research Association*, Chicago, IL.

Thomas, S. (2006). *Education policy in the media: Public discourse on education.* Teneriffe, Queensland: Post Pressed.

Thompson, S. (2004). Leading from the eye of the storm. *Educational Leadership*, 61(7), 60–3.

Tuana, N. (2003) Moral competency. *Online Research/Penn State*, 24(2). Available at http://rps.psu.edu/0305/competency.html

Turner, B. S. (2002). Cosmopolitan virtue, globalization and patriotism. *Theory, Culture & Society*, 19(1–2), 45–63.

Uphoff, J. K. (2001). Religious diversity and education. In J. Banks & C. A. M. Banks (Eds.), *Multicultural education: Issues & perspectives*, 4th ed. 103–21. New York: Wiley.

Van Berkum, D. W., Richardson, M. D., & Lane, K. E. (1994). *Professional development in educational administration programs: Where does it exist?* Educational Resources Information Center (ERIC No. 026 260).

Wallace Foundation (2003). *Beyond the pipeline: Getting the principals we need, where they are needed most.* A policy brief by the Wallace Foundation. New York: Wallace Foundation.

Wanous, J. P. (1980). *Organizational entry: Recruitment, selection and socialization of school administration.* Reading, MA: Addison-Wesley Publishing Company.

Weber, E. (2007). Globalization, "glocal" development, and teachers' work: A research agenda. *Review of Educational Research*, 77(3), 279–309.

Welner, K. G., & Weitzman, D. Q. (2005). The soft bigotry of low expenditures. *Equity and Excellence in Education*, 38(3), 242–8.

Wenzel, J. (2000). Grim Fairy Tales: Taking a risk. In A. Amireh & L. Suhair Maja, (eds.), *Imaginary maps. Going global: The transnational reception of Third World women writers*, 229–51. New York: Garland.

Willinsky, J. (1998). *Learning to divide the world: Education at empire's end.* Minneapolis: University of Minnesota Press.

Winter, P. A., & Dunaway, D. M. (1997). Reactions of teachers, as applicants, to the principal recruitment practices in a reform environment: The effects of job attributes, job information sources, and school level. *Journal of Research and Development in Education*, 30(3), 144–53.

Wolcott, H. F. (2003). *Teachers versus technocrats.* Walnut Creek, CA: AltaMira Press.

Wolcott, H. F. (1991). Propriospect and the acquisition of culture. *Anthropology and Education Quarterly*, 22(3), 251–73.

Yin, R. K. (1994). *Case study research.* 2nd ed. Thousand Oaks, CA: Sage.

CHAPTER 9

Spiritual and Religious Leadership

This chapter investigates the spiritual dimension within educational leadership practices. We draw our working definition of spirituality from the literature (e.g., Dalia, 2007; Miller, 2006; Thompson, 2000) and argue that spirituality is a phenomenon which enables leaders to find deeper meaning in their work. Further, we support the argument that spirituality is a significant dimension of human existence that is often silenced in the public school system and support the notion that it is time to release the spiritual dimension of human existence out of the boxes in which it is often imprisoned (Riaz & Normore, 2008; Shields, Starratt, Sayani, Edwards, Langlois, & Fraser, 2004). For our purposes, spirituality is characterized by a heightened awareness of one's self and the desire to establish a connection with a transcendent source of meaning. A focusing theme of spirituality shapes our review of the literature on ethical decision making that exemplifies ethical and spiritual leadership. Spirituality provides the overall conceptual link among the different bodies of literature that we examined.

Given the definitions of spirituality and religion, the educational leader will be sensitive to the notion that regardless of religion, and, even in the absence of an espoused religious denomination, all people can have spiritual experiences. Consistent with other chapters in this book we focus on *learning* by articulating what the moral good of learning entails. We introduce an ethical paradigm of care, and show how religious and spiritual leaders can cultivate communities of trust and cooperative relationships within the workplace. The chapter embraces *leadership* with particular emphasis on the educational leaders' ability to influence the religious and spiritual dimension of educational leadership through formal and informal means. It emphasizes respiriting, renewal, religious respect, and respecting religious diversity. *Literacy* and a set of *reflective questions* are articulated in a discussion forum at the end of the chapter. The discussion is designed to help readers identify and analyze the way our concepts are practiced in schools, local communities and throughout the world. It further intends to serve as questions and prompts to help the reader understand the personal, interpersonal and organizational consequences of their actions.

Within the above-mentioned context an extant review and analysis of the literature focused on four predominant linkages between leadership, ethics and spirituality. These are: (1) the use of a multi-ethical paradigm for the moral good of learning, (2) the human element in leadership practice, (3) organizational integrity and authenticity, and (4) spirituality as the foundation for an individual's ethical framework. The balance of the chapter is devoted to a discussion of each of these themes or linkages in turn. Among key concepts highlighted throughout this chapter are:

- Spirituality
- Organizational integrity
- Organizational authenticity
- Servant leadership
- Religiousness
- Existential intelligence.

The Multi-Ethical Paradigm for the Moral Good of Learning

Shapiro and Stefkovich (2005) argue for a multifaceted approach to resolving ethical dilemmas. Their multiple ethical paradigm approach incorporates the paradigms of justice, critique, care, and the profession. These authors contend that, by applying the paradigm of professional ethics, an individual in a professional setting may mitigate clashing ethical codes. They state, "if there is a moral imperative for the profession, it is to serve the 'best interests of the student' . . . consequently, this ideal must lie at the heart of any professional paradigm for educational leaders" (p. 25). The tenet of serving the "best interests of the student" may be the essential ethical obligation for educational leaders. Starratt (1996) concurs with this notion, suggesting that leadership must be transformed from one that is focused on efficiency and technical problem-solving to one that pursues an organization's vision. Starratt (2007) warns that the traditional "functional" approach to leadership might exclude the obligation to "pursue *the good intrinsic to the work*, intrinsic to the *practice* of the profession" (p. 166). He further argues that, although the moral good of the learner is important, it is inevitably intrinsically related to the moral good of learning. Thus, a more "substantive" (Starratt, 1996) approach toward relieving ethical dilemmas would embrace spirituality as an additional ethical perspective. He argues that spirituality provides leaders the opportunity to model the ethic of care within the workplace for it provides individuals with the strength to prevail over difficult situations.

In practicing the ethic of care, spiritual leaders cultivate a community of trust and cooperative relationships within the workplace (Northouse, 2004; Riaz & Normore, 2008). Caring for others proves to be an essential component within an effective ethical framework and within spiritual-based leadership. Gilligan (as cited in Northouse, 2004) concurs with this notion identifying the *ethic of caring* and personal relationships as the foundation for ethical behavior. Ethically responsible educational leaders focus on the human element—relationships, values and actions of individuals within the school community. The need to cater to the human element is evermore present in today's workforce (Leonard, Schilling & Normore, 2014).

A New Pedigree of Leadership: Spirituality and the Human Element

The emergence of faith-based principles in the workplace (Hillard, 2004) suggests a growing trend to mitigate moral and ethical dilemmas with decisions based on the spiritual domain. The shift from a capital-centered to a human-centered workplace has spawned a new pedigree of leadership. It is within the nexus of the ethic of care where the shift to a spiritual focus for leadership emerges (Fairholm, 1997). This focus on spirituality is one closely aligned with the need to find meaning within one's work. Fairholm suggests infusing spirituality within one's leadership is a vital adaptation to the shifting dynamic within today's workforce. He states, "People are hungry for meaning in their lives. They feel they have lost something and they don't remember what it is they've lost . . . it has left a gaping hole in their lives" (p. 60). Fairholm believes individuals are integrating spirituality within their everyday work lives to fill the void. In contrast, Klenke (2006) argues that the purpose of spirituality is not to serve work. Instead, work is to serve spirituality. From a leadership perspective, spirituality enables administrators to provide the meaning and passion that individuals are eagerly searching for (Houston, 2002; Houston & Sokolow, 2006). In his study of "good-to-great" companies, Collins (2001) argues that great organizations have the uncanny ability of providing work that is significant for its individuals. He states "the idea here is not to stimulate passion but to discover what makes you passionate" (p. 96).

Covey (2004) posits that our current workforce is undergoing a dynamic transformation as it shifts from an Industrial Age mindset to one focused on the Knowledge Worker. The Industrial Age's main asset was capital and focused on things. In contrast, our evolution to a Knowledge Worker society has shifted the focus to the human element, that is, the workers themselves. Covey believes, "Quality knowledge work is so valuable that unleashing its potential offers organizations an extraordinary opportunity for value creation" (p. 14).

Influence of Spirituality

Discussing the influence of a leader's spirituality, Heifetz and Linsky (2002) state: A sacred heart means you may feel tortured and betrayed, powerless and hopeless, and yet stay open . . . the power of a sacred heart helps mobilize others to do the same— to face challenges that demand courage and to endure the pains of change without deceiving themselves or running away (p. 230). Spirituality provides the vehicle by which educational leaders model the appropriate behavior to the individuals within the school community by setting an example for their colleagues through their approach to daily work tasks (Solomon & Hunter, 2002). The term spirituality encompasses several perspectives including: making sense of situations; significance of life; deriving purpose; beliefs, standards and ethics that one cherishes; increased awareness of a connection with self, others, spirit, and nature; an unfolding of life that calls for reflection and experience including a sense of who one "is" and how one "knows"; and experience, awareness and appreciation of a "transcendent dimension" to life beyond self (Martsolf & Mickley, 1998). Although the concept of "transcendence" is underplayed within the literature, it represents an integral aspect used to define spiritual leadership. The ability to establish a connection with something beyond mere physical experiences provides leaders with the inner strength to deal with difficult situations (Miller, 2006; Miller, Dantley, Denith, Brady, Shapiro, Boncana, & Engel, 2007; Wheatly, 2002). Fairholm's contention that individuals utilize spirituality to find meaning in their work is of great consequence for leaders within the educational milieu.

Effective leadership entails a deliberate attempt to provide experiences that will allow them to evolve first as individuals and then as practitioners. Palmer (1998) attests to this theory, indicating that teachers participating in programs designed to allow them to explore the spiritual dimension have reported to be better grounded with their inner being and more likely to flourish. These teachers have accounted such spiritual explorations for improving their teaching ability and enhancing their rapport with their students.

Organizational Integrity and Authenticity: The Spiritual Dimension

Klenke (2003) contends that the roots of effective leadership may be grounded within the spiritual dimension. She argues that spirituality provides leaders the opportunity of aligning personal and organizational values. It provides an "integration of, rather than separation between, the "private life of spirit" and the "public life of work" . . ." (p. 58). Aligning values for educational leaders reinforces individuals' needs to find meaning through purpose or contribution. Most importantly, it benefits the entire workplace by providing organizational integrity. Evans (1996) maintains that "Integrity is a fundamental consistency between one's values, goals, and actions . . . at the simplest level it means standing for something, having a significant commitment and exemplifying this commitment in your behavior" (p.185). For the school leader, the first moral lesson that they teach is that they have valuable beliefs and are willing to take action that demonstrate integrity, self-honesty, and practice authenticity (Begley, 2006; Bhindi & Duignan, 1997; Evans, 1996; Hodgkinson, 1991). If leaders do not act from a place of integrity then their authenticity will be questioned (Evans, 1996). Authentic leaders are those who are believed in because they fulfill their obligations, meet their commitments, and are trustworthy (Evans, 1996; Houston & Sokolow, 2006; Leonard, 2005).

The primary principle of moral leadership and courage for the educational leader is complemented by authenticity—acting in accord with one's beliefs—or as the colloquial expression goes, "If you talk the talk, then you better walk the walk." For example, Nucci (2001) explains that a school leader who believes in Kohlberg's concept of a "just community" may create a structure for joint decision making and democratic participation that involves all stakeholders, demonstrating in action his/her belief in cooperative power sharing. Such a structure will communicate to the community a very strong message about the leader, but even more so it will communicate that the climate, culture and community are founded on such values. The communication of values is a difficult, yet important task—one that requires balance.

Establishing organizational integrity is essential to the concept of community building within the workplace. Spiritual leaders view the relationship between the leader and those being led as a reciprocal one in which both parties are guided by the need for self-development. As suggested by Sizer and Sizer (1999), in order to find the covenant of any organization all that's required is to see how people spend their time, the relationships they build and how they approach ideas. These authors further suggest that we "look for the contradictions between words and practice, with the fewer the better . . . try to estimate the frequency and the honesty of its deliberations . . . though it will always want to spruce up for visitors, its hour-by-hour functioning is what is important . . . judge the organization not on what it says but on how it keeps" (p.18). Spiritual leaders attend to their workers' needs, continually encouraging them to become more autonomous (Northouse, 2004). In turn, this relationship harbors a feeling of spiritual wholeness among all stakeholders (Fairholm, 1997). Individual relationships seem to be enhanced when spirituality is shared throughout the work community. Ultimately, spiritual leaders understand that their effect on the organization is greater than themselves. Referring to the spiritual leader, Barton (2003) asserts, "Authority, like love, is useless until it is given away" (p. 7). Covey (2004) argues that effective leaders understand that making a sacrifice denotes "giving up something good for something better" (p. 316). Covey further elaborates by quoting Albert Schweitzer, "I know not what your destiny will be, but one thing I know: the only ones among you who will be truly happy are those who have sought and found how to serve" (p. 316).

Servant Leadership

We support Greenleaf's concept of the servant leader as essential in defining spirituality. Greenleaf (1988) argues that if a better society were to emerge, it would be one predicated upon the care for others. In *Spirituality for Leadership*, he articulated:

> If a better society is to be built, one more just and more caring and providing opportunity for people to grow, the most effective and economical way, while supportive of the social order, is to raise the performance as servant of as many institutions as possible by new voluntary regenerative forces initiated within them by committed individuals, *servants*. Such servants may never predominate or even be numerous; but their influence may form a leaven that makes possible a reasonably civilized society. (p. 1)

Still, an important notion not explicitly stated within Greenleaf's concept of servant leadership is that of the "authentic leader". Bhindi and Duignan (1997) argue that a framework for effective leadership must be based on authenticity. If the concept of servant leadership is to be used as the foundation for spiritual-based leadership, it is vital for spirituality to stem from authentic relationships. Servant leadership engages individuals in meaningful relationships and attempts to make connections with something greater than the self. Greenleaf's (1970) concept of servant leadership is at the core of the spiritual leader. He asserts that leadership emerges within an individual's capacity to serve others. Thus, leadership is achieved through authentically giving of oneself in the service of others (Sanders, 1994). Fairholm (1997) maintains that servant leadership provides the transformational dynamic that is required for individuals within today's organizations. This transformation entails shifting leaders' values from the material to the spiritual. To be effective, leaders must change their heart, or spirit, and "put those they serve first and let everything take care of itself" (p. 26). Thus, the servant leader is one driven by spirituality. Fairholm further asserts that "Spirituality stretches the leader's mind toward vision, reality, courage, and ethics. The spirit leadership mind is touched by the unconscious. It lets us get in touch with external questions of the spirit" (p. 26). Servant leadership suggests that individuals should treat others as *they* would like to be treated (Beckner, 2004).

The tenets of servant leadership are aptly described within Covey's "paradigm of interdependence." Within this paradigm, Covey (1989) argues for the power of collaboration and cohesiveness among individuals within an organization. He states that organizations that practice empathic listening and rally individuals toward a common goal establish synergy. Northouse (2004) claims that interdependence suggests that true leadership emanates from being a servant. Servant leaders focus their attention to the needs of their workers, emphatically listening and providing them the guidance necessary to become free, more autonomous, and ultimately, more like servants themselves.

This notion of serving others before serving the self is also manifested in the Golden Rule found within the other major religions and faith traditions (i.e., Prophetic Christian, Catholic, Jewish, Buddhism, Hinduism, and Muslim traditions). For example, in keeping with the notion of serving others, one can turn to the Buddhist tenet of respect for the sanctity of life. The Soka Gakkai Buddhists (SGI), an NGO that promotes peace, culture and education work in ways appropriate to local cultures and customs to promote human rights and sustainable development, raising awareness and moral responsibilities, and forging links at the grass-roots level to foster personal change, social contribution and a culture of peace. SGI has its roots in Soka Gakkai, an organization originally founded to promote educational reform in Japan in 1930. SGI sees education "as the key to a healthy society and is committed to promoting humanistic education aimed at fostering the unique potential of every human being and a deeper understanding of human life and the world we live in" (Soka Gakkai International, 2008).

Empathic listening is an essential quality to the servant leader and integral in establishing interdependence within the workplace (Northouse, 2004). Covey (1989) defines empathic listening as the process of listening with the intent to *understand*. Empathic listening allows leaders to get into an individual's "frame of reference" (p. 240). Covey claims individuals not listening at the empathic level fail to reach an authentic understanding of others. Greenleaf (as cited in Beckner, 2004) contends that empathic listening builds strength in other people.

Spiritual Meaning

Spiritual leadership may be credited with enhancing individuals' perception and utilization of their inner strength. Individuals in the workplace benefit from applying personal spiritual meanings to construct and frame their approach to work (Solomon & Hunter, 2002). Greenleaf's (1996) concept of *entheos* describes how leaders may adhere to spirituality to enhance their leadership and establish their own ethical convictions. *Entheos* refers to being driven by one's spirit. It is the "power actuating the person who is inspired" (p. 82). Greenleaf explains: Entheos is an imperative if the ethical obligation to develop *strength* is accepted. To accept this as a binding ethic when society at large does not accept it calls for sustained inner prompting—entheos. New ethics evolve not from idealistic pronouncements but because determined individuals practice them, in opposition to the prevailing sentiments of society if necessary, and demonstrate their validity. (p. 82). The ability to find strength within one's spirituality to construct new ethical convictions parallels Kohlberg's postconventional levels of moral judgment. Kohlberg (as cited in Beckner, 2004) asserts that individuals within this level practice the highest form of ethics and follow self-chosen principles indicating a higher degree of moral virtues. The empowerment of teachers is a high priority for spiritually oriented educational leaders (Barton, 2003). These leaders understand that their role is to promulgate collaboration among individuals within the school community. Lambert (2003) suggests the power of establishing this community lies in an organization's ability to lead itself and to sustain this leadership capacity when key individuals have left. Thus, spiritual leaders place less emphasis on formal authority and choose to distribute power among those being led.

According to Keyes, Hanley-Maxwell and Capper (1999), a school leader who creates a supportive environment for critique, encourages autonomy and risk-taking, while communicating trust that teachers can succeed. These authors indicate that leader behaviors are undergirded by a spirituality grounded in valuing personal struggle, recognizing the dignity of all people, blending the personal and the professional, believing that people are doing their best, listening and dreaming. However, using one's personal spirituality as the foundation for modeling the appropriate actions within the workplace may seem daunting.

One may question whether their own beliefs will be sufficient for others during difficult times. Sokolow (2002) and Tolle (1999) argue that the enlightened leader utilizes a set of universal principles, or spiritual truths available to all leaders. Leaders are able to acclimatize themselves to these principles by strengthening their "spiritual muscles" and relying on what Covey (2004) coined "spiritual intelligence" (p. 54). He insists human beings are endowed with four intelligences at birth including mental, social, emotional, and spiritual. Covey asserts that spiritual intelligence is essentially superior because of its guiding role in directing the other intelligences. According to Covey spiritual intelligence is "linked to humanity's need for meaning, an issue very much at the forefront of people's minds . . . spiritual Intelligence is what we use to develop our longing and capacity for meaning, vision, and value" (p. 54).

The Foundation of an Ethical Framework: Spirituality

Researchers assert that spiritual leaders provide the transformational power to influence change in the context of ethical principles (Dantley & Tillman, 2006). Dantley (2005) applies Cornel West's notions of prophetic spirituality along with the tenets of principled, pragmatic and purposive leadership to serve as the foundation for progressive transformation of educational leadership. According to Dantley (2005), the application of personal spirituality to community issues of social change and social justice may provide a direction for educational leadership. Aligned with Dantley's work, Klenke (2004) identifies spiritual leaders as having the "ability to transcend their own interests and needs and for the sake of the followers, which motivates them to pursue higher moral standards" (p. 58). Thus, spirituality provides an effective paradigm for basing ethical decisions.

Fairholm (1997) contends that spirituality "moderates and contains the day-to-day life challenges that often cause us to question "right or wrong" choices" and "serves as the basis for decision making and subliminally shapes the opinions that we see as viable" (p. 77). Thus, spirituality is essentially the foundation for an individual's ethical framework. Individuals with greater spiritual convictions may boast a deeper and more complex set of ethical paradigms attained from their relationship with the divine. The spiritual domain manifests itself within the core of one's value system (Covey, 1989) and provides the framework by which one thinks and acts according to one's values (Fairholm, 1997). To revisit Greenleaf's work (1996), he suggests *entheos* is crucial to uncertainty during decision making:

> Entheos is seen as a basic spiritual essence. It is the sustaining force that holds one together under stress. It is the support to venturesome risk-taking action. It provides the prod of conscience that keeps one open to knowledge when the urge to be comfortable would close the door. It provides a linking concept by whatever religious beliefs one has are kept in contact with one's attitudes and actions in the world of practical affairs. It nurtures a powerful concept of the self. (p. 82)

Finding clarity during tumultuous times is possible with an identity emanating from the divine (Thompson, 2004). Spirituality provides the source for clearing one's mind of preconceived judgments and honing in on one's value system. Thompson proposes that spirituality allows leaders to move toward clarity and perceive what is truly important during trying ethical situations. In his study determining the relationship between knowing scripture and using ethical reasoning, Nelson (2004) found that college seniors' Bible knowledge wasn't positively correlated with Kohlberg's postconventional levels of ethical reasoning. Moreover, Nelson discovered a negative correlation between Bible knowledge and Kohlberg's preconventional levels of reasoning. The study revealed that a student's knowledge of scripture was attributed to high levels of moral reasoning. Covey (2004) maintains the highest manifestation of spirituality is the development of a conscience. He defines conscience as one's moral sense or inner light and claims that it is a universal phenomenon, independent of a singular religion. Covey asserts that "the spiritual or moral nature of people is also independent of religion or of any particular religious approach ... Yet all of the enduring major religious traditions of the world are unified when it comes to basic underlying principles or values" (p. 77). Thus, it appears that the spiritual dimension provides the essential foundation for ethical, principle-based leadership. It is evident that ethical decision making is influenced by an individual's degree of spirituality (Fairholm, 1997; Miller, Dantley et al., 2007; Nelson, 2004). However, the literature fails to differentiate between the religious and secular spiritual domains (e.g., Normore, 2012; Sanders, 1994). There appears to be a significant need to further identify and delineate the role each of these domains contributes as the foundation for ethical decision making that resonates with ethical and spiritual leadership (Jean-Marie & Normore, 2010).

Religion and Spirituality

Skepticism is sometimes expressed about the legitimacy of spirituality in the workplace, especially in public education (Fairholm, 1997). However, Thompson (2004) attests that spiritual-based leadership does not challenge the separation of church and state delineated in the United States Constitution's Establishment Clause. Klenke (2006) offers the following explanation:

> Spirituality is often defined by what it is not. Spirituality . . . is not religion. Organized religion looks outward; depends on rites and scripture; and tends to be dogmatic, exclusive, and narrowly based on a formalized set of beliefs and practices. Spirituality, on the other hand, looks inward, tends to be inclusive and more universally applicable, and embraces diverse expressions of interconnectedness (p. 59).

Research asserts that spirituality is the ability to lead from deeper levels of experience, meaning, and wisdom (Sokolow, 2002; Thompson, 2004). Fairholm (1997) concurs stating that "Spirituality does not apply to particular religions, although the values of some religions may be part of a person's spiritual focus. Said another way, spirituality is the song we all sing. Each religion has its own singer" (p. 29). Solomon and Hunter (2002) argue that spirituality is better understood as a meaning system. Fairholm (1997) argues that as individuals begin to differentiate religion from spirituality, the role of spirituality within individual and organizational life becomes clear. He concludes:

> Our spirit is what makes us human and individual. It determines who we are at work. It is inseparable from self. We draw on our central values in how we deal with people every day. Our values dictate whether we set a good example, take care of people, or try to live the Golden Rule. Our spirituality helps us think and act according to our values (p. 77).

Spirituality's role in aligning a leader's actions with their values is a distinctive characteristic not shared by religion. Religion guides by specific doctrine whereas spirituality is generic and affords the leader a dynamic quality capable of capitalizing on the diverse belief systems operating within an organization. Gardner (1999) identifies the possibility of an "existential intelligence" (p. 60) and differentiates it from religiousness. Citing the profound experience of loving another person, Gardner argues "existential intelligence" may qualify as a provisionary addition to his original list of multiple intelligences. It is within this definition of existential intelligence where spiritual leaders may identify with the ethic of care (love for another) and the need to serve others. Gardner's reluctance to willingly incorporate existential intelligence within his index of multiple intelligences implies the ill-conceived notion that spirituality or existential intelligence does not mesh well with the secular world. His definition of existential intelligence as a profound loving experience for another person presents a limited understanding of spirituality. Spirituality is not, as Gardner contends, the ability to express profound love. Instead, it is the capacity to strike a personal and meaningful relationship with the divine (Bhindi & Duignan, 1997; Sokolow, 2002). It is the sustainability of this relationship that is integral to ethical leadership.

Renewal and Spirituality

Ethical leadership entails a persistent renewal of one's spirituality. Thompson (2004) argues that spiritual leadership calls for a continual "renewal of mindfulness" (p. 62). Renewal of mindfulness is imperative for leaders as it mitigates the probability for habitual practices evolving into common routines. The monotony of everyday decision making may pose a threat to the reliability and validity of one's principles and values. Renewing one's spirituality provides leaders with the medium through which they may realign their personal values and redefine their passions. Covey (1989) stipulates that renewal also provides leaders the opportunity to reinforce their personal leadership. He states:

> You increase your ability to live out of your imagination and conscience instead of only your memory, to deeply understand your innermost paradigms and values, to create within yourself a center of correct principles, to define your own unique mission in life, to rescript yourself to live your life in harmony with correct principles and to draw upon your personal sources of strength (p. 304).

Covey criticizes contemporary beliefs claiming the relationship between self-esteem to matters of the mind, or attitudes. Instead, he posits that self-esteem and personal security are fostered by the persistent renewal of spirit. In other words, renewal is essential to an individual's matter of emotion. He claims individuals are at peace with themselves when their lives are in harmony with their true principles and values. This harmony with one's self builds integrity and harbors interdependent living. Spiritual renewal manifests itself within a myriad of activities. Meditation, prayer, reading great works of literature, listening to music, and communicating with nature are a few examples of activities spiritual leaders may utilize in renewing their spirituality (Covey, 1989). Thompson (2004) describes the method of *self-talk* as an effective means of renewing one's spiritual dimension. *Self-talk* entails "conversing with oneself in positive terms about one's performance" (p. 61). He contends this process allows individuals to realign their personal values and principles and redefine the meaning they derive from their work.

Renewing teachers' spirits is a central task of the spiritual leader (Fairholm, 1997; Jean-Marie & Normore, 2015; Palmer, 1998, 1993). Educational leaders must provide teachers with opportunities to grow and learn within the school community. However, leaders must be aware that sources of spiritual renewal are highly individualistic (Thompson, 2004; Tolle, 1999; Woods, 2007). Leaders must be cautious inculcating spirituality in the workplace. Attention to the needs and private thoughts of the individuals must be the primary objective (Fairholm, 1997). Fairholm suggests that "any activity that challenges us to listen, share, and review our value system with others builds our spirits" (p. 84). Furthermore, he makes a distinction between the different varieties of spirituality that may be present within the workplace. He contends "in-spirit" (p. 84) activities are ones designed for group socialization. These activities provide workers the opportunity to engage in discussions pertaining to the meaning of life and work-related issues. Individuals' spirituality is fostered through bonding and participating with their colleagues. Group brainstorming and staff meetings provide the venue for individuals to collaborate in planning and decision making.

In contrast, "respiriting" (Fairholm, 1997, p. 84) activities provide opportunities for praxis and personal reflection. Praxis is used by educators to describe a recurring passage through a cyclical process of experiential learning such as the cycle described and popularized by Kolb (Smith, 2001). Research indicates that praxis is key in spirituality due to the inability of the finite mind (and its tool, language) to comprehend or express what is infinite (Normore, 2012; van Gelder, 2006). Quiet contemplation, reflection, and challenging study are appropriate activities for engaging individuals in spiritual strengthening activities. Respiriting activities are vital to an organization's success as they provide employees with an emotionally rewarding experience. Furthermore, respiriting establishes work as a spiritually meaningful practice.

Discussion

In a narrow sense, spirituality concerns itself with matters of the spirit that help form an essential part of a school leader's holistic health and wellbeing. By attending to other's needs, these leaders may define the shared values and purposes necessary for revitalizing the school's community. The following questions are intended to guide activities and discussion:

1. We presented an argument that spirituality is a viable component that connects school leaders and their leadership practices. We contend that spiritual leadership enables leaders to find deeper meaning in their work by heightening self-awareness and the desire to establish a connection with a transcendent and metaphysical source of meaning. How does a school leader navigate the complex cohesion of inspiration, encouragement, multiple paradigms of ethics, authenticity, morality, relationship building, reflective self-honesty, and the renewal of spirituality? How do these dimensions of leadership provide organizational integrity and authentic leadership practices that can influence thinking and understanding of individual and collective values, not only in school settings but in the greater society?

2. By incorporating the spiritual dimension in leadership practices, school leaders are able to think more holistically, to act responsibly in judgments, to challenge others, to learn more clearly their own worldview and points of view, and to regard their own professional work as one that builds and enhances not only their own character and identity but those with whom they interact. Toward this end, how can school leaders serve as the spiritual guide to their teachers, students and the larger learning communities in which they serve?

3. Adding the dimension of spirituality to their leadership can be helpful for leaders who search for life-sustaining contexts while simultaneously empowering themselves as agents of transformative change who align everyday practice with core values in ways that will make a significant difference in their professional and personal lives. How does a school leader fulfill this mission? How does the leader understand and connect with the spiritual dimension of school leadership and re-energize those who are committed to giving their full physical and moral energy to the profession?

Could it serve as an impetus to increase student achievement, closing gaps, and taking the next step in engaging the entire learning community?

4. The literature supports the notion that spirituality is a "meaning system" (Solomon & Hunter, 2002, p. 38) that has a broad ranging impact on how leaders think and act in daily life routines. It is a sense of profound internal connection to things beyond and/or within one's self. If school leaders make this connection how can they be guaranteed the likelihood of motivating others?

5. We concur with Houston's theory that leaders get their work done, not through mandate and fiat, but by gathering people together and persuading them to do what is right. To carry this out requires a higher connection than the direct line to the state department of education or the president of the school board, and perhaps through the connection with a higher power. The result is people feel more engaged and present, not only in their work life but also in their personal life. In addition to Stokley's (2002, ¶23) useful examples of spiritual school leadership experiences that leaders might consider (e.g., inspiring a student to voluntarily assist those in need, such as the elderly or disabled; comforting the student who recently has lost a close friend or relative) discuss examples such as encouraging students to visit an infirmed classmate at home or in the hospital; attending wakes, memorials and funeral services of colleagues, parents and students; giving heartfelt sendoffs to those who are leaving for new positions or retiring; collecting and distributing food for those less privileged; voluntarily working in food kitchens, and; accepting the differences of others based on sexual orientation, race, ethnicity, physical stature, social and economic status, and gender.

6. We propose that the metaphysical dimension of school leadership may be the antidote for improving work environments in schools. It is common knowledge that educational leaders face ongoing series of dilemmas and challenges and often find themselves in need of constructive strategies to ensure smooth functioning of the complex organizations they manage and lead. Metaphysically-oriented educational leaders put a premium on establishing genuine connections with those who work with them including fellow school leaders, administrators, teachers, parents and the larger community who look to them to set the tone for the district. How do these dimensions create a safe and trusting environment where personal risk-taking is valued and where leaders find themselves surrounded by people who are invested in what they do? How do school leader engage in ongoing reflection on the human condition and cultivate rich, deep and complex understandings of different subjects and make conceptual connections between them? How will teachers who are encouraged to fuse spiritual connections more likely to pass such a spirit of inquiry to those who matter most—their students.

7. Metaphysical leadership can provide opportunities for students, teachers and administrators to reflect upon their lives, beliefs, traditions and experiences that have shaped their lives and its transcendent purpose. Education emphasizes not only "objective" learning of knowledge (Hunter, 2002, p. 39) but also the personal connection and relevance that knowledge has to a student's life. According to Miller (2006) the transcendent purpose is: a creative, self-guiding energy which we ought not attempt to suppress. No ideology, no social order devised by wealth- or power-

seeking factions should be allowed to corrupt the delicate, miraculous unfolding of this creative energy. How is the spiritual worldview a *reverence for life*, an attitude of wonders and awe in the face of the transcendent source of our being?

REFERENCES

Barton, M. D. (2003). School spirit. *Delta Kappa Gamma Bulletin*, 69(2), 10–13.

Beckner, W. (2004). *Ethics for educational leaders*. Boston: Pearson.

Begley, P. T. (2006). Self-knowledge, capacity and sensitivity: Prerequisites to authentic leadership by school principals. *Journal of Educational Administration*, 44(6), 570–89.

Bhindi, N., & Duignan, P. (1997). Leadership for a new century: authenticity, intentionality, spirituality, and sensibility. *Educational Management & Administration*, 25(2), 117–32.

Bredeson, P. (2005). Building capacity in schools: Some ethical considerations for authentic learning and leadership. *Values and Ethics in Educational Administration*, 4(1), 1–8.

Carley, K. (1992). *Coding choices for textual analysis: A comparison of content analysis and map analysis*. Unpublished Paper.

Collins, J. (2001). *Good to great*. New York: HarperCollins.

Covey, S. (2004).*The 8th habit: From effectiveness to greatness*. New York: Free Press.

Covey, S. (1989). *The 7 habits of highly effective people*. New York: Fireside.

Dalia, D. (2007, September). *Spirituality and school leadership*. Paper presented at the 12th Annual Values and Leadership Conference. University Park, PA.

Dantley, M.E., & Tillman, L. C. (2006). Social justice and moral transformative Leadership. In C. Marshall & M. Oliva (Eds.), *Leadership for social justice: Making revolutions in education*, 16–30. Boston, MA: Pearson Education.

Dantley, M. (2005). African American spirituality and Cornel West's notions of prophetic pragmatism: Restructuring educational leadership in American urban schools. *Educational Administration Quarterly*, 41(4), 651–74.

Evans, R. (1996). *The human side of school change: Reform, resistance, and the real-life problems of innovation*. San Francisco: Jossey-Bass.

Fairholm, G. (1997). *Capturing the heart of leadership: Spirituality and community in the new American workplace*. Westport: Praeger.

Gardner, H. (1999). *Intelligence reframed: Multiple intelligences for the 21 century*. New York: Basic Books.

Greenleaf, R. (1970). *The servant as leader*. Indianapolis: Robert K. Greenleaf Center for Servant-Leadership.

Greenleaf, R. (1988). *Spirituality as leadership*. Indianapolis: Robert K. Greenleaf Center for Servant-Leadership.

Greenleaf, R. (1996). *On becoming a servant leader*. San Francisco: Jossey-Bass Publishers.

Heifetz, R., & Linsky, M. (2002). *Leadership on the line: Staying alive through the dangers of leading*. Cambridge: Harvard Business School Press.

Hillard, J. C. (2004, May 24). Inspired by the Golden Rule: Business ethics titles bring religions principles into the workplace. *Publishers Weekly, 21*. S12.

Hodgkinson, C. (1991). *Educational leadership: The moral art*. Albany: State University of New York Press.

Houston, P., & Sokolow, S. (2006). *The spiritual dimension of leadership: 8 key principles to leading more effectively*. Thousand Oaks: Corwin Press.

Houston, P. (2002). Why spirituality, and why now? *School Administrator, 59*(8), 6–8.

Jean-Marie, G., & Normore, A. H. (2010). The impact of relational leadership, social justice, and spirituality among female secondary school leaders. *International Journal of Urban Educational Leadership, 4*(1), 22–43.

Jean-Marie, G., & Normore, A. H. (2015). Relational leadership, social justice, and spirituality among female secondary school leaders in urban and suburban contexts. In J.S. Brooks & M. Brooks (Eds.), *Urban educational leadership for social justice*, 275–302. Charlotte, NC: Information Age Publishing.

Keyes, M., Hanley-Maxwell, C., & Capper, C. (1999). Spirituality? It's the core of my leadership: Empowering leadership in an inclusive elementary school. *Educational Administration Quarterly, 35*(2), 203–37.

Klenke, K. (2006). The "S" factor in leadership: Education, practice and research. *Journal of Education for Business, 79*(1), 56–60.

Lambert, L. (2003). *Leadership capacity for lasting school improvement*. Alexandria, VA: Association for Supervision and Curriculum Development.

Leonard, P. (2005). The ethics of practice: Navigating the road of authenticity, journey interrupted. *Values and Ethics in Educational Administration, 3*(4), 1–8.

Leonard, P., Schilling, T., & Normore, A. H. (2014). Towards a holistic approach to moral development of educational leaders. In C. Branson & S. Gross (Eds.), *An international handbook for the development of ethical educational leadership*, 533–76. New York, NY: Routledge/Taylor & Francis.

Martsolf, D. S., & Mickley, J. R. (1998). The concept of spirituality in nursing theories; differing world-views and extent on focus. *Journal of Advanced Nursing, 27*, 294–303.

Miller, R. (2006). Reflecting on spirituality in education. *Encounter, 19*(2), Summer.

Miller, P., Dantley, M., Dentith, A., Brady, J., Shapiro, S., Boncana, M., & Engel, M. (2007). *Critically prophetic leadership in the public square: Examining faith-inspired practice from diverse traditions*. Symposium presented at the 21st Annual Convention of University Council for Educational Administration, Alexandria, VA, Nov. 15–18.

Nelson, D. (2004). Bible knowledge and moral judgment: Knowing scripture and using ethical reasoning. *Journal of Research on Christian Education, 13*(1), 41–57.

Normore, A. H. (2012). *Educational leadership and religious diversity: How to support students and teachers of different faiths*. Paper presented at the East Asia Regional Council of Schools (EARCOS), Kuala Lumpur, Malaysia, Nov. 1–4.

Northouse, P. G. (2004). *Leadership: Theory and practice*. Thousand Oaks: Sage Publications.

Nucci, L. P. (2001). *Education in the moral domain*. New York: Cambridge University Press.

Palmer, P. (1998). Evoking the spirit in public education. *Educational Leadership, 56*(4), 6–11.

Palmer, P. (1993). *To know as we are known: Education as a spiritual journey*. San Francisco, CA: Harper.

Riaz, O., & Normore, A. H. (2008). Examining the spiritual dimension of educational leadership. *University Council for Educational Administration (UCEA), Journal of Values and Ethics in Educational Administration, 6*(4), 1–8.

Sanders, J. (1994). *Spiritual leadership: Principles of excellence for every believer*. Chicago, IL: Moody Press, The Moody Bible Institute of Chicago.

Shapiro J. P., & Stefkovich, J. A. (2005). *Ethical leadership and decision making in education: Applying theoretical perspectives to complex dilemmas*. Mahwah: Lawrence Erlbaum Associates.

Shields, C., Starratt, R., Sayani, A., Edwards, M., Langlois, L., & Fraser, D. (2004, April). *Exploring the meaning and significance of spirituality for educational leadership*. Paper presented at the annual meeting of the American Educational Research Association, San Diego, CA.

Sergiovanni, T. J. (2006). *The principalship: A reflective practice perspective.* Boston, MA: Pearson.

Sizer, T. R., & Sizer, N. F. (1999). *The students are watching: Schools and the moral contract.* Boston, MA: Beacon Press.

Smith, M. K. (2001). *David A. Kolb on experiential learning, the encyclopedia of informal education.* Available [online]: http://infed.org/b-explrn.htm

Soka Gakkai International (2008), Retrieved from, http://sgi.org/do/do.html

Sokolow, S. (2002). Enlightened leadership. *School Administrator, 59*(8), 32–6.

Solomon, J., & Hunter, J. (2002). A psychological view of spirituality and leadership: Finding meaning through Howard Gardner's notion of existential intelligence. *School Administrator, 59*(8), 38–41.

Starratt, R. (2007). Leading a community of learners: learning to be moral by engaging the morality of learning. *Educational Management Administration & Leadership, 35*(2), 165–83.

Starratt, R. (1996). *Transforming educational administration: Meaning, community and excellence.* New York: McGraw Hill Publishers.

Stokley, F. (2002). What it means to be a spiritual leader: A superintendent sees special moments in day-to-day operations. *The School Administrator, 59*(8), 46–8.

Thompson, M. C. (2000). *The congruent life: Following the inward path to fulfilling work and inspired leadership.* San Francisco: Jossey-Bass Publishers.

Thompson, S. (2004). Leading from the eye of the storm. *Educational Leadership, 61*(7), 60–3.

Tolle, E. (1999). *The power of now: A guide to spiritual enlightenment.* Novato, CA: New World Library.

van Gelder, S. R. (2006). *Spiritual uprising: holy impatience. an interview with Matthew Fox.*YES! Magazine. Available [online]: http://yesmagazine.org/article

Wheatley, M. (2002). Spirituality in turbulent times. *School Administrator, 59*(8), 42–6.

Woods, G. (2007). The "bigger feeling": The importance of spiritual experience in educational leadership. *Educational Management, Administration & Leadership, 35*(1), 135–55.

CHAPTER **10**

Temporal Leadership

> "Issues of time and timing are absolutely central to modern management: 'Where did the time go?' 'Time flies.' 'We must have this ready on time.' 'Does anybody know what time it is?' 'Time is money.' 'How long will it take?' 'I never seem to have enough time!' But despite the near preoccupation with time on the part of practicing managers, students of organization and management theory have until recently paid relatively little attention to the topic of time."
>
> (Bluedorn & Denhardt, 1988)

In the most basic sense, temporal leadership has to do with being able to read, understand and shape the history, present and future of people and institutions. Several leadership scholars have noted the importance of understanding the history of an organization (Fullan, 2001; Deal & Peterson, 1991; Schein, 1992), but we argue that it is important for leaders to extend their understanding beyond the schoolhouse, while also looking more carefully within it. Without an astute understanding of the history of a school and community, leaders run the risk of getting the school stuck in the rut of policy churn, a cycle of negative or ineffective action that yields no substantive or continuous improvement (Hess, 1999). This deep and nuanced understanding of history should inform educational leadership practice as schools seek to implement various reforms and initiatives (Brooks, 2006). A solid understanding of an organization and community's history should inform contemporary practice by suggesting which types of change were successful and which failed. Moreover, considered in glocal perspective, an understanding of history at local, national, and global levels—and an understanding of how all of these histories have been and continue to influence one another (Friedman, 2005)—allows a leader to avoid repeating the mistakes of the past.

While being an historian is important, it is equally important that leaders develop their ability to examine the way that time operates in the present. This demands not only a deep and rich understanding of the significance of time as a resource, but also as a cultural phenomenon. When viewed as a resource, time is something that leaders often have the ability to influence. Put differently—*school leaders can change time.*

In saying this, we mean that school leaders can shape: (a) who meets with whom, (b) how long and how often they meet, (c) the purposes for which they meet, and (c) under what circumstances they meet. This means that school leaders can influence and support—or ignore—short-term and long-term work of the school, both on a day-to-day basis and over a span of many years.

Much of the research on school leaders deals with the future—with the processes and outcomes of planning, crafting visions, articulating missions, identifying and achieving goals, setting aims and establishing benchmarks as indicators of success and failure (Fullan, 2005). In this sense, a large part of school leaders' work is conceptual, that is, leaders must develop the ability to see what is not there and help plot a path that will lead to intentional improvement. While this may seem a matter of imagination, in today's schools such future work is often the result of deep understanding of trends, extant data, the community and changes happening throughout the world. Moreover, leaders must develop their ability to communicate a vision that no one can see, and this is no small matter.

In this chapter, we discuss content that leaders need to *learn* in order to be *literate* with respect to temporal *leadership*. This includes understanding several ways to think about and shape the way that time works in educational organizations. In the most basic sense, this means being able to "read" the past, present and future, and to understand the ways that these can be guided by thoughtful leadership. The chapter concludes with discussion points the reader can consider and explore to *reflect* on their assumptions and practice about time. Some key concepts discussed in this chapter include the following:

- Pretext (History)
- Context
- Post-text (Future)
- Visions, missions and change.

Time: The Visible and Invisible Language

When many people think of time in their mind's eye, they see a clock. However, this is only one narrow way of thinking about something that is not absolute, but rather shaped by culture. Many schools are chock full of other objects that indicate time. These can come in the form of artifacts that show how people think about and use time: calendars, lesson plans, meeting minutes, trophy cabinets, sports schedules, the sequence of academic periods, bells, announcements of upcoming events, commemorations of past students, faculty and administrators and so on. Each of these tells us not only how we spend our time in minutes, but they are also an expression of what we value. How we spend our time, and how leaders shape the way that teachers, staff and students spend their time, communicates a great deal about the core and superfluous work of the school.

It is important to know that not everyone views time in the same way, and that these differences can be due to culture, perspective or position. Cultures can view time in many different ways. For example, in discussing anthropologist Edward Hall's (1989) work, Bluedom and Denhardt (1988) explain that:

Events may either be scheduled as separate items—one thing at a time—or people may be involved in doing several things at once. Hall describes the former as monochronic, typically associated with North Europe, and the latter, polychronic, associated with Mediterranean cultures.

Certain people and organizations are better or worse at approaching their work as a monochronic or polychromic endeavor. Moreover, Hall, Bluedom and Denhardt all acknowledge that this is only one way, albeit useful, of understanding time. Many people throughout Asia, South America, Africa, Australia and other parts of the world will see time in still different ways. Moreover, there is certainly great variation within each of these cultures as to the importance and value of time.

An astute leader will look around a school and ask themselves these types of questions:

1. Do we acknowledge past and current achievements in a meaningful and appropriate manner?
2. Is the school day organized in a way that honors tradition, or in a way that maximizes teaching and learning?
3. Are teachers inundated with tasks and responsibilities that allow them to focus on teaching and learning or are they forced to focus on rigmarole?
4. Do teachers meet with other teachers who can challenge and improve their classroom work or do they meet with people because of convenience or tradition?
5. Could the time before and after the school day be better used?
6. Are meetings efficient, informative and inspirational?
7. Is the school calendar aligned with the community and national calendar in a way that optimizes teaching and learning?
8. Is the school day teacher-centered or student-centered?
9. How often, in what ways and about what content do parents, guardians and community members have an opportunity to collaborate with the school on policy, teaching and learning?
10. How often, in what ways and about what content do students, staff, faculty and administration communicate?

Of course, these are only a few of the time-related questions a leader will ask about their school. The important issues are to (a) not make assumptions or uncritically accept traditions around time, (b) question and consider changing current daily, weekly, term, year and multiyear practice cycles, (c) seek deeper understanding of plurality of perspectives on time in school and community.

Educational Leadership and History

Educational leadership is in some ways future-oriented work. Leaders seek to improve educational processes and outcomes by supporting, challenging and encouraging students, staff, faculty, the organization and organizational groups. This demands a focus on individual and collective forward progress. As such, the field of educational leadership has rightly been built around concepts such as vision, mission, aims, goals, benchmarks, monitoring and the like. However, in order to effectively lead people and schools toward a brighter future, it is critical for leaders to understand the past.

There is no one "history"—instead there are multiple histories, as each group and person's experiences are unique given their circumstances and worldview. When we try to understand or study history, it is helpful to keep in mind that we are not only looking at events, but also into the various meanings and significance that people ascribe to those events. It is therefore important that leaders seek out information from multiple sources and understand that a program that greatly improved some students and teachers' educational experience may not have had an impact on others and, for some, may have even been negative. Leaders should not obscure or suppress individual negative experiences as outliers within positive institutional trends—if we are truly committed to the notion that every student's education is important, it is incumbent on leaders to embrace a pluralistic approach that means understanding that there are few initiatives that are positive for every teacher, student, school, community and family (Placier, 1998).

Educational Leadership and Individual History. When I was conducting the research that led to publication of the book, *The Dark Side of School Reform: Teaching in the Space Between Reality and Utopia* (Brooks, 2006), I was struck by the way that individual people experienced the same event in different ways. My research focused on school reform initiatives, and the school I studied had been through quite a few: adopting, adapting and abandoning programs, instructional practices, reporting structures and other forms of change at breathtaking pace. While the principal viewed all of the action as an indicator of how hard they were all working on improvement, the teachers' experiences were more varied. My first round of interviews suggested there were basically three ways that teachers viewed change in the school. To some, especially those at the beginning of their career, the school was exciting—a high-energy environment characterized by excitement. Every day was new! This is what they signed up for and they were up for it. A second group were less enthusiastic about change, but no less enthusiastic about their students and their jobs. This group, generally teachers who had between 4 and 15 years of experience, was change weary and mainly wanted to be left alone to do their work with the students and their peers. They worked very hard on their classroom and curricular work, but found much of the governance work in which they engaged a distraction from the core work they were there to do. A third group had been at the school for over 20 years, so they saw their work in the context of longer trends, developments and changes in school and community. These teachers had seen principals, superintendents, students, staff and faculty come and go. In some, this manifest as healthy skepticism, while others were irascible curmudgeons and a few were enthusiastic but perplexed as to why the school kept leaving behind things that worked and then rolling out a nearly identical initiative a decade or two later. From a young researchers' perspective, things were falling into place nicely. I would be able to write about these three groups, identify how people in each of them worked and hopefully suggest some lessons that leaders might learn.

But then I did my second round of interviews . . . and another, and then a fourth. The more I met with teachers over a prolonged period of time (2 years, in this case) the more I came to appreciate that the differences in the private ways people experience a common event are as important as the public activities that they share. The individual histories that shape people's lives and who they are as a student or teacher are, in many ways, intensely personal—existing in the context of preschool development, out-of-school experiences, songs that they love, sports in which they competed, games they liked to play, foods that give them comfort, individual teaching and learning moments that failed or succeeded, and the like. To one teacher, the school's efforts at common assessment were a revelation, and to another they were the tinny echo of superior efforts the school had made 20 years ago. There is great diversity of history in any school, and it is critical that leaders not lose sight of the fact that individual experience is as important as the collective—perhaps more important than the collective—and that no one narrative about what a school is, or was, should dominate and obscure the plurality of discourses in a community.

Educational Leadership and Dyadic History. A dyad is comprised of two people. As leadership is essentially a relational endeavor (Eacott, 2013), the connections that we establish, maintain and lose with individual people are of critical importance. Individual relationships shape our worldview and in many instances teach us lessons that stay with us for the duration of our work in an organization, and indeed for the rest of our lives. Many leaders explain that their approach was, in part, shaped by positive and negative experiences they had in their past—family members, coaches, community members, role models, leaders in organizations where they were followers, mentors, leaders they admired, and so on. (Alston & McClellan, 2011). Thus, reflecting on the importance of past relationships can help a leader understand why they believe what they believe and why they behave in a certain manner.

Moreover, no matter how intimate or far removed, a leader develops some kind of relationship with each follower, other leaders and stakeholders in their school community. For those who lead schools, this means that it is important to pay attention to the establishment, maintenance and growth of individual relationships throughout the organization. Leaders must be mindful of the ways their words and actions may strengthen or weaken relationships throughout the organization (Eacott, 2015). One of the most common mistakes leaders make is focusing their relationship-building activities on people who agree with them, people who tell them what they want to hear, people who share certain characteristics with them (such as race or gender) and with those in close physical proximity to them. Leaders must be mindful of not falling into this trap—it will undermine morale, increase the possibility of unintended cronyism, limit the leaders' access to insights and institutional wisdom and likely make it harder for leaders to earn trust and acceptance when they seek to implement new initiatives (Tschannen-Moran, 2014). Reaching out to connect with individuals throughout the school who are contrarian, or whose personality make it difficult to connect with is important—both in terms of the specific relationship, but also because such activity communicates to all organizational members that everyone is important.

Educational Leadership and Small Group History. Much of the work and social activities in schools happens in small groups—for example committees, grade-levels, departments, athletic teams, clubs, parent-teacher organizations. Each of these has a history that is discrete and also one that connects to the larger history of the school and community. This history can be a mix of positive, negative and mixed contributions to the school—of course, it is also important to keep in mind that people will look at the same group as a failure or success given their perspective and personal connection (Friedman, 2010). It is helpful for leaders to understand both the history of various small groups throughout the school, and their overall place in the decision-making structure of the school. That is, it is important to know more than just what a group does, but to also know their overall status and importance in the school's work and decision-making processes. Are they autonomous? Are they advisory or do they take action on their own? Do they have budgets? Are their approval processes that provide oversight for their work?

Educational Leadership and Institutional History. Institutions have histories, both internally and within the community. This is reflected in the policies, procedures, norms and culture of the school. Leaders must understand the significance of institutional history within the school, so they have a deep understanding of where the school has been as they seek to lead it forward. Internal and external institutional history may include issues related to the marginalization of people around dynamics such as race, class, gender, age, sexual orientation and position. It also has to do with the way that information has been communicated throughout the school and between the school and community (Epstein, 2001).

Educational Leadership and Local History. As schools are part of the local community, it is important for leaders to have a working understanding of the area's history. While this may mean something different in each context, knowing the issues, community leaders and political actors that have shaped local history will give a leader insight into why things are in their current state, and how that history constrains of facilitates possibilities for change.

Educational Leadership and National History. Leaders should have a working and critical knowledge of national history to help them better understand the degree to which national history has influenced local educational practice. This can be manifested as educational processes, outcomes or policy and it is helpful to know how the school and local histories map onto national priorities. For example, in many countries there was a recent boom around using digital educational technologies in schools but some schools have been left behind due to a lack of resources. Understanding which conversations and trends a school and community have been part of (or excluded from) will help a leader identify specific resources or strategies they might employ in situ.

Educational Leadership and Global History. All students, teachers, communities and school leaders are part of a global history of educational practice both because schools are increasingly diverse and because of the many ways we are linked. Developing an understanding of the ways that certain ideas and educational practices developed and then moved transnationally can help a leader understand both the past and future of educational practice. Importantly, leaders should strive for a deep understanding of global history as it allows them to identify and project future trends by mapping and extending those from the past (Brooks & Normore, 2010).

Educational Leadership and the Present

It is obvious to most leaders that they need to understand their context in order to be effective. While this is certainly true, few leaders look to time as a dynamic that might give them insights that are helpful in their work. Moreover, in order to make informed decisions in a school, it is important to develop an understanding of the ways that students, teachers, staff and families spend their time as well.

How Do Principals Spend their Time?

As Grissom, Loeb and Mitani (2013) explained:

"Managing time or making effective use of time requires techniques and good planning behaviors. Past studies and numerous how-to books suggest that one can use time efficiently and productively by setting short-term and long-term goals, keeping time logs, prioritizing tasks, making to-do lists and scheduling, and organizing one's workspace."

They go on to mention two studies that identified characteristics of effective time management, Britton and Tesser's (1991) three facets of time management:

1. Short-range planning. For school leaders, short-range planning is the ability to organize the time in a day and week so as to complete the technical, relational and conceptual tasks that facilitate the work of the school. Importantly, this is not only the organization of personal time, but also organization of time throughout the school—insuring that everyone contributing to the school's work has adequate time to complete their work.
2. Long-range planning. For school leaders, long-range planning usually takes place over a term, semester, academic year or over several years. Typically, this includes setting goals, establishing benchmarks, organizing a schedule of meetings and deliverables, and generally projecting the work of the present into the work of the future.
3. Time attitudes and behaviors. Attitudes and behaviors in relation to time have to do with establishing and maintaining a disposition toward time that positively influences the organization's work. Schools where the culture is characterized as "time poor" operate in a deficit mentality that increases anxiety and undermines productivity and collegiality. These are the schools where the answer to the question "How are you doing?" is commonly met with the response, "I'm so busy!" Every school and most educators are "busy" because education is the facilitation of an ongoing process, not the production if a single outcome. In "time-rich" schools, work is scheduled at a sensible pace, including time for planning and reflection rather than just time for "doing." Meetings are productive, interactions are at a comfortable rather than hurried pace, and each day's accomplishments help the school make incremental progress toward short and long-term goals.

Grissom and colleagues also discussed Macan's (1994) work that added mechanics —meaning the making of lists, agendas, schedules and so on, and a "preference for organization" which is prioritization of items in said lists. In sum, it is important for leaders to keep in mind that their approach to time has a profound influence on the effectiveness, culture, educational processes and educational outcomes of a school (Grissom, Loeb & Matani, 2014). Sadly, many school leaders are driven by the need to show that they are doing everything they can possibly do to help their schools. While this is admirable in intent, it can mean imposing an impossible regime of initiatives and changes without discussion, negotiation or even pausing to consider if change and new ways of doing things are necessary. The result are hurried schools where educators and students are not afforded the time to teach and learn (Wolcott, 1970). School leaders would do well to remember that it is often more effective to remove responsibilities from teachers and students' roles in order to give them more time to focus (Brooks, 2007).

How Do Teachers, Students, Staff and Families Spend Their Time?

People in school communities spend their time in a variety of ways—some of these complement the rhythms of the school calendar and others cause friction. Importantly, there is a great deal of research that indicates students and teachers will perform better if they are able to spend more time on teaching and learning. While this may seem obvious, many school leaders implement policies and procedures that decrease the amount of time spent on these activities and increase the demands on teachers and students to do everything but teaching and learning—serve on committees, fill out paperwork, input data, attend non-educational events, participate in professional development activities that do not relate to their core duties (Brooks, 2006). It is important for leaders to understand that they can change this dynamic—by restructuring tasks, carefully considering timelines, and by seeking to ensure that the right people are in the right space at the right time doing the right work. Often in schools, leaders do not think about this last point—but it is the one that should guide nearly every structural and organizational decision in the school.

As a final note, it is important for school leaders to develop an understanding of the ways that people in the school community spend their out-of-school time. Are they in technology-rich environments? Do they work outside of school? Are they homeless? Is the family situation difficult? What pressures are affecting the local economy that might shape out-of-school and in-school experiences? These and still other issues are critical to an understanding of the educational context in which leadership happens, as it has both direct and indirect effects on school experiences and academic performance (Hallinger & Heck, 2010).

Leadership and the Future

Traditionally, the orientation for understanding the future in leadership studies has been strategic planning (Kaufman & Herman, 1991), yet educational researchers in globalization studies suggest that a more appropriate approach might be found in future trends (Green, 1997). There is ample evidence that strategic planning was never effective in business, and that educators likewise have reaped little, if any, benefit from the process despite ongoing enthusiasm for the approach (Mintzberg, 1994). As an alternative to strategic planning, future trends instead looks at longitudinal data and, rather than looking at them in isolation (treating the school as a closed system), integrates these data with other longitudinal data to promote connected leadership via a future trends framework. Marx (2006a, 2006b) identified 16 distinct future trends of immediate concern to educational leaders:

1. For the first time in history, the old will outnumber the young. (Note: This aging trend generally applies to developed nations. In underdeveloped nations, just is opposite is true: the young will substantially outnumber the old.)
2. Majorities will become minorities, creating ongoing challenges for social cohesion.
3. Social and intellectual capital will become economic drivers, intensifying competition for well-educated people.
4. Technology will increase the speed of communication and the pace of advancement or decline.
5. The Millennial Generation will insist on solutions to accumulated problems and injustices, while an emerging Generation E will call for equilibrium.
6. Standards and high-stakes tests will fuel a demand for personalization in an education system increasingly committed to lifelong human development.
7. Release of human ingenuity will become a primary responsibility of education and society.
8. Continuous improvement will replace quick fixes and defense of the status quo.
9. Scientific discoveries and societal realities will force widespread ethical choices.
10. Common opportunities and threats will intensify a worldwide demand for planetary security.
11. Polarization and narrowness will bend toward reasoned discussion, evidence, and consideration of varying points of view.
12. International learning, including diplomatic skills, will become basic, as nations vie for understanding and respect in an interdependent world.
13. Greater numbers of people will seek personal meaning in their lives in response to an intense, high-tech, always-on, fast-moving society.
14. Understanding will grow that sustained poverty is expensive, debilitating, and unsettling.
15. Pressure will grow for society to prepare people for jobs and careers that may not currently exist.
16. Competition will increase to attract and keep qualified educators. Marx (2006, Winter) explains the importance of these trends:

All organizations, especially education systems, are of this world, not separate from it. To earn their legitimacy, they need to be connected with the communities, countries, and world they serve. Unless they are constantly scanning the environment, educators will soon find themselves isolated . . . and out of touch . . . Understanding these forces is the key to unlocking rigidity and reshaping our schools, colleges, and other institutions for the future. In a fast-changing world, looking at tomorrow and seeing it only as a little bit more or a little bit less of today won't cut it as we move into the future. As educators and community leaders, we need to use powerful trends data, coupled with imagination, as we plan ahead. A challenge will be to not only develop a plan but to turn it into a living strategy—a strategic vision that will help us lead our students, schools, and communities into an even more successful future (p. 4).

Transformational Leadership: Visions, Missions, Objectives and Aims

Over the past 40 years, educational leadership scholars and practitioners have developed a vocabulary for talking about the future. Much of this revolves around four concepts: vision, mission, objectives and aims. Vision is the conceptualization and communication of a projected future. Visions can be personal and collective, and it is important for educators in general and educational leaders in particular to understand this distinction and to reflect on, develop and critique both. Often, leaders poorly communicate their vision for the school and/or confuse their personal vision with the collective vision. This means that they impose their vision on people by fiat when a school's vision should be co-constructed by all members of faculty, staff, students and the community. Failing to authentically facilitate an ongoing process of visioning can at best result in confusion and at worst make people throughout the school community feel a sense of alienation—that they have no connection to the work of the school (Brooks, Hughes & Brooks, 2008).

The mission articulates the basic purposes of a school, and often goes a bit further by making a statement about the role of the school in the lives of people who work and study in it, and it's role in the community. A school's mission can be helpful in orienting the work of a school so they do not experience "mission creep" and start to shift their purpose unintentionally.

Objectives are more specific and less abstract than a vision or mission. They make clear benchmarks that the school is working toward. This might be in improving educational processes, achievement outcomes, organizational culture, internal and external communication, technology integration, or any other tangible aspect of the school. An objective can be attained—it is measurable and specific. Aims are the components of an objective that help leaders and followers identify the various formal and informal changes that need to occur in order to achieve an objective.

Change Leadership: Shaping Ongoing Experiments in Schools

The concept of change has had a tremendous influence on the way we think about the future in education. Michael Fullan (2014) in particular has been particularly influential in this area, but rather than rewrite his work we offer a model that embodies some key aspects of change (Figure 10.1).

The figure suggests a multifaceted conceptualization of leaders' work in relation to change:

1. Moral Purpose. Leaders must talk and act with moral purpose, always putting students at the center of their decision making and moving the school toward a just and equitable future.

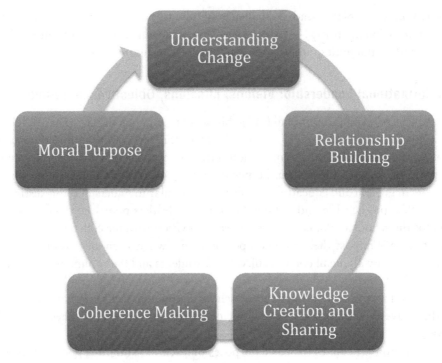

FIGURE 10.1 Change Process

2. Understanding Change. Leaders must help people throughout the organization understand the necessity for change, the nature of the change on a day-to-day basis and the future toward which they are working.
3. Relationship Building. Leaders must establish, maintain and grow relationships with staff, students, faculty and community members as a way to co-construct rather than impose change.
4. Knowledge Creation and Sharing. As information about the change become available it is important for leaders to both share and solicit input on the interpretation of information. Leaders who share the work of change will find much greater understanding of the initiative and willingness for participation.
5. Coherence Making. As schools are complicated systems, changing one aspect of the work routinely changes others. As change is implemented it is important for leaders to make sure that the intended and unintended consequences of change are indeed moving the school toward intended and positive changes.

As leaders do this work, Fullan (2014) reminds us that they are most effective when they offer hope, bring energy to the work and practice in an enthusiastic manner. This leader-centered work then influences the internal and external commitment of followers and ultimately yields changed processes and outcomes. The bottom line is that change is difficult, complicated and ongoing in schools. Each content area experiences continued change and student, teachers, staff, administrators and community members cycle into and out of the school. Critically, Fullan's work reminds us that change has no end, and is instead a process that leaders should invite a school into rather than demanding their participation.

TEMPORAL LEADERSHIP: A SUMMARY

We encourage school leaders to deepen their literacy in relation to time and to understand that they can change time in the sense that they can help put the right people in the right space at the right time doing the right work through their structural and organizational decisions. Whether it be an immediate, short-term or long-term issue, the ways that a leader understands history, the present and future will help them make more informed decisions as they lead a school toward improvement and seek to avoid mistakes of the past.

DISCUSSION

1. Interview five people who have a perspective on the history of an educational institution. Contrast their recollections and interpretations of events, and of what the institution stood for (and stands for today). Do these differences fall along racial, ethnic, gender, language (or other) lines?
2. What do you think are the most important contextual cues that help you understand the present situation in a school? Are there formal and informal issues to which you pay more attention?
3. How does the past, present and future of education relate to the past, present and future of a community? In what ways are they related and unrelated?
4. How do people throughout the school and community envision the future of education and of local schools? What is happening at local, state, national and global levels that make them think these things will come true?
5. What is the role of leadership in shaping perspectives on the past, present and future?

REFERENCES

Alston, J. A., & McClellan, P. A. (2011). *Herstories: Leading with the lessons of the lives of black women activists*. Peter Lang.

Bass, B. M., & Riggio, R. E. (2006). *Transformational leadership*. Psychology Press.

Bluedorn, A. C., & Denhardt, R. B. (1988). Time and organizations. *Journal of management*, 14(2), 299–320.

Brooks, J. S. (2006). *The dark side of school reform: Teaching in the space between reality and utopia*. Lanham, MD: Rowman & Littlefield Education.

Brooks, J. S., Hughes, R., & Brooks, M. C. (2008). Fear and trembling in the American high school: Educational reform and teacher alienation. *Educational Policy*, 22(1), 45–62.

Brooks, J. S., & Normore, A. H. (2010). Educational leadership and globalization: Literacy for a glocal perspective. *Educational Policy*, 24(1), 52–82.

Deal, T. E., & Peterson, K. D. (1991). *The leader's role in shaping school culture*. Washington, DC: United States Department of Education.

Eacott, S. (2015). *Educational leadership relationally: A theory and methodology for educational leadership, management and administration*. Springer.

Eacott, S. (2013). "Leadership" and the social: time, space and the epistemic. *International Journal Of Educational Management*, 27(1), 91–101.

Epstein, J. L. (2001). *School, family, and community partnerships: Preparing educators and improving schools*. Westview Press, 5500 Central Avenue, Boulder, CO 80301.

Friedman, T. L. (2005). *The world is flat: A brief history of the twenty-first century*. Macmillan.

Friedman, W. A. (2010). Leadership and history. *Handbook of Leadership Theory and Practice*, 291–304.

Fullan, M. (2001). *Whole school reform: Problems and promises*. Chicago, IL: Chicago Community Trust.

Fullan, M. (2005). *Leadership & sustainability: System thinkers in action*. Corwin Press.

Fullan, M. (2014). *Leading in a culture of change personal action guide and workbook*. John Wiley & Sons.

Grissom, J. A., Loeb, S., & Mitani, H. (2013). *Principal time management skills: Explaining patterns in principals' time use and effectiveness*. Standford University: Center for Education Policy.

Hall, E. T. (1989). *Beyond culture*. Anchor.

Hallinger, P., & Heck, R. H. (2010). Collaborative leadership and school improvement: Understanding the impact on school capacity and student learning. *School leadership and management*, 30(2), 95–110.

Hess, F. M. (1999). *Spinning wheels: The politics of urban school reform*. Washington, DC: Brookings Institute.

Green, A. (1997). *Education, globalization and the nation state*. New York: Macmillan.

Kaufman, R., & Herman, J. (1991). *Strategic planning in education: Rethinking, restructuring, revitalizing*. Lancaster, PA: Technomic Publishing.

Marx, G. T. (2006a). *Sixteen trends: Their profound impact on our future*. Alexandria, VA: Educational Research Service.

Marx, G. T. (2006b). *Future-focused leadership: Preparing schools, students, and communities for tomorrow's realities*. Alexandria, VA: Association for Supervision and Curriculum Development.

Mintzberg, H. (1994). *The rise and fall of strategic planning*. London: Prentice Hall International.

Schein, E. H. (1992). *Organizational culture and leadership*. 2nd ed. San Francisco, CA: Jossey-Bass.

Placier, M. (1998). Uses of history in present-day qualitative studies of schools: The case of the junior high school. *International Journal of Qualitative Studies in Education*, 11(2), 303–22.

Tschannen-Moran, M. (2014). *Trust matters: Leadership for successful schools*. John Wiley & Sons.

CHAPTER 11

Holistic Health Leadership[1]

Educational leadership textbooks have tended to neglect issues related to holistic health including mental and physical wellbeing, even though research has long established a link between physical health, mental health and learning. This chapter will explain this research and link it to the various school-level factors that educational leaders can influence. The focus of our inquiry is holistic leadership, particularly in terms of examining holistic approaches to the development of educational leaders. We first provide a brief review of the scholarly literature pertaining to holistic health and literacy leadership. Second, drawing from earlier work of Leonard, Schilling and Normore (2014), we present "lived experience" (Chase, 2011, p. 422) of two educators. Both educators are involved in educational leadership projects. Their experiences help us provide a backdrop for examining and understanding holistic literacy and leadership.

Consistent with previous chapters, we begin with an introduction to the *learning* about holistic leadership concepts such as physical health, wellbeing, and mental health. Next, we will demonstrate how health and holistic *literacy* is analyzed through the use of case studies. The cases are designed to help readers identify and analyze the way that the key concepts are practiced in schools, the level of sustainability, and the environmental impact they have in local communities and throughout the world. Then, we focus on an educational *leader's* ability to influence the health dynamics of a school through formal and informal means. It emphasizes skills that include spirit, mind and body health garnering community support for health issues and ethical issues related to health. Finally, we offer a series of *reflective* discussion questions to help decipher how holistic health literacy is practiced on a daily basis for educational leaders.

HOLISTIC LEADERSHIP THEORY

Popper (2004) asserts that leadership is a relationship that extends beyond the properties of leaders and followers, because "the conceptualization of leadership as relationship permits an integrative view of leaders, followers, and circumstances, and thus reduces the bias . . . of giving too much weight to the leader" (p. 118). According to Popper, influence is a central feature of leadership and it arises from the emotive force that emanates from leadership relationships. It is this emotive force that creates the leadership mandate of charismatic leaders which has evolved into its operationalized and most researched form—transformational leadership.

In describing the three forms of relationship that leadership can produce, Popper (2004) noted that *developmental* relationships are characterized by the ability to create an environment of psychological safety that allows participants to engage in developmentally oriented behaviors, including those most closely associated with transformational leadership: individualized consideration, autonomy reinforcement, and the promotion of trust, self-confidence, self-esteem and achievement orientation.

However, even this interpretation remains constrained by the very limitation that it exposes: that is, positioning the leader as the locus of causality in the leadership relationship. Popper (2004) hints at the solution by referring to the routinization of charisma, noting that this process breaks the bond between follower and a specific leader and converts it into a property of the institution or organization. Thus, the glaring conundrum in the leadership literature lies in how to successfully instigate this routinization process. Holistic leadership theory suggests that the answer lies in defining the unit of analysis not as the leader, the follower, the circumstance or the relationship, but rather as a holistic system of development.

Holistic leadership proffers seven fundamental assumptions about the nature of effective leadership:

1. Successful outcomes result from an orientation toward development.
2. The healthiest and most productive development is done collaboratively.
3. The leadership unit shapes the context of collaboration.
4. The core leadership unit is the individual, which makes every participant a leader within his or her own sphere of influence.
5. The intrinsic desire for meaningful purpose suggests that every individual wants to realize his or her best potential.
6. Holistically-led collaboration requires that the participant's right to self-determination be respected.
7. The exercise of self-determination in a way that realizes the individual's best potential, results from an iterative process that must be supported.

Holistic Development

The theory and resulting definition of holistic leadership presented here is not the first or only one attempted. On her website, Orlov (2003) describes holistic leadership as a methodology focusing on systemic development that impacts "oneself as leader, others as followers, and the environment" all resulting in "a journey that leads toward transformation at the individual, team, and organizational/community levels" (p. 1). Taggart (2009) offers a holistic leadership model on his website that he refers to as an "integrated approach to leadership." It includes components such as organizational teaching, personal mastery, reflection, inquiry, stewardship, visionary and strategic action, results orientation, thought leadership, power-sharing, collaboration, and nurturing. Similar to Orlov, Taggart's model also addresses a psycho-spiritual triad of personal wellness focused on mind, body, and spirit.

Wapner and Demick (2003) maintain that holistic development is inherently systems-oriented and identify the "person-in-environment" as the system state. This interface is contextualized according to three dimensions that relate to both person and environment: the bio-physical, the psychosocial, and the sociocultural. A holistic system's features are interactionistic, involve a process of adaptation, reflect change as a feature of transformation, and require synchronization and coordination of its operating elements (Magnusson, 2001). From this perspective, leader, follower, and circumstance are not jockeying for a position of control but are instead discrete components of a series of interconnected systems that continuously "adapt, transform, coordinate and synchronize" with each other throughout the leadership process.

Lips-Wiersma and Morris (2009) add to this construct by emphasizing the role of meaningful work in framing the holistic development process, stating that "a sense of coherence and wholeness is particularly important in experiencing meaningfulness" (p.502). Based on research into the elements of meaningful work, they produced a model of holistic development comprised of four quadrants—developing and becoming self, unity with others, expressing full potential, and serving others—that, it can be argued, orient the person-in-environment system state. Popper (2004) also addresses the role of meaning in symbolic leadership relationships by highlighting the impact that leaders have on followers' self-concept and motivation for self-expression. Leaders in positions of formal authority have the opportunity to project values that followers can internalize as prized components of their self-concept and sources of motivation through linkages to an idealized vision articulated by the leader.

Lips-Wiersma and Morris's (2009) theory of holistic development asserts that leadership does not, and in fact cannot, manufacture or manage meaning for others. It is instead challenged to find ways to promote the integration of self-defined meaningful purposes that emerge organically from the individual and are subsequently aligned with the broader goals and objectives of the organization. This view is embodied in the definition offered by Rogers, Mentkowski, and Hart (2006) in which holistic development is described as "a further integration of the meaning making self" (p. 500). In their investigation of the relationship between holistic development and performance, Rogers, Mentkowski, and Hart (2006) conducted a meta-analytic review of research studies in support of their meta-theory that "person in context" and intentional focus of meaning converge to create a framework for holistic development and performance. Their meta-theory forms a matrix in which the structures of the person and external contextual frames such as the working environment intersect a plane of internal vs. external foci of meaning. This matrix yields four domains of growth: reasoning, performance, self-reflection, and development. Several concepts emerged from their analysis that would be germane to an emerging theory of holistic leadership. When combined, these theories coalesce as a leadership imperative highlighting the need for:

- An assemblage of self-directed participants.
- Environments that promote the development of meta-cognitive skills like reflective thinking and pattern recognition to support the active use of mental models that will sustain constructive, autonomous decision making.

- Leaders that engage participants in ways that demonstrate respect for the autonomy and individual capacities of their members.
- A collective approach to the development of member capacities in a way that seeds meaningfulness into the work environment.

These perspectives on holistic development map to elements of the leadership theories that have retained their salience and applicability over time. They include the relationship between leader personality traits and leadership performance; personal and organizational values and leadership behavior; leader influence and follower motivation; and follower motivation and organizational performance. Further, this convergence of holistic development and integrative approaches to leadership presage the type of learning organizations described by Senge (2006).

Current educational leadership discourse is typically characterized by discussions that serve to broaden our conceptualization of what constitutes effective leadership. Moreover, this turn in the leadership discussion has served to promote "dialogue across local, national, and international boundaries" (Normore, 2010, p. xiii), with the goal of "cross-fertilization of ideas and experiences" (p. xiv). One important outcome of this cross-fertilization is the increasing interest in exploring the multidimensionality of leadership and leadership development. From the perspective of the business world, it has been suggested that the recent high-profile corporate failures have raised many questions about the narrow focus of traditional leadership programs (Quatro, Waldman, & Galvin, 2007). Similarly, in education, Branson (2007) suggests that the uncertainties inherent in today's world have caused people to "want their leaders to act morally" (p. 469). As a result, the role of moral judgment and, more recently, moral literacy (Tuana, 2007), are now widely identified in the educational leadership literature.

While there may be increasing emphasis on the moral dimension of leadership in education, less sustained attention has been given to other non-traditional dimensions that characterize holistic health literacy and leadership. Nevertheless, a review of the literature revealed that holistic leadership, as a concept worthy of study, is gaining momentum. References to leadership development programs are beginning to include examining ways to "integrate mind, body, and spirit to become more effective leaders" (Shinn, 2010, p. 58). For example, Quatro et al. (2007) propose that corporate leadership development programs and initiatives, which traditionally have focused on the analytical aspects of leadership, should be "more holistic in scope" (p. 248). Alternatively, spiritually enlightened leaders would be skillful in enabling followers to connect their work to moral and ethical values. Accordingly, cultivating the spiritual domain would include a focus on self-reflection and meditative thinking, similar to Branson's (2007) structured self-reflection for educational leaders.

Discussions of holistic leadership vary in terms of which aspects of humanity appear to warrant our focus and sustained attention. For example, based on her academic background in organizational learning and social work, as well as her experiences with leadership training in a variety of organizations, Julie Orlov (2003) states that holistic leadership is "being able to lead from the mind, the heart, and the soul" (p. 1). Clearly, there is no reference to the physical (i.e., the body) aspect of holistic leadership development. In stark contrast, Sinclair (2007), in her treatise on how to become an enlightened leader, emphasizes the importance of paying attention to the body for gaining new insights for leadership. Alternatively, Taggart (2010), a self-described student of leadership for over 20 years and creator of a leadership consulting organization, omitted any references to mind, body, and spirit in presenting his model of holistic leadership. Therefore, we may infer that the apparent lack of consensus regarding holistic leadership may be the result of authors' use of different terminology, at least to some extent.

Inherent in discussions of holistic—mind, body, spirit—leadership development is the challenge of countering criticisms from those who may conceptualize effective leadership solely as an activity of the disembodied mind—one where ration, reason, cognitive mastery, and objectivity prevail (Sinclair, 2007). Riaz and Normore (2008) acknowledge that challenge in their examination of the spiritual dimension of educational leadership: "spirituality is a significant dimension of human existence that is often silenced in the public school system" (p. 1).

On the "body" front of the holistic leadership development discussion is the challenge of resisting or subverting the dominant paradigm that leadership is just a cognitive activity; it is also a physical one. According to Shinn (2010), effective leaders understand the connections among their physical, mental, and emotional capabilities. Consequently, some innovative leadership training programs are incorporating physical exercise and personal reflection into the curricula. Similarly, Sinclair (2007) claims that, traditionally, leaders have been seen as a bodiless activity of the mind. She also advocates that focusing on breathing in a conscious way can help foster composure and attentiveness, and may even change the practice of leadership.

Despite the differing definitions and terminology embedded in discussions of holistic leadership, there is growing consensus that leadership is more than an activity of the mind. Moreover, there is increasing recognition that leadership development programs need to be broader in scope to incorporate the multidimensionality of humanity.

TRANSLATING THEORY TO PRACTICE: VOICES FROM THE FIELD

What follows is an account of experiences of two professors of education at a university who attempted to connect theory and practice. In relating their reflections on these processes, a major goal is to underscore the lack of attention to, as well as the importance of, addressing the *holistic* development of moral leaders.

Educator A

In 2003, the educational leadership faculty in our department designed and implemented a new educational leadership master's program. As our educational leadership team collaborated to develop the program, many of us shared our struggle of authenticity—reconciling beliefs with practice. We faced a tremendous challenge in developing the program within redesign guidelines, national and state standards, as well as our own conflicting views of what a leadership preparation program should look like for real-world applications. What was quite interesting, upon reflection, is that, as a committee, we took our responsibility very seriously, but the nature of that responsibility often differed. In applying Starratt's (2004) work on ethical leadership and the ethics of responsibility, I was able to more fully understand that process.

Starratt (2004) has stated that educational leaders must be morally responsible, not only in a preventative sense but in a proactive one as well. Responsibility, in the latter sense, is three-dimensional in that the leader is: (i) responsible as; (ii) responsible to and, (iii) responsible for. I believe that the educational leadership team members felt responsible in all three of these ways, with each member being responsible in different ways on different issues. One example is that of meeting the redesign guidelines, particularly the request for identifying the empirical basis for educational practices and teaching methods covered in the newly developed courses for the program. There was considerable deliberation about which research studies to include with some of the program development team members placing substantial importance on integrating studies from journals and organizations that were reportedly considered to be embraced by the State Board of Regents and Board of Education. This position suggested they felt a primary responsibility *as* state employees, *to* state governing agencies, *for* developing an educational program based on strict adherence to state guidelines. Alternatively, other team members expressed dismay at such an approach, and advocated that there was enough expertise on the committee to locate, examine, and utilize empirical studies that were deemed most appropriate for meeting course and program goals and objectives. This stance indicated that they felt a primary responsibility *as* program developers, *to* prospective program candidates, *for* developing an educational leadership program informed, but not constrained, by state guidelines.

In my work as a member of the educational leadership team, I was able to experience first-hand the challenges of working collaboratively to develop a new program. And while there were differences in how we conceptualized our responsibilities as, to, and for when developing the program, reflecting upon the process allowed me to ask important questions about how we worked through our differences while remaining true to our beliefs. The experience, and reflection upon the experience, has helped me realize the importance of knowing who we are, of attempting to clarify our identity, and of understanding whom we are responsible as, to, and for. The quest for authenticity demands that we participate in this process.

Structured Self-Reflection

While my work in the area of administrator preparation program development has tended to focus on emphasizing the moral aspects of leadership, my involvement in teacher preparation program development evolved to include an emphasis on the *holistic* development and wellbeing of teachers (Ryan & Deci, 2000). This emphasis on holism emerged from the realization that there existed a lack of cultural and ethnic diversity among graduates of teacher education programs, which necessitated our focusing on culturally responsive teaching. In an effort to address that challenge, we explored the notion of the reflective practitioner as being very powerful in the process of cultivating whole teachers. Branson's (2007) deeply structured reflective process provided an avenue for facilitating the process of preservice and inservice teachers in connecting their respective life experiences to their stated teaching behaviors.

As an example, in 2008, a colleague and I conducted a qualitative case study (Leonard & Basinger, 2008) to field test an instructional technique—structured self-reflection—based on Begley's (2003) values framework and Branson's (2007) components of Self. The instructional technique was a modified version of Branson's (2007) deeply structured reflective process, which we implemented in a required teacher education course. The instructional technique assisted teacher candidates in the process of critically reflecting on their life experiences and the impact of those experiences on the development and interaction of their respective self-components: self-concept, self-esteem, motives, values, beliefs, and teaching behaviors. The findings supported the premise that facilitating teacher candidates' understanding of self through structured self-reflection enhances moral literacy and helps to create *whole* teachers who are culturally responsive in their teaching.

Holistic Health Development

The essential message in sharing the preceding examples is that (i) I have always tried to connect and align my work and responsibilities as a professor-teacher, a professor-scholar, and a professor-administrator; and (ii) while my efforts have been rewarding in many ways, I realize that I have fallen short in terms of conceptualizing and exploring a fully *holistic approach to leadership*. Moreover, my contention is that this is the norm and providers of administrator preparation programs typically have focused on the intellectual aspects of leadership development to the detriment of other important aspects of our humanity, all of which are integral for the holistic development of moral leaders. In other words, I propose that sustainable effective leadership performance is best achieved when leaders recognize the critical interdependence of mind, body, and spirit (Quatro, Wladman, & Galvin, 2007) and the importance of purposefully aligning, developing, and integrating these domains as essential components of organizational culture.

As I reflect on my journey as a faculty member and administrator, I realize that, typically, I have tried to separate or compartmentalize the emotional, mental, physical, spiritual, and intellectual experiences or aspects of my being. For example, invariably my "to do" lists are categorized under personal and professional, even though some clearly impact both private and public life. This begs some important questions. Would not taking 10 minutes to meditate, sit quietly in silence, during the workday improve my ability to think more clearly and, perhaps, make more enlightened professional decisions? Shouldn't a 15-minute walk mid-morning get me away from my computer, help keep me physically fit, and perhaps positively increase my energy for teaching a class that evening? Would not taking time to emotionally connect with colleagues help engender trust and, perhaps, enhance collaborative initiatives? In examining the spiritual dimension of educational leadership, Riaz and Normore (2008) suggest that leaders can strengthen their "spiritual muscles" (p. 4). The authors also claimed that "human beings are endowed with four intelligences at birth including mental, social, emotional, and spiritual" (Covey, 2004, cited in Riaz & Normore, 2008, p.4). While perhaps not an "intelligence" as such, I would add the physical realm to these four dimensions of leadership. Informed by my recent deliberations and beliefs about the significance of holism for human growth and development, I am currently engaged in facilitating faculty involvement in departmental visioning and strategic planning through the incorporation of activities that engage mind, body, and spirit. This process is in its preliminary stages and we are all neophytes in terms of how best to approach the holistic development of our professional learning community. However, to some extent we have attended, at least on a superficial level, to addressing the physical realm (e.g., instead of sitting to discuss an educational initiative during a professional learning initiative meeting, we walk with a partner and return to discuss whole group). We have also shared quotes and poetry to spark our "spiritual muscles."

Suffice it to say, these experiences I share pertaining to the holistic development of moral leaders are elementary attempts to explore and understand the notion of holism and its implications for creating and sustaining professional learning communities. Furthermore, these deliberations about holistic leadership underscore emerging and still unanswered questions. For example, should we address the challenge of examining current leader preparation programs for ways to integrate holistic approaches to the development of moral leaders? And, if so, how?

Educator B

Prior to my current position, I worked for 10 years with underserved youth in responsibility-based afterschool physical activity programs. I am now heavily involved in Louisiana Gaining Early Awareness and Readiness for Undergraduate Programs (GEAR UP). The mission of LA GEAR UP is to increase the number of low-income students who enter and succeed in post-secondary education (Louisiana Board of Regents, 2005). Accomplishing the program's mission requires a multifaceted approach including summer learning camps (SLC), professional development of teachers and counselors (PD), and year-round Explorers Clubs in schools. In addition to directing summer camps, I serve as the leadership coordinator for LA GEAR UP. In this role, I develop leadership and Explorers Club activities each year as options for all SLC and also conduct PD activities with teachers and school counselors. As such, I have had the opportunity to refine my philosophy on the development of youth leadership.

Leadership training for LA GEAR UP is designed to help students learn and practice personal and interpersonal leadership skills within a supportive community of peers and mentors. The leadership style that I espouse is empowerment- and service-oriented. We want students to experience leadership as an opportunity for "voice" and "choice" and to consider the importance of raising others up with them as leaders. This is a different philosophy than some of the more authoritarian leadership styles (and ones which our kids have likely been exposed to the most).

The short-term nature of summer camps, and the larger scale of LA GEAR UP, necessitated a much more intensive and strategic approach to leadership development. I incorporated more team-based challenges that would dismantle walls of discrimination, prejudice, and insecurity, and compel diverse participants to work cooperatively to achieve success. Some of the activities are associated with Adventure Education.

Adventure experiences generally consist of physical team-building challenges that encourage the development of specific leadership skills like trust, communication, and cooperation in a fun environment. The activities elicit different feelings for different individuals and some participants may initially be uncomfortable participating in certain activities. Participants are encouraged to engage fully in the experience with the understanding that, ultimately, each person can choose their level of participation and challenge. This concept is called Challenge By Choice (Project Adventure, 1995, p. 9). Another important concept is the Full Value Contract (Project Adventure, 1995). This is, essentially, an agreement to respect and value all participants and their contributions.

At the beginning of each leadership session, we discuss our Full Value Contract as the following guidelines or expectations:

1. Be respectful (of yourself, others, equipment and space).
2. Be safe (physically and emotionally).
3. Be here now (be focused and "in the zone").
4. Let go and move on (persistence; the key is how you respond to challenges).

These guidelines, and the adventure activities, set up an environment ripe for leadership development. However, it is the use of debriefing after the activities, and at the end of each session, that provides the most powerful opportunities for processing the emergence and display of leadership skills, challenges or barriers to success, and strategies for transfer of leadership skills to other settings.

Across my experiences in promoting youth leadership, a consistent set of beliefs have emerged and been reinforced. These are described below.

Belief in the Capacity of Young People to be Leaders

With continued emphasis on disempowering curriculum and standardized testing, and the beat-down of even our most effective teachers, the most critical roles of students may be as educational leaders and active participants in changing the current school culture. After all, teachers often remain in the profession because of the inspiration of their students. In our programs, I have seen numerous youth participants demonstrate surprisingly mature resilience and moral leadership. For me, the challenge continues to be helping all youth participants see in themselves what we see and nurturing motivation to explore that capability. This process cannot be top-down nor can you pour leadership rhetoric on kids and hope it sticks. They need to experience personal meaning in the process and feel that there is some benefit to being courageous enough to step up as a leader.

Belief in the Use of the Physical Domain as a Medium for Holistic Development

The physical challenges that we use in LA GEAR UP stimulate cognitive development in terms of strategic problem solving. Additionally, physical activity promotes unique opportunities for personal and social development (Hellison, 2011). Participating in physical activities or challenges facilitates body, space, and self-awareness and requires the courage to put your body and physical ability on display. Since we are typically in a gym with a variety of different types of equipment, some participants may initially perceive challenges through the lens of competition. This can elicit a higher level of emotions (e.g., pressure on oneself and others to be first to finish). These situations provide us with powerful teachable moments where we can reinforce the importance of focusing on your group, the positive results of cooperation, and the notion that all of us can be, and are, winners in the challenges. Contrary to popular belief, this is a good thing.

Belief in Reflection as a Key to Continual Leadership Development

As noted earlier, debriefing is an important component following the team-building challenges. Debriefing provides opportunities to use analogies in reflection. For example, in our Stepping Stones activity, five or six students work together using life support vehicles (wood blocks) to transport their group across the toxic land to another planet that has food, water, and most importantly, available technology use. This is a challenging activity that requires balance and physical support as students must share blocks in order to advance across the toxic land. At the end of this activity, we often consider their destination on the court as students' postsecondary aspirations (i.e., where do you see yourself after high school?). We discuss barriers, or challenges (toxic land), and sources of support (life support vehicles) in achieving their goals.

Deeper reflection about morality and values is also important and occurs at the end of the leadership session. In some years, I have focused on a theme such as "take your place," which was emphasized by Cicely Tyson's character in the *Madea's Family Reunion* movie. In other years, I have been inspired by something I have read. For example, in Wayne Dyer's 1996 book, *Your Sacred Self*, he discusses the three most difficult things in life: (i) return love for hate (positive for negative); (ii) include the excluded and (iii) admit when you are wrong. These points are conducive for jump-starting students to consider how these might be put into action in their own lives and for discussing serious issues in schools like bullying and our role as leaders in addressing bullying.

Belief in the Importance of Empowerment in Leadership Development

For leadership to develop, youth must feel empowered. This requires adults to respect youth and their right to ownership in the process. It also means that we need to be genuine in our empowerment and listen to the voices of youth, even if we do not necessarily agree with their perspective all the time. As Hellison (2011, p. 27) notes, this does not mean, "caving in to everything kids want or demand." We must be courageous in standing up for our core values and in confronting kids when warranted. The key is in how we confront them—with respect and valuing what they can positively contribute and how they respond to the situation.

In other work (Schilling, Martinek, & Tan, 2002), my colleagues and I have articulated principles of empowerment that affect leadership development including: (i) one size does not fit all; (ii) various contexts dictate the type and potential for leadership of youth participants and (iii) leadership development is a dynamic process marked by grand successes, disappointing failures, and, sometimes, average experiences. This process necessitates an understanding of the balance for knowing the best situations and potential for empowerment, and times when empowerment is not effective and could even be detrimental.

As a final discussion point, small and barely recognizable windows of opportunity for empowerment can result in remarkable possibilities for youth leadership. It is important not to discount such windows. The story of Ja'Marcus Goudeau is a notable example. Ja'Marcus (also known as Turbo) attended LA GEAR UP Sports Medicine Camp one week in 2012. The entire group that week was strong and cohesive, but there was something else remarkable under the surface about this group. After graduation dinner and our awards ceremony, Ja'Marcus was granted his request to share his poetry about camp, **Pass the Message**. I wasn't sure about the exact meaning of the poetry but felt it was powerful. Buoyed by the strength of his own words and voice, and by the positive response to his poetry, Ja'Marcus asked if he could share another one about his brother, titled, **Understanding**. Opening this small window of opportunity, and trusting in Ja'Marcus, fueled his courage to share his poetry and his pain. In turn, other campers felt empowered to embrace their own pain and fears, which resulted in a tremendous release of deep, pent-up emotions. This experience significantly impacted the high school students, our college student counselors, and the adult staff. The impact on Ja'Marcus continues as he, along with some classmates, have started a poetry club at his school.

Developing Self-Awareness/Reflection

In each of the experiences, self-awareness and reflection were critical for opening doors for leadership development. Educator A discussed the importance of Branson's (2007) structured reflective process for preservice and inservice teachers as well as faculty. Debriefing following the team-building challenges in Educator B's LA GEAR UP camps enhanced self-awareness and reflective skills of youth leaders. Self-awareness and reflection are also critical for those leading the initiatives. Through critical reflection of our needs, experiences, and behaviors, we grow as people and professionals, develop consistency between what we say and do, and refine strategies for enhancing holistic literacy development.

Fostering a Safe and Empowering Environment

According to Maslow (cited in van Linden and Fertman, 1998), individuals have *deficiency* needs including survival, safety, self-esteem, and belonging and love. Once these needs are met, individuals can fulfill *being* needs, such as knowing and understanding and self-actualization. The environment is critical in meeting all needs and also influences behavior as noted in Bandura's (1986) social cognitive theory. Whether working with underserved youth, or teacher education students and faculty, a safe, supportive, and empowering environment that values all participants' voices was warranted for leadership development. Participants are only able to let go and experience their full leadership potential if they can fully trust the people and situation. This was particularly evident for marginalized populations that reside on the fringe of mainstream society and have limited opportunities for stability, growth, and leadership.

HEALTH LEADERSHIP: REUNITING THE MIND, BODY, AND SPIRIT

As a result of the increased emphasis on efficiency, technology, and commercial entertainment, development in the physical domain has suffered greatly in our society. Due to her background in physical education and kinesiology, utilizing the physical domain in leadership development is a natural undertaking for Educator B. Her experiences have reinforced strong beliefs in the power of physical activity in holistic development. For youth participants, the activities compel them to understand and utilize their bodies strategically and cooperatively with other participants to achieve the team-building challenges. For many participants, it is an introduction of mind, body, and soul in symphony and for others a reunion. It is evident in her professional life, and in her work with faculty, that Educator A also seeks this reunion.

Also embedded in each narrative, and worthy of note, are references to the spiritual dimension—the soul—of leadership development. For example, Educator A explicitly indicates that she has transitioned to a realization that leadership and leadership development should be a holistic process, which would include a focus on integrating the spiritual dimension. She fully acknowledges that her recent attempts to incorporate holism and spirituality in her approach to leadership fall short of having any real impact. Nevertheless, she believes that the concept warrants attention and study. Educator B's references to spirituality are more implicitly stated. In sharing her beliefs about the importance of reflection and empowerment in cultivating student leadership, she describes the relationships that develop between and among the students and the adults in the LA GEAR UP camps. There is an undercurrent of spirituality that resonates in her storytelling, which is clearly evident when she relates the event of Ja'Marcus reading his poem, *Understanding*, to the group. The images and concepts he captured in his poem suggest that he was able "to establish a connection with a transcendent source of meaning" (Riaz & Normore, 2008, p. 1), an important feature of spirituality.

FINAL REFLECTIONS: HOLISTIC SCHOOL LEADERSHIP

We contend that the holistic component of leadership enables leaders to find deeper meaning in their work by heightening self-awareness and the desire to establish a connection with a transcendent source of meaning. In a narrow sense, "spirituality concerns itself with matters of the spirit that help form an essential part of a leader's holistic health and wellbeing . . . By attending to other's needs, these leaders may define the shared values and purposes necessary for revitalizing their community" (Riaz & Normore, 2008, p. 8). As supported in the literature, leadership involves the complex cohesion of inspiration, encouragement, multiple paradigms of ethics, authenticity, morality, relationship building, reflective self-honesty, and the renewal of spirituality (Starratt, 2007). It is within these dimensions that leadership provides integrity and authentic leadership practices that can influence thinking and understanding of individual and collective values, not only in educational settings but also in the greater society. We concur with Riaz and Normore (2008) that by incorporating the spiritual dimension in leadership practices, leaders in any discipline and at any level are able "to think more holistically, to act responsibly in judgments, to challenge others, to learn more clearly their own worldview and points of view. They are able to regard their own professional work as one that builds and enhances not only their own character and identity but those with whom they interact" (p. 7), while simultaneously empowering themselves as agents of transformative change who align everyday practice with core values in ways that will make a significant difference in their professional and personal lives.

The literature supports the notion that spirituality is a "meaning system" (Solomon & Hunter, 2002, p. 38) that has a broad ranging impact on how leaders think and act in daily life routines. It is a sense of profound internal connection to things beyond and/or within one's self. When leaders have made this connection in all likelihood, they will be able to motivate others. Solomon and Hunter further claim that "approaching work tasks and colleagues with humility and respect not only provides important models for how others should conduct themselves but also establishes a tone, or ethos" (p. 41), that tend to the moral imperative of communities.

Our two educators shared poignant and relevant experiences that were shared through the lens of growth and self-reflection about three leadership development projects in the United States (e.g., teacher leadership, youth leadership). Engaging learners and leaders in authentic learning experiences (e.g., self-reflection, ethics of responsibility, moral literacy, spiritual development and connectedness) signifies critical steps toward a holistic educational approach to moral and leadership development. As initially highlighted by the educators, these projects were intended to engage in critical reflection and to cultivate development of morally literate and responsive leaders in education. Participants ranged from PK-12 teachers, administrators, to higher education faculty, community and youth leadership. The process of reflecting critically on shared experiences, as both inquirers and respondents (see Lincoln et al., 2011), presents a series of discussion questions for holistic leadership development.

Discussion Questions

1. Quatro et al. (2007) holistic leadership model focused on analytical, conceptual, spiritual, and emotional components of leadership where significant skills, practices, and behaviors not only embrace moral and ethical values but also serves as a catalyst of trust, self-reflection, and meditative thinking. How do educational leaders create an organizational social covenant whereby integrity and trust are built? How do the same leaders nurture, sustain, and honor its integrity? How do they support and foster a safe and psychologically secure environment for holistic development?

2. There are various definitions and terminology embedded in discussions of holistic leadership. However, a growing consensus exists that leadership is more than an activity of the mind. Leadership is a multi-dimensional activity, which invokes action of the mind, body and spirit.

3. Caring for others and self-care prove to be an essential component within an effective healthy and holistic leadership paradigm. Holistic leaders focus on the human element: relationships, values, and actions of individuals within the community. When this happens, opportunities to learn about ways in which leaders and learners are developed and prepared to take leadership roles in communities are enormous in scope. How do learners and leaders both individually and collectively, bring knowledge, strategies, skill sets, research understanding, and practical experiences that promote and foster holistic educational leadership?

4. When education programs encourage learners to explore the spiritual dimension of "who" they are, then, in all likelihood, they will be better grounded with their inner being and more likely to flourish. In the words of Fairholm (1997), "Our spirit is what makes us human and individual. It determines who we are at work. It is inseparable from self." How does a leader's spirituality help them think and act according to values?

5. How do leadership development training personnel incorporate the multidimensionality of humanity into programs so that holistic health literacy including mind, body, and spirit are critical components?

NOTE

1 Copyright Permission granted to publish portions of the following article in this chapter: Candis-Best, K. (2011). Holistic leadership: A model for leader-member engagement and development. *The Journal of Values Based Leadership*, 4(1). College of Business Administration, Valparaiso University, 1909 Chapel Drive, Valparaiso, Indiana 46383.

   Copyright Permission from Taylor & Francis is granted to reprint portions of this chapter from the following source: Leonard, P., Schilling, T., & Normore, A.H. (2014). Towards a holistic approach to moral development of educational leaders. In Branson, C., and Gross, S. (Eds.), *An international handbook for the development of ethical educational leadership* (533–76). New York, NY: Routledge/Taylor & Francis.

REFERENCES

Bandura, A. (1986). *Social foundations of thought and action: A social cognitive theory*. Englewood Cliffs, NJ: Prentice-Hall.

Branson, C. (2007). Improving leadership by nurturing moral consciousness through structured self-reflection. *Journal of Educational Leadership*. 45(4), 471–95.

Begley, P. T. (2003). In pursuit of authentic school leadership practices. In P.T. Begley & O. Johansson (Eds.), *The Ethical Dimensions of School Leadership*, 1–12. Boston: Kluwer Academic Publishers.

Best, K. C. (2011). Holistic leadership: A model for leader-member engagement and development. *Journal of Values-based Leadership*, 4(1). Retrieved from, http://valuesbasedleadership journal.com/issues/vol4issue1/holistic_leadership.php

Dyer, W. W. (1996). *Your sacred self: Making the decision to be free.* New York: HarperCollins Publishers.

Frankl. V. E. (2006). *Man's search for meaning.* Boston, MA: Beacon Press.

Hellison, D. (2011). *Teaching personal and social responsibility through physical activity.* 3rd ed. Champaign, IL: Human Kinetics.

Leonard, P. (2005). The ethics of practice: Navigating the road of authenticity: Journey interrupted. *Values and Ethics in Educational Administration, 3*(4), 1–8.

Leonard, P. (2007). Moral literacy for teacher and school leadership education: A matter of Attitude. *Journal of Educational Leadership. 45*(4), 413–26.

Leonard, P., & Basinger, D. (2008). Educating the whole teacher. *The Beacon, 4*(2), 1–8.

Leonard, P., Schilling, T., & Normore, A. H. (2014). Towards a holistic approach to moral development of educational leaders. In C. Branson & S. Gross (Eds.), *An international handbook for the development of ethical educational leadership,* 533–76. New York, NY: Routledge/Taylor & Francis.

Lincoln, Y. S., Lynham, S. A., & Guba, E. G. (2011). Paradigmatic controversies, contradictions, and emerging confluences, revisited. In N. K. Denzin & Y.S. Lincoln (Eds.), *The SAGE Handbook of Qualitative Research,* 97–128. Los Angeles: SAGE.

Lips-Wiersma, M., & Morris, L. (2009). Discriminating between meaningful work and the management of meaning. *Journal of Business Ethics, 88,* 491–511.

Louisiana Board of Regents. (2005). *Request for proposals for Louisiana GEAR UP summer/ academic year learning projects.* Baton Rouge, LA: Author.

Normore, A. H. (November, 2010). Introduction: Global perspectives on educational leadership: The development and preparation of leaders and learners of leadership. In A. H. Normore (Ed.), *Advances in Educational Administration: The Development, Preparation, and Socialization of Leaders of Learning and Learners of Leadership: A Global Perspective,* xiii–xiv. Bingley, WA: Emerald Group Publishing Limited.

Orlov, J. (2003). *The holistic leader: A developmental systemic approach to leadership.* Retrieved January 16, 2017 from http://julieorlov.com/docs/holistic_leader_article.pdf

Popper, M. (2004). Leadership as relationship. *Journal for the Theory of Social Behaviour, 34,* 107–25.

Project Adventure, Inc. (1995). *Youth leadership in action.* Dubuque, IA: Kendall/Hunt Publishing Company.

Quatro, S. A., Waldman, D. A., & Galvin, B. M. (2007). Developing holistic leaders: four domains for leadership development and practice. *Human Resource Management Review, 17,* 427–41.

Rshaid, G. (2009). The spirit of leadership. *Educational Leadership, 67*(2), 74–7.

Rogers, G., Mentkowski, M., & Hart, J. R. (2006). Adult holistic development and multi-dimensional performance. In C. H. Hoare (Ed.), *Handbook of adult development and learning,* 498–534. New York, NY: Oxford University Press.

Ryan, R. M., & Deci, E. L. (2000). Self-determination theory and the facilitation of intrinsic motivation, social development, and well-being. *American Psychologist, 55,* 68–78

Schilling, T., Martinek, T., & Tan, C. (2002). Fostering youth development through empowerment. In B. Lombardo, K. Castagno, T. Caravella-Nadeau, & V. Mancini (Eds.), *Sport in the 21st century: Alternatives for the new millennium,* 169–79. Boston, MA: Pearson Custom Publishing.

Senge, P. M. (2006). *The fifth discipline: The art & practice of the learning organization.* New York, NY: Doubleday.

Shinn, S. (2010). The holistic leader. *BizEd, May/June,* 58–63.

Sinclair, A. (2007). *Leadership for the disillusioned: Moving beyond myths and heroes to leading that liberates* [DX version]. Retrieved from http://amazon.com

Solomon, J., & Hunter, J. (2002). A psychological view of spirituality and leadership: Finding meaning through Howard Gardner's notion of existential intelligence. *School Administrator*, *59*(8), 38–41.

Starratt, R. J. (2004). *Ethical leadership*. San Francisco: Jossey-Bass Publishers.

Starratt, R. (2007). Leading a community of learners: learning to be moral by engaging the morality of learning. *Educational Management Administration & Leadership*, *35*(2), 165–83.

Taggart, J. L. C. (2010). *Becoming a holistic leader: Strategies for successful leadership using a principle-based approach*. 2nd ed. Retrieved from http://changingwinds.files.wordpress.com/2010/10/becoming-a-holistic-leader-2nd-edition.pdf

Taggart, J. L. (2009). *Holistic leadership*. Retrieved, from http://leadershipworld connect.com/holistic.pdf

Tuana, N. (2007). Conceptualizing moral literacy. *Journal of Educational Administration*, *45*(4), 364–78.

van Linden, J. A., & Fertman, C. I. (1998). *Youth leadership: A guide to understanding leadership development in adolescents*. San Francisco: Jossey-Bass Inc., Publishers.

Wapner, S., & Demick, J. (2003). Adult development: The holistic, developmental, and systems-oriented perspective. In J. Demick, & C. Andreoletti (Eds.), *Handbook of adult development*, 63–83. New York, NY: Kluwer Academic/Plenum Publishers.

Copyright permission granted to publish portions of the following article in this chapter.

Candis-Best, K. (2011). Holistic leadership: A model for leader-member engagement and development. *The Journal of Values Based Leadership*, *4*(1).

College of Business Administration, Valparaiso University, 1909 Chapel Drive, Valparaiso, Indiana 46383.

CHAPTER 12

Bringing It All Together: Dynamic and Synergistic Leadership

The previous 10 chapters of this book presented and explored key concepts that can orient readers toward a twenty first century vision of educational leadership. Some of these concepts are classic, found throughout the literature, and some are cutting edge, pushing the field into new, research-based spaces. That said, one of the most important things for a leader to realize is the dynamic inter-relationship between these concepts. Put differently, all of these literacies are constantly changing and simultaneously in reciprocal influence with all of these others.

Everything that leaders do is connected and dynamic—leaders *both* influence education and are influenced by education.

This basic idea has implications for leaders in that their work in one area influences many others, whether that is their intention or not. Leadership has far-reaching intended and unintended consequences. At the same time, there are many inter-related dynamics that influence the ways that they practice leadership. Some of these constrain leadership and some of them facilitate leadership.

Recognition that leadership is infinitely complicated and constantly changing can elicit three basic responses. First, it may feel overwhelming and make a leader scared. How can a leader possibly hope to understand a protean web of expanding and contracting concepts, relationships and technicalities that make up educational leadership? By embracing it and accepting that leadership is not the work of any one person; leadership is instead about building relationships, empowering others, advocating for those in need and expanding and improving opportunities for students, educators and communities. While leadership demands moments of bravery and individual accountability, organizations will best realize their potential, if collective wisdom informs action. Don't feel you need to make sense of complexity on your own, and never feel it is up to you to enact leadership. Knowing when to step to the back and follow subordinates with more expertise in a particular area is one of the marks of a learned leader.

The second response a leader can have to complexity and dynamism is unreserved enthusiasm. Such leaders are excited by the daily twists and turns of leadership. They understand that the best designed plans will need to change course as new evidence comes in, and that relationships, concepts and the technical work of schools is in constant motion. To these leaders, change is the norm and their work is about supporting people to conceive and implement processes that will sometimes be ineffective and at other times fail altogether. This is the leader that many leadership books write about—an optimistic spirit filled with boundless energy who moves forward over success and obstacle.

A final reaction to complexity and dynamism is somewhere in between these two: a mixture of fear and confidence, of optimism and skepticism, of resolve and open-mindedness. Most of you reading this will fall into this third category. Importantly, no one decides to be one way or another—we shape and are shaped by our context. We can influence people, processes and outcomes but are also influenced by them, so our leadership grows as we enact it in a particular space.

In this final note, we want to encourage you to do a few things as you move into leadership:

1. **Continue to learn.** Many "leadership gurus" have suggested something along the lines of "if you don't read, you can't leave." Leaders keep current on best practices in education from around the world, they learn from their colleagues and seek out ideas contrary to their assumptions. They make time to read, debate, test and grow.

2. **Action without critical reflection is not leadership.** Leaders constantly take stock of their work and seek out evidence that will help them understand of what they and their organization is doing is effective. Leaders who do not reflect are dangerous in that they are destined to repeat mistakes and are more likely to act on their uncritical assumptions about people and processes.

3. **Map your leadership.** As leadership influences and is influenced by each of the topics we identified for the chapters of this book, they are in reciprocal relationship. Use the "map" in Figure 12.1 to think through the implications of your proposed decisions and implemented initiatives. How does the political influence the spiritual? What are the cultural implications changes in time? What are the moral dynamics of a political decision? The map is meant to be a guide for reflection and research in that working your way through it will remind you to consider aspects of leadership that may not be readily apparent. While working through the boxes in the map may be difficult or ask you to re-examine issues you have not considered, it is important to know that nearly every leadership decision made in a school can be mapped into every box in this matrix. As such, this map is meant to be a way to help you systematically think about complexity.

4. **The silent skills are as important as those on display.** Thinking, listening and looking are among the most underdeveloped skill for most leaders. They are physically present without being fully engaged in the moment, or they do not make an effort to authentically try and understand a situation from someone else's perspective. Likewise, making the time for thought and examination are absolutely critical to a leader's success—those who make time for such activities will practice a more intentional leadership.

5. **Leadership is an act of love.** At its heart, leadership and education are both acts of care. Leadership is about building relationships of mutual benefit that facilitate

growth in people and organizations. That is not to say that there aren't tough times and moments that require making difficult decisions that will hurt some people, but the core value that defines a leader's relationship to a follower in education is care and a sense of commitment to a common goal. Students do not learn best when they are fearful or afraid, and educators do not teach best when they are miserable or mistreated.

6. **Don't follow trends unless they are in the best interests of students and teachers.** Every decision in educational leadership has to come back to this central idea. It seems obvious, but it is clear that without learning, literacy, leadership and reflection, people can make decisions that move schools further away from their goals rather than closer to them.

7. **Leadership is not propaganda.** While style is important, true leadership is about substance. Creating new slogans or altering appearances without change that actually makes a difference in processes and outcomes is a distraction from work, not sound leadership.

8. **Lead with and for the many, not with and for the few.** Leadership is best practiced as a distributed endeavor—one in which the collective wisdom of the organization informs decisions of collective importance. There is no room for self-promotion or cronyism in educational leadership. This is doing the wrong things for the wrong reasons, and ultimately compromises the education of students.

9. **Leadership is a great responsibility and a great opportunity.** In the writing of this book, we reviewed and presented an enormous body of research that shows leadership makes a difference in schools. Whether it makes a positive and/or negative difference is up to the organizations in which leadership occurs.

10. **Seek critique.** It is important for educational leaders to seek constant constructive critique of their leadership. What went well? What went poorly? Where can I improve? What voices am I including and excluding when I make decisions? It will be best if this critique is both public and private, depending on the nature of the issue. The point here is that leadership is not about hiding, but rather it is about choosing to make oneself vulnerable. Leaders who avoid or deflect constructive criticism are likewise rejecting learning and development.

	Political	Economic	Cultural	Moral	Pedagogical	Information	Organizational	Spiritual and Religious	Temporal	Holistic and Health
Political	■									
Economic		■								
Cultural			■							
Moral				■						
Pedagogical					■					
Information						■				
Organizational							■			
Spiritual and Religious								■		
Temporal									■	
Holistic and Health										■

FIGURE 12.1

In the end, we are strong advocates for a leadership that is reflective, that involves learning in the form of reading research, involving others and re-examining context, and that is comprised of strong yet loving action. We admire and respect those who have chosen a leadership journey and thank them for their service. We hope you have found this book compelling, challenging and helpful and we encourage you to take the ideas forward in creating your own form of dynamic leadership.

Index

Abdelaziz, Abid 10
assessment literacy 97–8

Banks, James 65
Bennis, Warren 135
Bernstein, Basil 94
Blase, Joseph 35
Bluedorn, Alan C. 166, 167–8
Bogotch, Ira 110
Boyd, William L. 2–3, 9, 117
Branson, Christopher 182, 184–5
Brooks, Jeffrey S. 45
Bruner, Jerome 94

Carlson, Richard O. 137, 138
Christians, Clifford 6, 74
Clark, Timothy 12, 134
Collins, James 153
Covey, Stephen 153, 155, 156, 157, 158, 160
cultural leadership: collegiality, contrived to
    comfortable 62; cultural levels 5; culturally
    relevant pedagogical practices 65–7; culture's
    interrelated components 55; exclusion to
    inclusion 62–3; healthy to toxic culture
    59–60; individualistic to collaborative
    culture 60–1; multiple culture participation,
    appreciation of 63–4; organizational
    development, leader's influence 55–6;
    propriespect, concept of 4–5, 64; school
    culture, roles within 56–8; school
    improvement, influential norms 57; stuck-in-
    a-rut to culture-in-motion 61; subcultures 4
curriculum development: capacity building
    programs 100; collaborative enhancement
    59, 61; culturally relevant 66; economic
    competence, broadening learning 45–6, 51;
    ethical factors 75, 79; homeland security
    education 78; information literacy 9;

information technology 111, 115, 116–17;
    social justice education 120

Dantley, Michael E. 13, 83, 109, 110, 157
Deal, Terrence E. 58
decision making: collaborative school cultures
    59, 60–1; destructive school cultures 60,
    61–3; leadership succession 137;
    micropolitical factors 32–3; organized
    groups, contributions to 170–1; structures
    and processes 37–9, 51, 56
Demick, Jack 181
Denhardt, Robert B. 166, 167–8
digital divide 8, 107, 108–9, 110–11

Earle, Jason 135
economic leadership: business ideas, cautionary
    use 46–7; capital: economic, human and
    cultural 47–8; capital resources, allocation
    and benefits 48; economic competence,
    broadening learning 45–6; economics, part
    of education 49; employment trends 50–1;
    global outlook for learning 43; glocalization,
    mixed impact 49; guiding principles 51;
    innovation economics, facilitating relevant
    skills 3–4, 44–6; liberalism's negativity
    49–50; poverty and affluence 50; school
    finance 48–9
ED Tech program 114
education: nature of 92; teaching theories 93–5
educational leadership: development framework
    18–20, 19; holistic leadership, gaining
    recognition 182–3; identified areas of study
    1; interconnectivity of systems 17, 18; inter-
    related dynamics, leader responses 195–6;
    progressive guidance 196–8, 197
educational opportunity: digital divide and
    career choices 107, 108–9; middle school ILS

and digital equity 115–17; poverty and student support 50; social justice, working towards 109, 114–15; youth leadership training 186–9
empathic listening 156
E-Rate program 114
Evans, Robert 154

Fairclough, Norman 10, 76, 118
Fairholm, Gilbert 13–14, 153, 155, 157–8, 160–1
Flessa, Joseph 31–2
Freire, Paulo 92, 94
Fullan, Michael 57–8, 61, 138, 175–7
Fyfe, Ian 2, 3

Gardner, Howard 159
GEAR UP leadership initiative 186–9
Gee, James 8
global education policy 36
globalization: education policy, effect on 2–3, 14–15; global outlook for learning 43, 45, 82
Greenleaf, Robert K. 155, 156, 158
Grissom, Jason A. 172–3

Heiftez, Ronald 153
Herbart, Johann 93–4
Herschell Paul 8
holistic health leadership: holistic development perspectives 180–3, 185–6, 190–1; leadership program development, case study findings 183–6; leadership theory and key assumptions 179–80; physical activity, power of 185, 187–8, 190; safe and empowering environment 188–90; self-awareness and reflection 184–5, 188, 189; spiritual contributions 183, 185–6, 190; varied interpretations 16; youth leadership training, case study findings 186–9
Hunter, Jeremy 159, 191

information leadership: digital access, class and racial factors 110–11, 112–14, 119; digital divide, global and national issue 107, 108–9, 113, 120; information literacy 9–10, 117–18; integrated learning systems (ILS) 111–12, 115–17, 119; media representations, power of 9–10, 118; middle school ILS and educational equity 115–17; non-profit and commercial IT investment 119–20; social justice education 109–10, 114–15, 120

King, Matthew 57
Klenke, Karin 13, 153, 154, 157, 158
Knowles, Malcolm 96
Kohlberg, Lawrence 154, 156–7, 158
Kruse, Sharon 135

Lee-Boggs, Grace 77
Lindle, Jane Clark 31, 33
Linsky, Marty 153
Lips-Wiersma, Marjolein 181
local community: groups, organizational connections 170–1; political role in school 36
Ludwig, Christine 8

MacIntyre, Alasdair 83
macroeconomics, school level 49–51
Marginson, Simon 74
Marshall, Catherine 109–10
Marx, Gary 43, 174–5
mass media: leader's morals, talking point 83; moral stance, influence of 6, 72, 74, 76; power and sphere of influence 9–10, 117–18
Miami-Dade County Public Schools 112, 115–17
microeconomics, school level 46–9
micropolitics, school level: defining factors 31; formal structure and processes 32; informal practices, good or bad 32; leader's power, use of 33, 35–6; open and closed systems 32–3; political actors and networks 33, 34–5
Mitchell, Douglas E. 2–3, 9, 117
moral leadership: administrative strategies, positive and negative 80–1; advocacy, working towards 85–6; citizenship and public responsibilities 76–8; discussion topics 84–5; ethical duties as educators 79–80; ethical responsibility domains 75; human responsibility and impartiality 75–6; moral action, reflective adaptions 73–4, 85–6; moral agency 83–4; moral literacy 74; morally literate citizenship, goal of 6–7, 72, 75; research areas 85; transformational education 81–3
Morris, Lani 181

national education policy 36
Nelson, Daniel 158
Nelson, Murry 78
No Child Left Behind Act 76, 114
Noddings, Nel 95–6

Normore, Anthony H. 45, 79, 139–40, 183, 185, 191
Northouse, Peter G. 99, 156

Oliva, Maricela 109–10
organizational leadership: academic training review 136–7, 141; organizational dynamics and patterns 11–12, 133, 134–5; organizational socialization 136–7; professional socialization 135–6; recruitment and selection practices 138–40; succession planning, focus for re-evaluation 137–8, 140, 141; systems perspective 12, 135, 140–1
Organization for Economic Cooperation and Development (OCED) 7
Orlov, Julie 180, 182

Palmer, Parker 95, 154
pedagogical leadership: accompanying role 95; assessment literacy 97–8; capacity building, program essentials 99–100; caring relations and social pedagogy 95–7, 109; critical literacy and learning 7–8; pedagogues, role of 92–3; pedagogy, modern revival and debate 94–5; practices model student program 100–1; special needs students 102
Pestalozzi, Johann 92, 95
Peterson, Kent D. 58
Plato 93
political leadership: decision making, structures and processes 37–9; globalization and educational policy 2–3; leader's power, use of 33, 35–6; macropolitics, role in 36; mesopolitics, community relations 36; micropolitical open/closed systems 32–3; micropolitics, definition and dynamics 31–2; negotiation and conflict resolution 38–9; political literacy, core element 2; political philosophies, potential influences 27–31; political savvy, decision guidance 37; reflective feedback 37; transparency and communication 38
political philosophies: anarchism 27–8; capitalism 28; communism and communitarianism 28; conservatism 29; democracy 30–1; fascism 29; feminism 29–30; meritocracy 30; tranactionalism 29
Popper, Micha 179–80, 181
propriespect, concept of 4–5, 64

Rawls, John 109
Riaz, Omar 183, 185, 191
Rogers, Glen 181–2

Saphier, Jon 57
Schein, Edgar 54–6
school cultures: collaborative, collective enhancement 60–1; collegiality, contrived or comfortable 62; culture-in-motion 61; exclusion or inclusion 63; healthy, collaborative 59; individualistic isolation 60; stuck-in-a-rut, self-reliance 61; toxic, destructive deceit 60
Senge, Peter 17, 134
Shapiro, Joan 152
Sinclair, Amanda 182–3
Sizer, Theodore R. 154–5
Smith, Mark K. 92–3, 94, 96
social justice leadership 109–10, 115
Soka Gakkai Buddhists (SGI) 156
Solomon, Jeffrey 159, 191
spiritual and religious leadership: *Entheos*, Greenleaf's concept 156, 158; ethic of care and spirituality 152; human-centered elements 152–3; inner strengths and guiding principles 156–7; metaphysical leadership 162–3; organizational integrity and authenticity 154–5, 161–2; servant leaders and interdependence 155–6; spiritual influence, integration of 153–4, 161–2, 183, 190–1; spirituality and religion 159–60; spirituality, foundation for ethical framework 157–8; spirituality, varied interpretation 13–14; spiritual renewal, individual and group 160–1
Spring, Joel 3, 4, 42, 46
staff, all levels: budgetary transparency 48–9; cultural reflection 65–6; destructive school cultures 60, 61–3; human and cultural capital 47–8, 66–7; political actors and networks 33, *33*–5; positive school cultures 59, 60–1; school culture 56–7
Starratt, Robert J. 73, 75–6, 79, 80, 81–3, 152, 184
Stefkovich, Jacqueline 152
Stolp, Stephen 56
students: cultural reflection 65–6, 81; digital divide and equity of access 108–9, 110–14; disadvantaged by school policy 80, 112; focus of school culture 57; human and cultural capital 47–8, 66–7; knowledge-based economy, preparing for 45–6; moral

reasoning skills 74, 77–8, 80, 81; moral responsibility, community vs. state 76–8; political actors and networks 33, *35*; positive school cultures 59, 60–1, 65; post-school guidance 49, 50–1, 75; poverty and student support 50, 82; social justice, working towards 109, 114–15; special needs 102; transformational education 81–2; youth leadership training, holistic approach 186–9

Taggart, James 180, 183
teachers: accompanying role 95; administrative career, rejection of 139; ancient Greek pedagogues 92–3; assessment literacy 97–8; civil liberties 76; collaboration in school culture 57–8, 59, 60–1, 62; cultural reflection 65–6; destructive school cultures 60, 61–3; educational assessment, critical evaluation 101–2; human and cultural capital 47–8, 66–7; leadership consultation, value of experiences 169–70; pedagogical tasks 96; political actors and networks 33, *34–5*; professional development 57; special needs students 102; teaching theories 93–5; transformational education 81–2
temporal leadership: change process, leader's role 175–7, *176*; future trends and planning 166–7, 173–5; institutional timeline 166, 171; personal to global histories, contributory discourses 168–71; principals and time management 172–3; relationship building 170; school community dynamics 173; teachers' experiences, value of 169–70; transformational concepts 175; understanding perspectives on time 167–8
Thomas, Sue 10, 118
Thompson, Scott 158–9, 160
Tillman, Linda 83, 109, 110
Tuana, Nancy 6, 72, 74, 118

Wapner, Seymour 181
Wolcott, Harry F. 5, 64

Zakaria, Fareed 74–5